A History of
PINNER

A History of
PINNER

Patricia Clarke

PHILLIMORE

2004

Published by
PHILLIMORE & CO. LTD
Shopwyke Manor Barn, Chichester, West Sussex, England

© Paricia Clarke, 2004

ISBN 1 86077 287 0

Printed and bound in Great Britain by
MPG BOOKS LTD
Bodmin, Cornwall

Contents

Foreword

To the people who live in Pinner the centre is 'the village'. If you take a look at the centre you will understand, for there is the High Street rising gently from the river crossing to the parish church which dominates the scene at the top. The church, built in flint, is typical of the 14th-century genre in Middlesex. On either side of the street stand houses of every century from the 15th to the 20th, and yes, there is even an ancient tavern. It all makes a fine picture, whether looking up or down the street. It is the most photographed view in Pinner, and it is this, and the annual fair, held in the street ever since 1336, that outsiders call to mind when they think of the place.

But the people who live in Pinner know that there is more, embedded, like the village, in the matrix of Greater London. There are still a few old houses where Pinner's hamlets used to be. There is a farm of over 200 acres close to the village, where cows still chew the cud. There are fragments of medieval woodland. There is a 14th-century manor house with a completely water-filled moat, and barns only a little less old.

Why is Pinner like this? What are these reminders of its rural past? Who has lived in these places? What did they do? And when did it all begin?

Can we 'give to airy nothings a local habitation and a name'?

Let us find out.

Acknowledgements

While the conclusions I have reached are my own, and much of the research, I could not have written this book without using the research of many members of the Pinner Local History Society, who have been generous in this respect. I must particularly acknowledge the late Jim Golland, Iris Long, Ken Kirkman, Graham Elcombe, the late Tony Venis, Hilary Thornley, Charmian Baker, George Stoddard, the late Eric Whittleton, and Bernard Harrison. To these I would add the owners of so many Pinner buildings who have, over the years, allowed me to study their homes in detail. And I must also recognise the help given over as many years by Bob Thomson and the staff of Harrow Reference Library.

The illustrations are reproduced by kind permission of the following, to whom any application for use should be made: Mrs Charmian Baker, 26; Baldwin's Auctions Ltd., 24; Charles Russell & Co., 19; Mrs Patricia Clarke, 2, 5, 8, 10, 13, 14, 17, 18, 23, 27, 29, 37, 40, 41, 44, 45, 46, 47, 63, 65, 78, 88; Clinton Dore, 83; English Heritage, NMR, 28, 31; Guildhall Library, Corporation of London, 49; Guy's & St Thomas' Charitable Foundation, 11, 20, 25; David J. S. Hallmark, 3; Mrs Janet Harris, 93; Harrow Heritage Trust, 12; Harrow Observer, 89; Imperial War Museum (IWM, CH.1391), 94; Ken Kirkman, 50; London Borough of Harrow Local History Collection, 6, 21, 22, 32, 33, 36, 42, 43, 52, 53, 54, 56, 57, 58, 86, 87, 90, 101, frontispiece; Mrs Iris Long, 9; Mrs Fiona Mallinson, 64, 67 (Jessie & Nelson Ward), 75; Frank Palmer, 76; Mrs Jette Parsey, 48 (including jacket illustration); Pinner Association, 16, 67 (West House), 73, 100, 103; Pinner Local History Society, 1, 7, 15, 35, 51, 55, 59, 60, 72, 79, 80, 81, 84, 85, 91, 92, 96, 97, 98, 99, 102; Mrs Helen Pugh, 66; Robin Richards, 39; John Scudamore, 34; Mark Seaman, 95; Mrs Claire Shaw, 61, 62, 74; Hilary Thornley, 4, 69, 77, 82; V & A Picture Library, 30; Mrs Susanna Vedel, 68, 70; Mrs Sylvia Venis, 38; Robin Weir, 71.

The Earliest Times

SAXON NAME

Pinner is a Saxon name meaning 'Pinnas settlement on the side of the hill'. Saxon place-names typically refer to a physical feature of the locality – to help people find it – or are a personal name, or both. The earliest written version of Pinner comes from 1231 in the Latin form *Pinnora*. The latest research considers that *Pinn* is a Saxon personal name, Pinna, not a pin or peg, which make no sense; and that *ora* is Saxon for a hill, not Latin for a river bank. The Saxons needed to identify the different silhouettes of hills and had exact words for them; an *ora* was an elongated, flat-topped hill rising to a shoulder at one or both ends. The word was often included in the name of a settlement growing up in its vicinity; Chinnor in Oxfordshire, Hedsor, Bucks., Bognor, Sussex, and Bicknor, Kent also signify settlements on the side of *oras*.[1]

Here the hill was Nower Hill, which is the right shape for an *ora*, and would have been obvious before modern development. It rises gently through Pinner Park from the north east, peaking at the top of Wakehams Hill. The drop of the shoulder is marked by the footpath to George V Avenue, Nower Hill, and Blackgates footpath/ Church Lane /High Street. The Pinn skirts its base from Moss Close via Avenue Road to Bridge Street and Marsh Road. Its side is best appreciated today from George V Avenue, and its shoulder from the crest of West End Avenue, preferably after leaf-fall. *Ora* persists in the name of Nower Hill, developing from *ora*, thus: – atten ora/ore (meaning at the hill) – atte nore – at Nore – at Nower. John ate Nore was mentioned in December 1315. By then Nower meant only the area from Wakehams Hill to Mayfield Drive, including Tookes Green. The addition of Hill to Nower was a sign that the original meaning was forgotten.

Who then was Pinna, the Saxon whose name we still use? He could have been the head of an extended family which settled here during the Saxon migrations, or the retainer of a king or leader who rewarded him with a grant of this land.

Ora was not much used in place-names after *c.*900, so Pinner was probably already in existence then, and the very name – Pinna's place by the hill – establishes that it began where its heart is still, against the slopes of Nower Hill, whose north, west and south sides are lapped by the stream named after the settlement.

Since 824 Pinner has been within the larger estate known as Harrow, and an understanding of the early history of Harrow is vital to any consideration of the origins of Pinner.

THE EXTENT OF PINNER

The old parish of Pinner is outlined in Map 1. Briefly, it was bounded on the north by Hertfordshire, on the west by Eastcote, on the south by Drake Road and Lucas Avenue. The eastern side was much more nebulous, and it varied. It was approximately Oxhey Lane, Headstone Lane, Pinner Park Avenue, and thence an uncertain curve down to the eastern end of Lucas Avenue. In the 19th century Pinner covered 3,782 acres of the 13,809 in Harrow as a whole.

THE LAND

Middlesex slopes down to the Thames from its northern boundary, where the highest point is Bushey Heath, 504 feet, in the north west. Not far away Harrow on the Hill stands detached from the northern slopes and reaches 408 feet. In Pinner the highest point is Pinner Hill, 430 feet, and the second is Wakehams Hill, 262 feet, on top of Nower Hill.

   The Pinner area is a geological sandwich of four or five layers, chalk and flint at the base; then a mixture of pebbles, sand and clay called the Reading Beds; then London clay; then a mixture of sand and clay called the Claygate Beds, and at the top a deposit of pebble gravel. Except at the summit of Pinner Hill the top two levels have been eroded away, leaving London clay as the predominant surface soil of Pinner today.

   Winding streams have made Pinner a landscape of hills and valleys, as anyone who walks very far soon discovers. The Pinn and its tributaries drain from the Pinner Hill/Harrow Weald slope, while the Yeading and its tributaries drain from both the

1   A centuries-old problem! The junction of Eastcote Road (right) and Marsh Road in May 1988 after the Pinn (far left) had burst its banks.

Weald and Harrow Hill. Part of Rayners Lane and Warden and Yeading Avenues run along the top of the most southerly hill in Pinner, which was called the High Worple in medieval times. Another, once called Middle Hill, crosses Rayners Lane at The Gardens, dividing the Yeading from its tributary, the Smarts Brook. Both of these are foothills of Harrow. North of the Yeading a steep outlier from Nower Hill runs from the Ridgeway across Rayners Lane to Compton Rise and dies out along Whittington Way. The view along Rayners Lane from one crest to the other is striking.

The Pinn and the Yeading never quite meet, because of the Ridgeway outlier. The Yeading flows on south and becomes the river Crane, while the Pinn bends sharply westwards and passes through Ruislip and Hillingdon to join the Colne at Yiewsley. Where it turns the Pinn has deposited alluvium or silt, creating a small flood plain, as residents know well. Before the 20th century this area was called Pinner Marsh, a recognition of its waterlogged condition.

PREHISTORY

Pinner is the locality created and evolved by the people who have lived here, so history has little meaning for it until regular occupation can be established. Most prehistoric remains in Middlesex have been found in the lighter soils along the banks of the Colne, and the south-western and Thameside areas. The exposed clays of the north, covered by deciduous forest of oak and hornbeam, may have been used chiefly as hunting grounds, though the absence of systematic excavation here means finds have been too few to be of much value.

A hand axe of the old stone age (paleolithic), found in a drain at Headstone Manor in 1986, counts only as a stray find. Middle stone-age (mesolithic) flints have been found in small quantity in several parts of Harrow, the best being just to the east of Pinnerwood House, where a small scatter suggests a camp site. In Pinner three bronze-age (c.2500-500 B.C.) items have been found; an early flint arrowhead in Montesole Playing Fields near Grimsdyke in 1957, a middle-period axehead of the palstave type at Pinner Green in 1956, and a flint arrowhead in a garden in Blythwood Road in 1997. (A bronze-age arrow head and domestic debris were found in Park Wood, Ruislip, in 1984.) These few objects are not enough to prove that there was a settlement; people may have been living here, or they may only have been hunting, or travelling through.

The iron age (600 B.C.-A.D. 43) is now recognised to be a period of forest clearance and increasing population, with a well-filled countryside and homesteads spaced a mile or two apart. It is possible that there may have been a few homesteads in Pinner, though not necessarily at the same time as each other. Once again, the finds are not enough to prove settlement – some sherds of late pre-Roman iron-age pottery beneath Grimsdyke at Montesole Playing Fields in 1957, and also in a similar situation near the *Grimsdyke Hotel* in 1979.

The occupants of iron-age Britain were Celts, who predominated in much of Europe. Celtic society owed strong personal allegiance to a chieftain, and fell naturally into a large number of kingdoms based on tribal connections. They did not need towns as we think of them, though forts formed regional centres for the exchange of goods and the performance of common religious or ceremonial rites.

THE ROMANS

In 54 B.C. Julius Caesar invaded Britain, crossed the Thames, and defeated the Catuvellauni at a place which is still a matter of dispute. The stronghold of Cassivellaunus, chieftain of the Catuvellauni, was near the present Wheathampstead. As no other Celtic centre of power nearer to Harrow is known, our area was very likely within the sphere of the Catuvellauni.

Verulamium was the nearest Roman town. Watling Street (Edgware Road) was the nearest Roman road to Pinner, with an important pottery works at the top of Brockley Hill which supplied the Roman military and London. There may have been a settlement at Sulloniacis, a way-station now thought to have been at the foot of Brockley Hill, or where Silk Stream, anciently called *Sulc*, crosses Edgware Road further south. At Canons Park there was a tile kiln.

Finds of Roman material in our area are ambiguous – building tiles in the medieval church towers of Harrow on the Hill, Kingsbury and Little Stanmore, perhaps salvaged from Sulloniac or Brockley, and a few coins. In Pinner, there is an unsubstantiated report of fourth-century coins found near Waxwell in the late 19th or early 20th centuries. A bronze coin of Constantine II (A.D. 337-61) was found west of Hatch End Station in 1955 and a few sherds of Roman pottery were later found behind 19-25 High Street, in Pinner Village Gardens, and at Headstone Manor, all unstratified and probably redeposited, so that they are not useful as evidence.

The Romans left Britain in A.D. 410 as their empire collapsed. Their administration foundered, having kindled no self-generating response in British society, and the unity of the land did not long survive their going.

EARTHWORKS

Grimsdyke is the major earthwork in Middlesex, stretching about six miles from the Ruislip side of Cuckoo Hill to Pear Wood at Brockley Hill. It is linear, a deep ditch with a spoil bank on its northern side. There is a break in the line to the east of Pinner Hill Road for a tributary of the Pinn, and another between Blythwood Road and Altham Road. Grimsdyke may have been one ditch from the start, or a series of extensions, or unassociated pieces. It conforms to no contour of height or geology, nor to the boundary of Middlesex.

The archaeological evidence of the pottery at Montesole Playing Fields and *Grimsdyke Hotel* places the western part of earthwork in the late pre-Roman iron age. The name is one which Saxons sometimes gave to works not built by them but which were so impressive in size that they attributed them either to the mighty Saxon god Woden, or to the devil, for both of whom the name Grim was used. Middlesex *Grimsdiche* was first documented in 1306.[2]

As the spoil was usually dumped on the diggers' side of the ditch to heighten the bank, Grimsdyke looks like a boundary for land on the north side, but for what purpose? As a defence it was weak at the breaks at Blythwood and Pinner Hill Roads, and at Old Redding, where its summit is below the level of the opposing land on the south – why not incorporate that piece or heighten the bank? It could have been a property boundary. It would have been unusual and difficult to drive a non-military earthwork through woodland, so the land on one or both sides must already have been cleared for grass or the plough, only to revert to woodland when abandoned later for reasons unknown. As we do not know what was going on at the time, no theory can be confirmed, though the area of Pinner was obviously outside whatever Grimsdyke defined.

There are no other early earthworks in Pinner. I discount Barrow Point as denoting a barrow, that is a tumulus raised over a burial in the bronze age or earlier times. No such shape has been recorded there. The name is probably medieval, based on *beorh*, another Saxon word for a hill, and first appears in the Harrow Manor court roll dated April 1399: 'the lord's weir or mill pond called the bery pond'. The pond was near the junction of Uxbridge Road and Old Hall Drive, at the foot of the low hill where Paines and Moss Lanes meet at the top, and where a hamlet formed using the same name, subsequently spelt in varying ways. The lord's old pond is recognisable on Messeder's map of 1759 in the greater width of the river at the north end of Paines Lane, and a pond was reinstated there in the 19th century by the owner of The Hall.

THE MAKING OF HARROW

The amount of strife associated with the Anglo-Saxon incursions, and the extent to which they ousted the indigenous people is still debated. England in Saxon times was well populated as a whole and north-west Middlesex need have been no exception, for the Saxon plough could cope with stiff soil. The British Museum has a gold coin of the Frankish king Theodobert I (534-48), found somewhere along the banks of the Pinn, which suggests at the very least that someone connected with the continent was in, or passing through, the area about that time.

Offa of Mercia (757-96) was the dominant Anglo-Saxon king of his day. In 767 he gave 30 hides of land, perhaps 3,500 acres, to Stidberht, a senior churchman. They were flanked on one side by the holy shrine of the Gumenings (*Gumeninga herga*), identified with Harrow Hill, and on the other by the river Lidding, identified with the Kenton Brook. Offa added six more hides east of the river, including a suitable residence for the owner, identifiable with the area of Barn Hill at Preston Road. Herga was a point of identification *outside* the land granted.

By 801 Stidberht's 36 hides were owned by Pilheard, a nobleman close to King Cenulf of Mercia (796-821). Pilheard bought two significant privileges from the king. The first was exemption from paying royal tributes except the *trinoda necessitas* (three great ones), that is, providing armed men for the king's service (one man per six hides), paying towards the upkeep of bridges, and towards the upkeep of highways. The second privilege was the right to receive the fines from legal jurisdiction in his lands, in place of the king's sheriff, and maybe even the right to exercise that jurisdiction himself. These were important and rare privileges, making Pilheard's one of the earliest Saxon estates with recognisable characteristics of the medieval manor, that is, a lord entitled to control most legal matters in his own domain and levy fines accordingly.

The land around Pilheard's estate, including Harrow Hill and the Pinner area, remained in royal hands and was given by Cenulf to his daughter Cwoenthryth, the royal Abbess of Southminster in Kent, who had other huge estates scattered over south-east England. Cwoenthryth has a lurid reputation in legend as the murderess of her younger brother St Kenelm. Her own end came, it is said, when in a fit of evil she recited a psalm backwards and her eyes fell out of her head.

In 824 Abbess Cwoenthryth was ordered to hand over a large chunk of land to Wulfred, Archbishop of Canterbury, as part of the settlement of a lengthy dispute between Canterbury and Mercia. It included 104 hides of land in 'Harrow, Herefrething Land, and Wembley, and Yeading' which, minus Yeading, scholars are satisfied are virtually the same as the 100 hides of the Manor of Harrow in Domesday Book. Wembley may be taken as being Wembley today. Harrow would have included the hill itself (*Herga*), and by implication other land roughly west of the hill (see above), including Pinner. The Stidberht/Pilheard land, not called Harrow, may have been the area called Herefrething Land. The king immediately extended the privileges of Pilheard's original portion to the whole of Wulfred's new estate which was always thereafter called Harrow, and had already taken the shape it kept for a thousand years. Its boundaries were influential; the northern one became the shire boundary, the western one the boundary between the Hundreds of Gore (covering Harrow) and Elthorne. And it stayed in the ownership of successive archbishops of Canterbury until 1547, except for a few years around 1066.

Offa, Cenulf, Cwoenthryth and Wulfred were, in turn, the earliest owners of the land on which Pinner lies whom we know by name. Cwoenthryth is the only woman ever known to have owned it.

FROM THE 9TH TO THE 11TH CENTURIES

In the manor of Harrow Wembley existed by 824, and Roxeth by 845. These were the only places in the manor separately mentioned before 1200. Yet there were certainly others. Considering who owned the manor there must have been a church, probably on the hill in place of the pagan shrine, which was the Christian way, and it would have been the centre of a settlement. And, as we have seen, the very name of Pinner implies its existence before 900.

In 1007 King Ethelred the Unready restored Oxhey and Batchworth on the northern boundary of Pinner to St Albans Abbey. Druett (p.16) claimed that this charter refers to a Saxon chapel on Pinner Hill, forerunner of Oxhey Chapel, but the claim is based on a mistranslation of Ethelred's document, because nowhere at all is there a reference to any structure, sacred or secular, which could have been a chapel. There was a crucifix somewhere on the boundary, which may have served as a boundary marker, or a wayside devotional cross, or even as a preaching point. Its logical site would have been on a track between Harrow and Watford, the likely candidates being Oxhey Lane or Potter Street Hill where they cross the boundary. Oxhey Chapel in Gosforth Road began as the chapel of the Tudor mansion called Oxhey Place.

Every charter or deed concerning Anglo-Saxon Harrow ignores Grimsdyke, either as part of the boundary or as a point of reference. Any significance it may once have had in this respect had obviously passed.

II

The Medieval Period

Domesday Book

THE ENTRY

With the victory of William I there was a large-scale replacement of the Anglo-Saxon landowners by his Norman supporters and a new hierarchy was established. The highest lords held directly from the king, his tenants-in-chief, swearing fealty as his vassals. All others held as sub-tenants of these, or as sub-tenants of the sub-tenants, and so on down the line.

Domesday Book was a catalogue of the estates of the tenants-in-chief and the human and economic resources available on them, which gave the king a basis for assessing taxes. It was compiled in 1086 and its attempt to describe a highly varied society in a few compressed terms makes interpretation difficult. The translated entry for Harrow in Domesday Book reads:

> In the Hundred of GORE
> Archbishop Lanfranc holds HARROW. It answered for 100 hides before 1066, and does so now. Land for 70 ploughs. 30 hides belong to the lordship; 4 ploughs there; 5 (more) possible. 45 ploughs between the Frenchmen and the villagers; 16 more possible.
> A priest, 1 hide; 3 men-at-arms, 6 hides, and under them dwell 7 men; 13 villagers with ½ hide each; 28 villagers with 1 virgate each; 48 villagers with ½ virgate each; 13 villagers with 4 hides; 2 cottagers with 13 acres; 2 slaves.
> Pasture for the village livestock; woodland, 2000 pigs.
> Total value £56; when acquired £20; before 1066 £60.
> Earl Leofwine held this manor in 1066.

The terms mean: *lordship* – land used by the lord for his own benefit; *hide* – either an area of about 120 acres, or a unit of taxation; *virgate* – one quarter of a hide. Land for 70 ploughs means the estimated number of plough teams needed to exploit the estate fully. Plough teams which were 'possible' shows what proportion of the allocated land was not being cultivated.

We see that one third of Harrow was directly used by its lord (*lordship* hereafter called *demesne*), another third was occupied by his tenants, from priest to cottagers, while the remaining third, not categorised, was presumably taken up with pasture for the animals of the villagers, the woodland, and waste, which was land not allocated to any other use. The pasture would have formed commons. The woodland lay across the northern part of Harrow – Bentley Wood, Harrow Weald

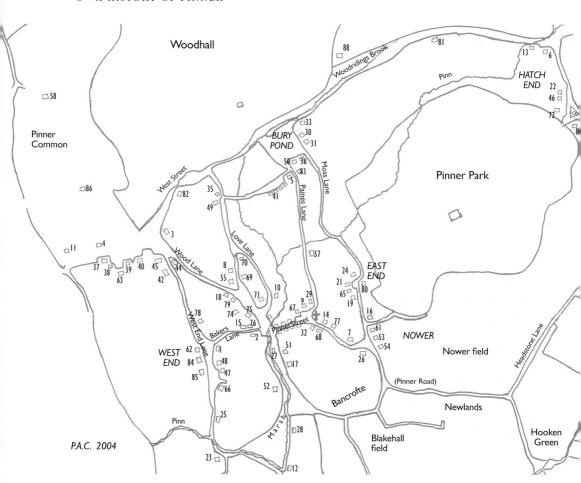

2 Buildings in Pinner. This includes buildings of many periods in Pinner prior to *c.*1800, though some had already gone, and many have gone since. The later Pinner Hill Farm, Lankers Brook Farm, Rayners Lane cottages, and Downs Farm have been added. See Appendix 1 and Appendix 2 (pages 205-9) for key to numbers. Map based on Isaac Messeder's Map of Harrow Manor 1759.

and Pinner Wood, of which remnants survive to this day – providing timber, fuel, and pig food in the form of acorns and undergrowth. With Enfield, Harrow was the most profitable place for pigs in Middlesex. The shortfall of 21 plough teams, 16 tenant, five demesne, represented unallocated land or future potential.

At 100 hides, about 12,000 acres, Harrow was the largest manor in Middlesex, almost the size of Ruislip, Great Stanmore, Little Stanmore and Harefield put together. Domesday Book does not mention Pinner because settlements inside a manor were irrelevant to its purpose – even Wembley and Roxeth were not mentioned.

THE PEOPLE

The lord's cultivated land at this date was Sudbury Manor, his residence when present. The size of the priest's holding signifies an important church whose incumbent would have been a capable, ambitious man hoping for preferment to higher episcopal or royal position.

The three men-at-arms, or knights, would have been some of those whom the archbishop, as a tenant-in-chief, was obliged to provide for the king's army. They had the largest holdings in Harrow with seven sub-tenants of their own – a knight usually sublet his holding and lived off the rents, or employed a steward. Though quickly lost to view in the early medieval land market the knights' holdings were probably represented by the earliest named and largest free holdings in the manor, particularly those which later used manor as part of the estate name. Two can be proposed in Pinner. The first is Headstone Manor, a freehold estate of around two hides, bought back by the archbishop at a relatively early date, 1344, a strong candidate on both counts. The second was the Manor called Pynnors or Females, a freehold hide situated north of the Pinn and west of West End Lane. The Pynnor family owned or tenanted part of it in the earlier 15th century, and their name is more likely to have derived from this estate than from the village.

The villager had a few acres around his house and the rest in the common fields, and from this he fed his family. Fifteen acres, a half virgate, is reckoned to have been needed to keep a family of five at subsistence level. Overall about half of the villagers were above subsistence level, and half at it, or below it.

The slave, a person without civil rights rather than the property of another, is difficult to pin down in Domesday Book because he had no property. They are sometimes thought of as officials, or important servants.

Using the commonly accepted multiplier of 4.5, the population of Harrow manor would have been about 530 if all the 117 people listed are treated as family men – even the priest would have had a household. There may have been more, like locally based administrators to run the demesne of an absentee landlord like the archbishop, unless the slaves did this work. There may also have been additional families, those of younger sons without a holding of their own, living with or renting from their fathers.

The Manor of Harrow

THE MEDIEVAL MANOR

The classic medieval manor was the possession of its lord, and the greater the lord the more manors he owned. The manor was his source of income, and all its resources – the land, streams, minerals, wild creatures – belonged to him. The manorial income fell into three parts. The first came from the demesne estate, which provided produce for his consumption or sale. The second came from his tenants, in the form either of money rent, or of unpaid labour on his demesne instead. The third part came from charges upon the tenants – for the use of resources such as the cutting of timber or digging of chalk, for exchanging or selling property, for special events such as inheritance or the marriage of a daughter, or as penalty for an offence like trespass or unneighbourly behaviour.

The lord's manor court was the place where matters between lord and tenant, between tenant and tenant, and the application of custom, were settled – where custom was in dispute or doubt a jury of tenants deliberated and declared the custom. It was called the court baron, dealing only with civil matters, chiefly inheritance, property transfers and local regulations, and was usually held every three or four weeks. There was no appeal from the court baron on customs of the manor – not even to the king's court.

Other matters, involving crimes, royal regulations, offences against the person or residents of other manors, were not a matter for the lord but for the hundred court, presided over by the sheriff of the county on behalf of the king. This was the king's justice. Good order was maintained by the system of frankpledge, groups of ten households called tithings, pledged to be mutually responsible for each other's good conduct, the head man or tithing-man having to report offences at the court. As time went by the number varied considerably from ten. The most common regulations were the assizes of bread and ale, which fixed the price and quality of those goods and monitored their application.

Some lords succeeded in obtaining the privilege of exercising all this jurisdiction themselves – and keeping the fines, of course – instead of the sheriff, holding a court leet once or twice a year. Pilheard and Wulfred had been among the earliest of these. Contrary to general belief, jurisdiction over serious crimes was seldom included, let alone the power of life and death; these rights a king guarded carefully.

HARROW MANOR

By the 13th century the usual settlement in a Middlesex manor was a village or nucleated community, with perhaps a scatter of hamlets further away, but few isolated homesteads.

At the time of Domesday Book no-one in Harrow was known by name or address, but by 1300 there were about a dozen centres of settlement within the manor, any of which could have existed at Domesday. Their first known dates are not an accurate guide to their age, though their names suggest how they began:

Harrow (767) the shrine; Wembley (825) 'Wemba's lea' or clearing; Roxeth (845) 'Hroc's marsh or pit'; Tokington (1171) the estate of Toca's family; Preston (1177/86) the priest's estate; Alperton (1199) Ealhbeorht's estate; Pinner (1231) Pinn's estate on the hillside; Kenton (1231) the estate of Coena's family; Uxendon (1257) the hill of the Wixan (a local tribe); Sudbury (1273) *beorh* or hill south of Harrow hill; Greenhill (1273) green hill; Weald (1282) in the wood; Norbury (about 1300) *beorh* or hill north of Harrow hill, perhaps the area from Pinner Road to Cunningham Park. Several had obviously grown out of farmsteads.

Each village had its own common open fields, except for Sudbury, and organised them independently of the others, but followed the same manorial custom and practice; the boundaries between them were significant only in relation to the fields. By the early 14th century Pinner, Weald, Roxeth and Sudbury had the largest populations, with the land spread rather more evenly between the inhabitants than in the other parts.

THE FIRST MENTION OF PINNER

This occurs in a dispute before the king's court between Godfrey of Pinner and Geoffrey of Batchworth, who must therefore have been knights holding land directly from him. In 1231 Geoffrey was sent to find out why Godfrey was risking imprisonment in the Tower of London by not appearing in court. Geoffrey subsequently made Godfrey a life grant of seven virgates in Pinner in return for one pound of cumin seed a year. Between 1237 and 1242, Geoffrey was contesting the ownership of 26 acres in Pinner with William, the son of (probably the same) Godfrey. The Pinner lands were held of the archbishop, of course, not the king, and were somewhere in the areas of freehold.[3]

THE SUB-MANORS

There was only one true sub-manor, that is, one created by the lord-archbishops and given some delegated powers. It was Harrow Rectory Manor, created sometime between 1086 and 1233 to enhance the rector's status and provide him with income additional to the tithes and glebe. The rector held his own courts leet and baron but was still a tenant obliged to attend the archbishop's court. Rectory Manor was made out of the priest's Domesday hide of some 120 acres, covering most of present-day Harrow on the Hill. (Subsequent references to Harrow Manor exclude Rectory Manor unless specified.)

There were four other so-called manors – Sudbury, Woodhall, Headstone, and Pynnors or Females. The first three were demesne estates where the tenants of the manor worked their services, and it was this manorial attribute which attracted the description 'manor'. They had no courts of their own for the archbishop was their owner and any business was dealt with in the Harrow court. Pynnors or Females was not demesne but was owned long ago by someone who also had large estates outside Harrow, all grouped under the name Manor of Females. The word manor remained in these estates, names long after the medieval period, giving a misleading impression that they had once been independent manors in their own right. The demesne of Pinner Park was different. By its non-agricultural nature it had no need of labour services, and was never called a manor.

HARROW MANOR COURT

Every male aged 12 or more, villager and free, had to attend court. The lord's steward presided and appointed a reeve and a beadle from names put forward by the villagers. The reeve was responsible for the economic side – organising the labour services, collecting rents and accounting annually to the archbishop, while the beadle's concern was with the enforcement of law and order as determined at the manor court. The tithing men, and the aletasters who reported the breakers of the assize of ale, were appointed from the tithings, which were identifiable with the Harrow villages by the 14th century. The work of all these was unpaid, took a great deal of time, and could bring unpopularity, for both the lord and their fellows were on the look-out for their mistakes.

Written on rolls of parchment, many of Harrow's manor court records survive from about 1315, though with gaps. They note matters decided at court, property transfers, and the names of persons and fees (called fines) involved.

FREE MAN AND VILLEIN

Free and unfree status was bound up with land tenure. The free man held by free hold, paid a money rent, and no work services, or very few, for his land in the manor, and could sell it as he wished. Though he must attend court he was not subject to

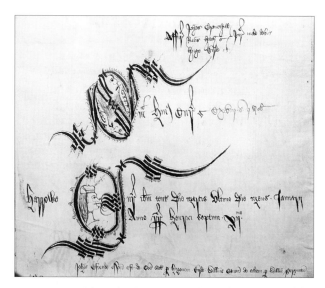

3 Part of a court roll of Harrow Manor, in Latin, with rare decoration of capital letters, showing the end of one court baron (25 October 1496) and the start of another (31 January 1497). Latin and English versions are shown below. The Latin was abbreviated by the scribe, as was usual, and most of the flourishes mark omitted letters. (Note that common suit was attendance at court.)

Latin: *Affur*   *Johes Grenehill*
                         Ricus Hach &
                         Hugo Bird   *Jur modo debit*
            Sma Huis Cur   *cxviijs jd et ob*

Harrowe   Cur ibm tent Die martis ultimo Die mens Januarij
           Anno r r Henrici septimi xijmo
           Johes Estende esson est de Coe sect p Hugonem
           Birde. Willms Canon de eodem p Willm Peryman

The Affeerors   John Greenhill Richard Hatch & Hugh Bird now swear what is owed. The total of this court is 118s. 1½d.

Harrow   Court held there Tuesday the last day of January in the twelfth year of the reign of King Henry VII. John Estend excuses himself from common suit via Hugh Bird. William Canon from the same via William Peryman

the will of his land lord but to common law. The unfree man, or villein, probably the villan or villager of Domesday Book, was required to give labour services for his land, sometimes very onerous ones, and had no power of independent disposal. He and his family were tied to the land and had recourse to no other authority but the land lord. The terms of tenure were copied into the court roll and the land was called copy hold. His protection lay in the customs of his manor by which, while he could not evade his obligations to his lord, neither could his lord oblige him to exceed them nor dispossess him of his father's holding. Villein holdings were therefore also called customary holdings.

The social and economic differences blurred as it became more and more the practice to substitute money rent for services, and by the time Lord North made his survey of Harrow in 1547 all services had been commuted. The essential distinction by then was that the freeholder could sell freely, while the copyholder still needed the lord's permission, and the change of owner was copied into the rolls.

THE CUSTOMARY HOLDINGS

There were three types of customary holding in Harrow. The most important was the head tenement, held directly from the lord himself, originally a hide, half hide or virgate of land, whose holder later considered himself a yeoman. The lord depended on the head tenants for most of his services, and it was they who were regarded as the most fit to exercise communal responsibilities, forming the pool from whom were chosen the reeve, beadle, and the juries set up to enquire into disputes or clarify custom. By the 14th century each head tenement had a name, and the tendency to repeat them in the rolls so that the lord could keep track of them was a practice which helps the researcher to trace their progress, though not consistent enough to be foolproof.

In Harrow at Domesday Book there were 38 holdings of head tenement size, totalling almost 13 hides. Lord North's survey of 1547 listed 70 head tenements, totalling 29 hides. In between, in a survey of 1285,[4] an unstated number of head tenements totalled the same number of hides, twenty-nine. Projecting backwards, the head tenements of 1285 and 1547 may well have been identical. Furthermore, over half of them were probably those of head tenement size in 1086. Where Pinner is concerned, it had 20 head tenements in 1547, and so also, presumably, in 1285. It was the highest number for any Harrow village – Roxeth was next with 13 and then Weald with twelve. All those 20 in the Pinner of 1547 can still be identified, but there is no means of telling which of them existed at Domesday.

The second type of holding from the lord was the cotland of five acres whose holder need not attend the court, paid no rent and no relief, but provided services. In Harrow the cotlanders were only at Sudbury.

The wastehold tenancy also came from the lord, a piece of land, usually less than an acre, granted from the waste in return for a small rent. Most grants regularised illicit encroachment upon the lord's waste by an adjoining tenant to make space for an extra outhouse. Rarely was a house built on one before the 16th century.

OTHER HOLDINGS

The underset was another type of holding, and not one granted by the lord but a sub-tenancy created by a head tenant out of his own holding. The relationship of the sub-tenant was with the head tenant, and his rent was due to him, not the lord. The head tenant remained responsible to the lord for the rent and services of the whole original holding. For this reason any underset existing in 1086 would not appear in Domesday Book.

They must have originated in dwellings provided for family members, usually comprising a house with a garden or toft of about an acre. Most eventually passed outside the family through sale or marriage and in time were recorded in the rolls as copyhold tenancies in their own right.

People who owned no land rented houses, which did not appear in the rolls, and the information is too vague to give a clear idea of them. People were sometimes confused about properties not in the rolls; Christine Godfrey, head tenant of Crouchers in Pinner Marsh (about 88-98 Marsh Road) thought she was entitled to several years' arrears of rent in 1394 from John Alverych, who lived in a cottage on Crouchers called Muggs (about 100-110 Marsh Road) but in court he was able to prove himself the owner, not a tenant.

Medieval Pinner

THE VILLAGE PATTERN

The main settlement of Pinner was on the south-west flank of Nower Hill near the river, with a few small hamlets further afield. This sort of settlement is called nucleated, typical of areas where agriculture was organised on a communal basis and so needed very large fields.

4 The ancient thoroughfare Cannon Lane, about 1934-6, contrasting the old rural lane and the distant Downs Farm with the suburban houses and Lulworth Drive at the left.

The arable land and hay meadows were in the south, covering two-fifths of the area. The common pasture was primarily Pinner Common (or Green), lying either side of Pinner Hill Road – in 1800 it was about 175 acres. The woodland lay in the north. About one-fifth of Pinner's area was taken up with three demesne estates; Woodhall, a farm of more than 300 acres north of Uxbridge Road; Pinner Park, a 250-acre reservation for deer; and Headstone, a farm of some 200 acres. Sizeable parts of Pinner were freehold, most notably Females Manor which blanketed the area north of the Pinn and west of West End Lane, and Thornburghs, which included a wide band south of Uxbridge Road from Pinner Green to the railway at Hatch End.

People lived in the middle area between the common and demesne of the north and the open fields of the south. Outside the main settlement, which contained the church, houses clustered in hamlets, probably for neighbourly security. The hamlets of Pinner were East End, West End, Hatch End, Nower Hill, Bury Pond Hill, Pinner Green, Wood Lane End and The Marsh.

5 (OPPOSITE) Medieval Pinner. The medieval topography: location of common fields, woodland, common, marsh, demesne estates, hamlets. Brackets show places with no particular medieval name. Some names have changed: Bakers Lane is Chapel Lane; Pinner Street is High Street, Church Lane and part of Bridge Street; West Street is Uxbridge Road; Wood Lane is Elm Park Road. See Appendix 1 and Appendix 2 (pages 205-9) for key to numbers. Map based on Isaac Messeder's map of Harrow Manor 1759.

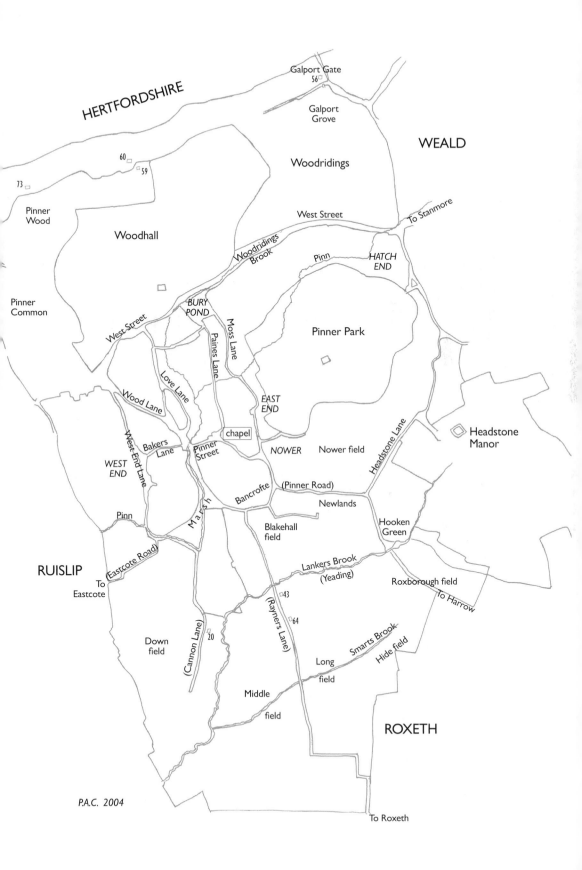

HERTFORDSHIRE

WEALD

Galport Gate
56

Galport
Grove

Woodridings

60
59

73

Pinner
Wood

Woodhall

West Street

To Stanmore

Woodridings Brook

Pinn

HATCH
END

Pinner
Common

West Street

BURY
POND

Pinner Park

Moss Lane

Paines Lane

Wood Lane

Love Lane

West End Lane

EAST
END

chapel

Headstone Lane

Headstone
Manor

Bakers
Lane

Pinner
Street

NOWER

Nower field

WEST
END

Marsh

Bancrofte

(Pinner Road)

Newlands

Pinn

Blakehall
field

Hooken
Green

RUISLIP

(Eastcote Road)

Lankers Brook

Roxborough field

To Harrow

To
Eastcote

(Yeading)

43

64

Down
field

(Cannon Lane)

20

(Rayners Lane)

Smarts Brook

Hide field

Long
field

Middle

field

ROXETH

P.A.C. 2004

To Roxeth

ROADWAYS

Pinner's road system was very clearly shaped to give access from the inhabited parts to all its resources, and it changed very little between medieval times and 1800. The Tudor roads are used today, some with the same names – Love Lane (earliest mention 1391) Headstone Lane (1397), Moss Lane (1432), Paines Lane (1536), Waxwell Lane (1539), West End Lane (1547). The High Street was called Pinner Street (1421) until the 18th century, and included Church Lane about as far up as Pinner House; Bridge Street and Elm Park Road were called Wood Lane (1514) and later Common Road; Chapel Lane was called Bakers Lane (1425), Marsh Road had no name before the 19th century; Uxbridge Road was West Street (1384) or Green Street(1416), or else the way to Rickmansworth or Stanmore; and Pinner Road was known as the road to Harrow. Marsh Road was so liable to flood and waterlogging that it was not dependable as a major route until well into the 19th century. The favoured route to Harrow and places beyond went via Church Lane, Nower Hill and Harrow Road. Cannon Lane and Rayners Lane were service roads into the common fields and were nameless. The latter met the road from Roxeth.

From the High Street there was no way out of Pinner which did not involve crossing a stream somewhere. Bridges were expensive to build and maintain and the lord usually accepted those on the public highway as his responsibility, though the villagers might have to press him hard to get the work done. All those in Pinner were likely to have been footbridges.

6 Rayners Lane c.1925, looking north from about Village Way, the ancient way from Pinner to Roxeth between the great common fields. Those shown were created at enclosure, 1803-17, the one further left being called Rayners Field in 1856. Daniel Hill's cottage for his workers shows through the trees.

The fording place at the foot of Pinner Street was wide, with space for a footbridge and a water splash for the passage of carts; even today buses can easily turn around at this spot. This, the town bridge, was first mentioned in 1451 as Elebrigge, which had developed into Yell Bridge by the early 16th century. Yell may come from the Old English word *ea* meaning river or water, which sometimes took the form of *eye* or *yeo*. Uxbridge Road had three bridges in May 1397, all in disrepair. Tannebrigge was just opposite Woodhall Gate, where the Pinn coming from the east joined a branch from the north to cross rushy land once called Tan Reading, now intersected by Woodridings Avenue. Berrypond bridge crossed a weir near the north of Paines Lane. Further east was Lowesbrygge (by Cornwall Road), alongside a field on the south which was called Lewces. Moryesbrygge in Moss Lane (1394) was probably identical with Leggersbrygge (1397) which stood near a lane (Little Moss Lane) leading to Lodge Field in Pinner Park. A bridge in Paines Lane was mentioned in 1572. A bridge in the marsh near West End Avenue was in poor state in 1574. Brokebrige (1468) was possibly at Hooken Green on the road to Harrow.

GREENS AND WOODS

A green was waste land used as common pasture. Many formed at road junctions, where plenty of space was allowed for backing and turning. The corners were rounded off by people and traffic and the remaining grass-covered area at the centre was called a green. All the hamlets had them, but they disappeared at the enclosure of Harrow and the only ones to be seen today are Tookes Green, originally Nower Green, whose formation is clearly preserved by the modern roadway, and a patch at the top of Waxwell Lane.

Hooking (Hooken) Green was not associated with any hamlet. It formed around the crossing point of the Yeading where it turned westward at modern North Harrow, forming a corner or hook. By the middle of the 17th century (1653) two acres had been made into a field called Hooken Green Close, which had grown to ten acres by 1810, and whose outline is today marked by Canterbury, Durham and Pinner Roads.

Most of the woodland had been felled by 1600, much of it in creating Woodhall Manor. Between Woodhall and Weald Common east of Rowlands Avenue was Woodridings, an equally large area also exploited for its timber during the 14th and 15th centuries. Its last remnant was Galport Grove, a five-acre grove of wood in the hands of Thomas Bird in 1616, but merely arable and meadow when he sold it eight years later. (The grove lay between Royston Park Road and Oxhey Lane Farm.) A wide strip bordering the county boundary was cleared by assarting, which is to say that it was let in freehold parcels to villagers, usually head tenants, for cultivation. Pinnerwood House, belonging to John Reading, began on one of these. Pinner Wood lay south of these and west of Woodhall, and was steadily eaten away from the south by the enlargement of Pinner Common.

Villagers were entitled to collect firewood, which was normally fallen wood, furze and bracken. No one was entitled to cut timber or any sort of wood without the lord's licence, but that did not stop a few from trying. John Ponder, who lived beside the park, felled four oaks the size of rafters in Pinner Wood in 1419; Gilbert

Downer and William Edlin made off with two cartloads of wood from Galport in 1421; in 1430 Thomas Neele, who had a head tenancy at the site of 32 West End Lane, felled an elm on the common, and John Downer took a cartload of brushwood from Woodriding in 1434. All were fined.

THE HAMLETS OF PINNER

The names of the Pinner hamlets were wholly topographical. End means a part or end of the main settlement. Hatch End derives from *hach*, the medieval word for gate or entrance, in this instance the chief way into Pinner Park, which was at the point where the footpath to the railway bridge leaves Chantry Place. Wood Lane End was the 17th-century name of the large green where Waxwell Lane joined Wood Lane; part is now ocupied by the police station and the *Oddfellows Arms*.

A few houses still survive in the hamlets. The major early buildings are listed in Appendix 1, and the following notes give the findings of the persons most likely to have built those still surviving.

East End Farm Cottage at East End was built by Roger of Eastend, head tenant, owner 1450 to 1497. Elizabeth Reading probably converted the open hall in readiness for the marriage of her son Richard in 1569 (see section on medieval

7 About 1500 East End Farm, a hall house, would have looked much like this Edwardian view. The chimneys and porch were added about 1600, and the brick infilling and window frames would be late 18th- or early 19th-century. There is a haystack at the rear.

houses for explanation). Tudor Cottage is on the site of Readings head tenement. Much of this house consists of genuine pieces brought from elsewhere in the 20th century, though whether any of it was in Pinner in 1592, the date on the chimney, is open to question.

Wood Lane End has three survivors in Waxwell Lane. William Street's head tenement, 18a/22a, has remnants of a smoke bay house built by him (owner 1519-26), or his son John, whose dates are not known. Orchard Cottage, a sub-tenancy dating from the time of John and Roger Durrant, 1510-58, also has a smoke bay. Bee Cottage, another sub-tenancy, was the work of Richard or John Ferne, owners 1572-1625, or of Richard Aylward, 1625-40.

At Nower Hill, Gardiner's head tenement is marked by Elmdene in Church Lane, which may contain work of about 1600. Bay House in Church Lane was built by Joseph Stanbrough about 1650, a sub-tenancy of Pinner House and a good size for a sub-tenancy.

At West End, Sweetmans Hall dates from the time of Henry Nicholas, head tenant, owner 1586-1611, or his son Thomas. Letchford House at Hatch End, a freehold sub-tenancy created by the Edlin family, is certainly the equivalent of a head tenant's, and similar in age to Sweetmans Hall. At Bury Pond Hill stands Moss Cottage, a sub-tenancy of Estends, the work of Robert Lawrence, owner 1584-1629.

A couple of survivors were never in a hamlet. Waxwell Farm (The Grail) at the north end of Waxwell Lane, was built by James Finch, owner 1598-1629, a member of the Mercers' Company. Pinnerwood House is a freeholder's house built about 1600 by the Leigh family, owners 1465-1734.

THE HIGH STREET

In the beginning there was no high street filled with buildings but just a lane linking a cluster of houses at the top of the slope with the river crossing at the foot.

The hamlet of Pinner on the side of its hill of origin had three head tenements and two freeholds ranged around the junction of Paines Lane, High Street and Church Lane. One freehold named Paynes bordered Paines Lane. Pinner House in Church Lane marks the other, called Strudlers in the 16th century. Of the head tenements, Blakes, Gulls and Rowheds, the house of Blakes still stands, called Church Farm and dating largely from the early 16th century.

At the foot, where five lanes met at the river crossing, two head tenements (Streets and Bowrings) and several sub-tenancies formed a hamlet focused upon the junction. Only the late 15th-century no.6 survives, just one wing of the original, but enough to show that the house faced Marsh Road, not the High Street, with a garden stretching back along the High Street to include the site of no.16.

The lane between the upper hamlet and the river is wide at top and bottom as was the case with road junctions, and narrows in the middle as both parts tail back towards each other. It gradually filled with houses and by the early 15th century was the most highly populated part of Pinner. It was called Pinner Street in 1421, and comprised the stretch from Blackgates in Church Lane to the end of Love Lane. In the 17th century it was called Pinner Town. Every house was formed out of the five head tenements and two freeholds already mentioned except for a shop built on the green or waste in front of the church, site of 58 High Street. The houses had no more than a garden attached, though the occupants usually had a few strips in the fields and either practised a craft or trade or were labourers.

Given the prime position of St John's church on the hill of Pinner's origin, there may have been a chapel of some sort there from very early times, though it is more likely that it reflected Pinner's growth. Surrounded as it is on three sides by the two freeholds, like a nut is held in a spanner, it is distinctly possible that the site was

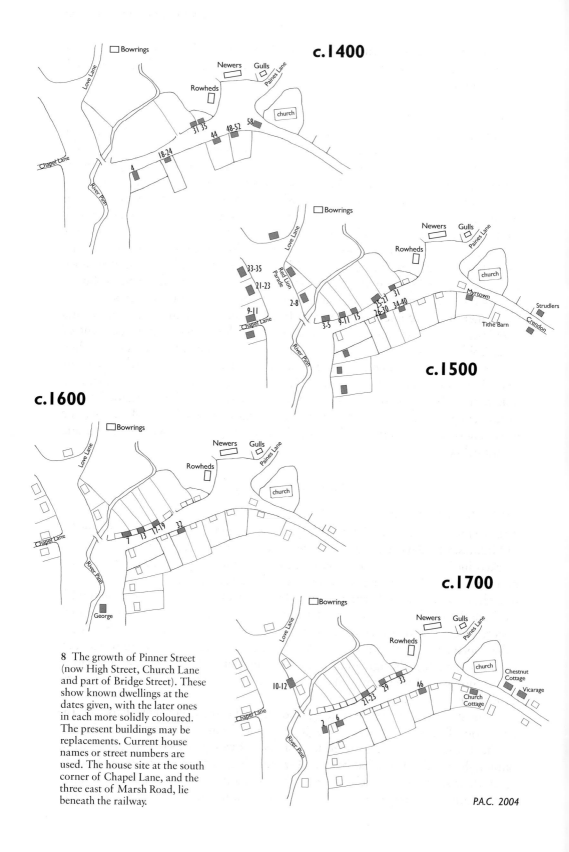

8 The growth of Pinner Street (now High Street, Church Lane and part of Bridge Street). These show known dwellings at the dates given, with the later ones in each more solidly coloured. The present buildings may be replacements. Current house names or street numbers are used. The house site at the south corner of Chapel Lane, and the three east of Marsh Road, lie beneath the railway.

P.A.C. 2004

given by one of them, which would also explain why the site is so small. This was not uncommon practice but unless more documents come to light the question will not be solved.

THE PRE-EMINENCE OF PINNER

The creation of Woodhall had a powerful and formative effect upon Pinner. Here was a great endeavour, needing labour over a long period of time to clear the wood and then more for cultivation – surely a major cause of the expansion of Pinner, and probably of nearby Weald also. There was plenty of space in Pinner for newcomers or younger sons to be granted fresh customary holdings in return for labour services at Woodhall. The new demesne work-place exerted a magnetic pull on the direction of the roads leading northwards from the village centre, where the customary dwellings were, drawing the ends of Moss, Paines and Waxwell Lanes towards its entrance in Uxbridge Road. The 357 acres of Woodhall, first mentioned 1236, were probably cleared between 1086 and 1285, and its field names show a remarkable continuity until the 19th century, when its area was 358 acres.

Pinner had become the largest village in Harrow manor in acreage and population – a sample survey of the court rolls shows that over 20 per cent of households can be considered as resident here (see Appendix 3). Pinner also had the largest amount of demesne in the manor. That Pinner had its own chapel by 1240 showed that even then it was the leading village in the manor. (A chapel at Tokyngton, the smallest settlement, had almost certainly been founded as the private chapel of the person who owned practically the whole of Tokyngton, and it was suppressed in 1547.) And in 1336 Pinner was granted a weekly market and an annual fair.

Getting a Living

THE AGRICULTURAL SYSTEM

The essential, almost the defining, occupation of a medieval villager was husbandry. In Middlesex land was cultivated by open-field farming in common, where villagers worked individual strips within large fields. In order to plough the fields it was necessary to pool the expensive equipment of the heavy plough and its team of six to eight oxen, and after harvest everybody's livestock was turned onto the stubble to share the invaluable animal feed and shed the equally valuable manure which resulted. Fences and hedges were inconvenient within such fields so they have been called open fields. With constraints like shared plough teams and common stubble-feeding controlling the agricultural round, operations and the crops grown had to be harmonised. Agriculture was a communal affair so the fields were said to be worked in common.

The strip in the field was long and thin, the most efficient shape for the procession-like plough team. Ploughing action formed it into a ridge. Within the fields the strips were grouped into shots or furlongs which were bordered by unploughed pathways called balks, allowing villagers to move about the fields to reach their strips. Each one's share of the common fields was made up of many strips scattered among the shots. In this way each had his share of good and bad

9 Pinner Village Gardens used to be part of Middle Field, and the ridges and furrows here may be medieval. Compton Rise is in the background. Photographed 1986.

soil, near and distant strips. Entitlement to use meadow, pasture and wood was commensurate with the allocation of arable land. Meadow provided the hay which would keep a few animals, especially the plough oxen, alive through winter and was usually located near a stream.

THE COMMON FIELDS

In Harrow the strip was called a sellion and averaged three-quarters of an acre. Traces of ridges are still to be seen in Pinner Village Gardens, about 15 feet across, straight and low, very likely 18th-century modifications of the medieval strips. Shots, which varied in size, had names but we know only a few vague locations. Thoroughfares in and through the fields needed no name since their primary purpose was to give access to ploughs, teams and carts; the words highway, wayside, greenway and worple way (or bridleway) sufficed.

There were seven common fields, which lay mainly south of the line of Cranbourne Drive, eastward along Lyncroft Avenue, Marsh Road and Pinner Road, and then going southward, roughly opposite Pinner View, as far as Lucas Avenue, and thence westward along Drake Road and Widdecombe Avenue. Nower Field was north of the line. Down, Middle and Long Fields were by far the largest.

Downfield (first mentioned 1316) lay west of Cannon Lane, a modern name for an access road of ancient origin ending short of the Pinner boundary in Roxbourne Park.

Middlefield (1393) lay between Cannon Lane and Rayners Lane, and Longfield (1389) lay east of that. Blakehall Field (1316) lay along the north of Middle and Long Fields and had been incorporated into them by the 16th century. Brancroste

(1547, later Bancroft) lying north of Marsh Road in the area of Cecil Park and The Chase, may have begun as part of Middlefield. Nower Field (1337) was north of Pinner Road, overlaid now by the playing fields of Nower High School, Hillview Gardens and Elmcroft Crescent. Newlands (1390), lying south of Pinner Road from about Melrose Road eastward to the Yeading, suggests by its name an area taken into cultivation later than the rest. Roxborough (1334) straddled the road eastward (the shopping area of North Harrow) and on into Harrow. Hidefield (1337) lay east of Longfield and south of Roxborough, and part of it belonged to Roxeth.

CROPS AND LIVESTOCK

We do not know how comfortable or hungry Pinner families were from year to year. The extreme difficulty of transporting foodstuffs any distance in large quantity made the villager dependent on what he or his neighbours in nearby villages could produce. Those with less than a virgate had little cushion against bad weather, accident, ill health, ineptitude, or even old age, any of which could push a family below the safety margin for a shorter or longer period.

The three-year system of crop rotation was practised. As late as 1601 the manor court ordered that all landholders must observe the rotation of crops 'as they were used to of old', which was set out as – the one year to grow wheat, oats, barley or peas, the next following to grow beans, oats or summer corn, the third year to let the field lie fallow.

The villager's stint, the number of animals he could put on common pasture and woodland, was related to his share in the common fields. In 1529 the sheep stint was five sheep for every acre of meadow and three for every acre of fallow held; in 1539 the stint of John Edlin, probably of Hatch End, was 50, and in 1555 for Thomas Rede of Bowryngs, twenty. But people were always trying to overdo the stint, especially with sheep, whose wool was a profitable commodity. Among the greatest offenders in Pinner were Thomas Bird of Crouchers who overstocked by 200 sheep in 1460, Richard Smyth, probably at Hatch End, 200 in 1532 and 40 in 1550, John Burton of Gulls, 100 in 1547. In September 1532 Thomas Downer and Robert Hatch were pasturing sheep for the vicar of Harrow under their own names – each was fined one shilling and the vicar had to pay £2 for this and similar offences.

The pig was reckoned the primary source of meat for the average villager. Villagers paid one penny per pig annually to the lord, called pannage, for letting swine run in the woods to feed on the beech mast and acorns which were the choicest pig food – collecting the acorns to take home was an offence. However, in 1315 only 52 per cent of the households of Harrow paid pannage for pigs (see Appendix 3). The leaders in Pinner were Emma at Parkgate in Hatch End with 13, neighbour Roger Elis with seven, John at Nore with six. The lord's demand for timber, particularly 'for the building of the college of the lord Henry Chichele at Oxford' (All Souls), progressively despoiled the woods so that there was nothing for the pigs after 1447 and the lord lost this source of income.

OTHER OCCUPATIONS

Even in a small community like Pinner there were a few who derived a part of their livelihood from other occupations, meeting the needs of those who lacked the special skills or facilities to make certain goods, or bringing in goods which could not be produced locally. There was always a baker in Pinner, and a butcher, a cobbler and a smith, often a victualler (for salt, spices, cheese, dried fruit, candles) and often a tailor. They usually had workshops in Pinner Street. Space permits only a few to be mentioned.

John Mogge and Walter Joliffe, bakers, were both fined in 1316; John Ponder, butcher, was selling rotten meat in 1421. Members of the Downer family were butchers for most of the 15th century, some living at 25-7 and others on the site of 42-46 High Street. John Gardiner was the first known victualler in 1420. Thomas Downer, victualler 1445-69 at the site of 46-54 High Street, also had some sort of cookshop. (It has been impossible to clarify the full relationships and ramifications of the Downer family.) Two generations of Edrops and Danbys kept Pinner in shoes and leather goods. John Edrop the younger was at 18-24 from 1468-74. William Danby owned cottages at 5-7, 18-24 and 31 High Street, though which was his workshop is a matter of guesswork. John Alverych was a weaver in 1419, perhaps at Muggs in Marsh Road. Among the tailors were John Edlin and Richard Edlin, probably related, who were round about 44 High Street in 1424-26. Richard Lane was the smith for a quarter of a century or so from 1440, situated in Marsh Road by the hill to the station. William Chamberlain had a smithy there in 1508.

The most widely sold commodity in the manor was ale. There were several alehouses in Pinner, and John Whash had something like an inn at 9-11 High Street in 1398. Lots of people brewed for sale and they were up to all the dodges. They used uncertified measures, or refused to let them be tested (Richard Smyth 1436), they overcharged (John Lynde 1422), sold lower grade as higher (William Danby 1425), sold without putting up the customary sign of the alehoop (John Danby 1419), sold after the sign was taken in (all of them in Pinner 1417), or refused to sell (Isabella Whash 1397). Richard Tanner (of Harrow Weald) adulterated his ale with filthy water from the ditch by his door in 1422.

Two Pinner men were named as millers between 1468 and 1478, Henry Whitberd (4 High Street) and Thomas Downer. Since the lord owned all mills they would have managed one of his, though the only ones recorded were a windmill on Harrow Hill and a watermill at Alperton.

Villagers with insufficient land to keep their families would have done paid work for more well-endowed neighbours, or for the lord, on the land, in the woods, on building sites or in the chalkpits.

Pinner had one mineral resource – chalk. It was needed for conditioning soil, and to make mortar and lime wash for buildings. It also contained bands of flint nodules, a difficult but usable building material. The chalk was close to the surface at the north end of Waxwell Lane, where it was quarried until exhausted sometime in the Tudor period, the activity over the centuries probably being steady and small in scale. The place was called the Marlpits and was probably worked by, or under licence from, the lord. The flint for St John's Church may well have come from here. The bumpy site is today filled by The Dell, and the uneven grounds of The Grail.

For a short and indeterminate period in the 13th century some itinerant potters set up in Potter Street Hill, where the remains of a kiln, cooking pots, bowls and jugs in South Hertfordshire greyware were found in 1975 during the construction of Potters Heights Close.

THE MARKET AND FAIR

There were a few alesellers and an occasional baker or butcher in other parts of the manor, but only Rectory Manor had a similar range of suppliers to Pinner. Both places were granted a weekly market and an annual fair – Rectory in 1261, Pinner in 1336 – and were well placed to serve the two sides of the manor. The other nearest markets were at Uxbridge, Watford and London.

King Edward III's grant in 1336 licensed 'one market each week on Wednesday at [the] manor of Pynnore ... and two fairs there each year ... one that is on the vigil and the morrow of St John the Baptist and the other on the day and the morrow of the Beheading of St John the Baptist ... in perpetuity.'[5] No further reference to Pinner market has been found since the day it was granted, and none to the fair – only the first one flourished – until the 18th century. The Harrow market lasted until the late 16th century, and its fair until 1872.

The top of the present High Street would have been the logical site for market and fair. The market offered local people an outlet for their surplus produce, and if it flourished would have attracted buyers and sellers from outside. A fair differed in being an annual or half-yearly event, attracting a wider range of goods and more

10 The High Street had seen more than 560 fairs by the time of this one in 1900. (The house at the extreme left is the bank, and next to it is the post office, run for more than 25 years by Robert Rowe.)

customers, and usually including some festivity. It was normally held on the day of the village's patron saint, in Pinner's case, John the Baptist, 24 June. The date was altered before1831, when a poster showed that it was held on the Wednesday after Whitsun.

WOMEN IN PINNER

Women were a large and important part of the agricultural force. They seldom traded in their own right, however, except as brewers or alewives. A female could inherit land in Harrow in the absence of male heirs, though on marriage it went to her husband, yet by the end of the 15th century it was usual to re-register it in their joint names.

The responsibility for office was associated with the property a man held, but, though there were several occasions when the tenant was female, no woman took public office until the 16th century. The first woman considered was Alice Newe of Blakes in Pinner, nominated in 1479 as reeve, no less, though passed over for a man. She was not merely the widow of a tenant, but had inherited it from her father John Blake in 1435, and must have been 60 years old or more. In 1515 Isabel Cosyn (residence unknown) became the first woman to hold office in Harrow manor when she was sworn in as beadle, and again in 1516. Agnes Canon of Alperton was beadle in 1528 and on four subsequent occasions, and became the first female reeve in 1541. Margaret Tanner of Dorsetts in Weald was reeve in 1545. All were probably widows.

For a short period each of the demesne farms of Pinner was in the hands of a widow, and then the second husband took over the lease until the eldest son came of age. At Pinner Park it was a little different because the deputy parker's unmarried daughter, Amy Bird, kept the lease after her father John died about 1555.

And while a woman was not regarded as a person in law, being incompetent to take any legal action, there was never any reluctance to take her to court for misbehaviour, as court records show. Only occasionally did her husband have to answer for her, as we shall see in the case of Hugh Elis' wife.

The Lord and the Outside World

RELATIONSHIPS WITH THE LORD

His Grace the Archbishop of Canterbury was one of the greatest magnates in the kingdom, a member of the king's council, often the holder of one of the high offices of state. It is no surprise, then, to find him living a life of constant travel, accompanied by a huge retinue of servants and secretaries and needing many manors to provide his income. His preoccupations seldom allowed him to make his presence felt in Harrow. Though some archbishops stayed at Headstone Manor, after 1344 Pinner residents would have had little chance to see their lord in person. His steward managed the manor.

The calamitous famines and pestilences of the 14th century, particularly the Black Death, sharpened resentment against having to perform labour services. The culmination was the Peasants Revolt of 1381. From Kent the uprising spread quickly through the south-eastern counties to London. In June the rebels snatched the chancellor, who was Simon of Sudbury, Archbishop of Canterbury, and the treasurer, Sir Robert Hales, from the Tower of London and beheaded them. In doing so they killed the lord of the Manor of Harrow.

What was the reaction of his tenants in Harrow? We do not know. They had already been excited enough to fall back on one of their favourite protests against the lord – trespassing in Pinner Park, for which the king instituted an enquiry, the archbishop being dead. One of the three commissioners was Thomas Pynnor, possibly of the Manor of Pynnors.[6] They may also have destroyed some court rolls, for a tenant of Rectory said in 1391 that the 1348 record of his copyhold 'was burnt in the time of discord', and there are indeed many big gaps in the 14th-century rolls of Harrow and Rectory manors. Richard Taillour of Harrow on the Hill was excluded from the general pardon of rebels. He cannot be properly identified so we shall never know whether he was a local ringleader or, which is more likely, had joined the trouble in London and been arrested there.

The court rolls hint at the mood prevailing during the 14th century. In May 1337 three tenants, who had married their daughters to free men without first having the lord's licence, were fined heavily. This particular fine, merchet, was one of the most hated signs of bondage. The offenders included John Swetman of Pinner who married his daughter to William Elis. The Swetmans were associated with two head tenements, Sweetmans Hall and another at East End, and the Elises were at Hatch End.

After the revolt tenants still pushed against the limits but the new archbishop and lord, William Courtenay, tried to reimpose his rights and keep the old system going, which had been slackening. Regarding unauthorised marriage, for instance, John Clerk was fined in 1385 for marrying Petronilla Duke, who stood to inherit land in Roxeth; Roger Marsh married off two daughters – Joan in 1385, and Alice in 1386 – the latter to someone outside the manor, which was very reprehensible. All the offenders were men of substance, either head tenants or from head tenant families – Marsh was head tenant of Gulls and owned much other land – people whom their neighbours would have respected.

At the same time there was a flurry of activity to find several men from Pinner, Weald and Roxeth who had left the manor without licence. From Pinner Roger Ball and John Schrobbe were called for in 1383. Roger Ball, holder of the virgate called Clobbes (in Chapel Lane), was never heard of again, and his son was allowed to take over his land. Two other absentees were being sought in 1386. The usual arrangement was for absence to be allowed in return for an annual payment and an annual report to the manor court.

Other lordly privileges continued to weigh upon the tenants. Roger at Dell was charged with using fishing nets in the lord's water – fishpond? moat? – at Pinner in 1462. In 1465 Thomas Smith, Richard Edlin, Roger Downer, and John Blackwell, all of the Hatch End area and all head tenants, or of such families, were fined for keeping greyhounds and hunting dogs, and Blackwell's dogs were to be put into the lord's pack. The message was clear – hunting was not a pursuit for yeomen or peasants and all game belonged to the lord. Digging for gravel or sand or chalk had to be paid for; Hugh Smith was fined in 1435 for having taken an unlicensed cartload of stones away from Pinner pond three years before. Yet when the lord, in the shape of his farmer, offended in the same way as any villager, with foul ditches for instance, there was no pressure the tenants could bring to bear.

WOODHALL, PINNER PARK AND HEADSTONE

By 1400 the archbishop was leasing his big estates to local men from the yeoman families. The lessee (or farmer) was expected to live on site, and to provide hospitality to the archbishop's officials when they came to take account.

At Woodhall the lessees came from the Street or Edlin families of Pinner. The earliest part of the present house there was probably built after the archbishop's time and contains an elegant late Tudor brick fireplace.

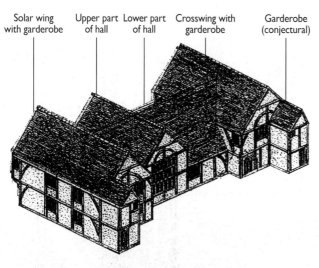

11 Pinner Park Farm with its moat, shown in A. Bowen's map of 1634. This was probably the original site of the keeper's lodge.

Pinner Park was a deer park, a luxury with which only a wealthy lord could indulge himself. It was not a hunting ground or chase, but a reserve to keep deer safely until the lord wanted some sent up for his table, or had them loosed into the countryside to be hunted. First mentioned in 1273, the park was enclosed by a bank and a double ditch, and at 250 acres was above the average reserve size of 200 acres.[7]

| Solar wing with garderobe | Upper part of hall | Lower part of hall | Crosswing with garderobe | Garderobe (conjectural) |

It formed a huge blockage isolating Hatch End from Pinner, a demesne closed to the inhabitants, who were obliged to go around it, for the path across its middle was gated and not for their convenience. They were regarded as potential trespassers or marauders.

The post of Keeper of Pinner Park was a perk given to an absentee holder – in 1383 it was the Abbot of Westminster – who appointed a deputy to do the real work, most deputies coming from the Pinner yeoman family named Bird.[8] There was a lodge where the deputy would have lived. A moat

12 The rear, or island side, of Headstone Manor is thought to have looked like this in the 14th century. The solar wing, upper part of hall, and garderobe are gone.

would have been sensible for keeping deer away, and the moated house shown at the centre in the map of 1634 had probably been the lodge. There were fishponds to provide fresh fish for the lord's table, situated where the Pinn leaves the park at Moss Close. Their earthworks are still discernible amongst the trees.

Headstone had belonged in about 1240 to Ailwin de la Hegge who derived his name from it – Heggeston is one of its early spellings, meaning an enclosed homestead. It had been twelve years in the hands of Robert de Wodehouse, a churchman in royal service, when Archbishop John Stratford bought it in 1344 and made it his Middlesex residence. In other respects it became demesne like Wood-hall, and its farmer always came from the Reading family of Pinner.

Headstone contains a marvellous group of medieval buildings. It has part of the oldest timber-framed dwelling house in Middlesex, which the technique of tree-ring dating puts at just before Wodehouse's purchase, a remarkable survival. It also has the third oldest and largest barn in Middlesex, and the only complete moat. We know that Simon Langham was at Headstone in 1367, ordaining deacons in the chapel, and probably Thomas Arundel in 1407, and Henry Chichele in 1434, when the manor court met there.

The house is of the open-hall type though only the hall and one two-storeyed cross wing are left (see Medieval Houses). The rafters of the hall are black to this day with the soot deposited from the medieval hearth. The house was very much larger, and had ancillary buildings including a detached kitchen, chapel, and dovecote. All these would have stood within the moat, whose chief purpose was to convey status and give some seclusion to the house. Stables, barns and a gatehouse formed

13 Headstone Manor House (then Moat Farm) and the great barn in 1927, drawn by Stanley R. Shepherd.

an approach courtyard west of the moat. Headstone Manor's large dimensions and moat confirm it as a house of high status built by someone wealthier than the yeomen and occasional London tradesmen to be found in Pinner. The great barn was rebuilt 1505-6 by Richard Boughton, probably the master carpenter of the Canterbury estates, who received £20 for his work 'and all woodworking necessities'. A further £24 11s. 8½d. was spent on wages for two other carpenters, for labourers and for carriage of wood with 'nails, lathes, wedges, tiles, bricks, lime, sand and other necessities'. The timber must have come from the Canterbury estates. The barn was never called a tithe barn before the 20th century, simply because the archbishop was not entitled to the tithes.

THE OUTSIDE WORLD

People were much more mobile in medieval times than is often supposed despite the restrictions, as the spread of surnames within neighbouring settlements shows. There were, for example, many names common to Ruislip and Pinner, even ignoring occupational names such as Smith and Baker. The most common reason lay in the need to find marriage partners, with its consequent movement and mixing of families. Pinner people travelled outside the manor to attend markets and fairs no doubt, and people came into Pinner for business, like aleseller John of Ruislip in 1334, and John Janyn of Uxbridge, baker in 1430.

Heirs, especially if female, might be far afield. Christine, one of William Croucher's heiresses, had married Stephen Godfrey, a member of the Founders' Company in London. The Londoners who occasionally owned land in Pinner were a mixture of relatives deriving from departed daughters, like Stephen Godfrey, or younger sons made good, or investors – freeholds were attractive to outsiders, having few manorial encumbrances, and were perhaps beyond the means of local people.

With two exceptions we know little but the names of investors. William Smith, ironmonger, owned the large freehold estate at Hatch End which later became Parkgate. His son John followed him into the Ironmongers' Company, while another son, Richard, was established as a smith on family land in Marsh Road near the foot of the High Street in 1440. Simon Sewale acquired Crouchers head tenement about 1415, which he would have let, plus a freehold somewhere near Pinnerwood House, and another called Leonards, covering Elm Park Court and more. Sewale, a member of the Saddlers' Company, had his shop and house close to Saddlers' Hall in Cheapside, and owned cottages and an alehouse called *The Horn* in Aldersgate. He also owned many silver items and several fur-trimmed robes. His failure to remember the church and poor of Pinner in his will suggests he had little contact with Pinner.

From Nuisance to Crime

AT THE MANOR COURT

The manor court was the ultimate arbiter of every local dispute except the most serious, and it was busy.

Arguments over boundaries and trespass predominated. William Aleyn's animals damaged John Reading's corn in 1387 so he had to pay compensation of 20s., though it took eight years to get it out of him; Robert Knyff did not like it when William Lowys ploughed up some of his land in spring 1398; Richard Rede and Richard Clerk cut and took away some of William Canon's wheat in 1478. (It went on – in 1524 George Canon's cart crushed some of his neighbour's wheat; and nobody liked it in 1591 when John Ferne ploughed up part of the greenway in Downfield.) The 14th-century peasant who admitted, in William Langland's *Piers Plowman*, that 'if I went to the plough I pinched so narrowly that I would steal a foot of land or a furrow ... and if I reaped I would over reap' seems to have been typical.

Claims of debt were plentiful, too, revealing that villagers were using money quite readily, that there were commercial transactions between them and with outsiders, and that goods were being purchased in London and produce being taken there for sale. Memories were long. In 1394 John Reading sued Richard Roxeth, who lived opposite Pinner church, for a 15-year-old debt. Next month Roxeth counter-claimed for two debts owed by Reading, one 12 years old, the other thirty. Some cases were tangled. On the Monday after Whitsun 1433, Agnes Bowryng went to the land of William Marsh, removed two horses and took them back to her place called Bowryngs, in Love Lane. They belonged to Richard Edlin, who owed Agnes rent for a property in the marsh called Huchens, and she had taken them in lieu. Edlin went round to Bowryngs and took them away again. Agnes sued for her rent plus damages but Richard said the rent was overstated. The court ruled in 1435 that Richard had retrieved the horses illegally and must pay something to Agnes.

Petty inconveniences escalated into nuisances. The most common by far was the blocked drainage ditch, high among the offenders being the lord himself. Obstruction of the highway was close behind, with heaps of dung, timber and so on often kept outside the house front. Then there were dogs, not pets but savage creatures to beware of, used to control stock and guard the homestead. Richard Peryman, head tenant of Woleyes at Hatch End, had a dog 'which bites everyone' in 1427, and in 1474 William Canon's vicious hound repeatedly went for the neighbour's sheep. Canon was at Canons. The dogs had to be put down.

Rowdiness was an offence and alesellers needed to watch out for it. Thomas Downer was fined in 1457 for allowing carousels on his premises at unlawful times. John Derewyn in Church Lane was summoned for harbouring 'players at dice and cards and other illegal games' in 1489. John and Cecily Kediar were to be evicted from their cottage opposite the chapel in 1467 because they harboured people of evil reputation.

PETTY VIOLENCE

Assault upon the person which drew blood was a crime and was penalised by a fine. Alan Rede, aleseller, was trouble, fined on four occasions for assault. In 1487 three people assaulted John at Vern in the course of his duties as aletaster, an offence which seems surprisingly uncommon. Richard Eastend took a weapon to Richard Blackwell in Pinner in 1498, and Thomas Body, an aleseller, ganged up with Henry Bird against John Clerk in 1504, slashing Clerk's hand with a short-sword during the commotion. Women were involved now and then. In 1337 John Alverych injured William Edlin's wife Ellen; Alice Crudde was assaulted by Alice Downer in 1383; in 1394 Alice Ponder clouted William Newman – she lived by the river where High

Street meets Bridge Street and he had a cottage near Canons. Though there were many more offences than these, their relative number was small, and Pinner was a peaceful place.

SERIOUS OFFENCES

Crimes were occasionally committed and no doubt provided excitement and horror at firesides and in alehouses. These cases were dealt with in the king's court, but the resulting conviction was reported at the manor court and then the lord was entitled to seize the convict's chattels, though not his land. Of 17 cases noted between 1315 and 1470 one was a murder, two were theft, ten were described as felony, while four were not characterised at all. Some of the culprits were from Pinner. It is a great pity that the records give never a hint of the passions behind the crimes, the wrongs, animosity, envy or poverty which provoked them.

The murder was the earliest, 1315, but was not a Pinner affair. Hugh Rede of Pinner and John Canon were hanged the same year, though the cause is not stated, and their crops were sold. Walter Crouch was convicted – for what? – at the Middlesex sessions, and in May 1337 his half-acre of beans fetched 15d. for the lord. There was a family named Brown in Pinner when Nicholas Brown was hanged in 1398. His goods were listed in 1399 as: a black horse, a sow, four pigs, one-and-a-half sheaves of oats, beans, hay, a pot, a woollen hide, a coverlet and pair of linen sheets, total worth 37s. 6d.

William Paltok, a Pinner victualler of five years' standing, committed a crime and took flight in 1425, leaving behind him a red bay horse and eight pigs. His place of business has not been identified. In 1425 four men were arrested in Pinner

14 St John's church before the churchyard wall was built in 1869. In 1880 the dormers were changed and a niche was discovered above the porch door. The wooden headboards have not survived.

on suspicion of felony and imprisoned in Windsor Castle – William Downer, Herman Dutchman, William Rowhed and John Roberd. Dutchman and Rowhed had no goods. Downer had a brown cow, three acres of land sown with wheat, 12 with beans, plus six bushels of wheat; Roberd had three acres sown with wheat, one with beans, one with hay, and a pot. Downer and Rowhed were from head tenant families, not the sort one would expect to be involved in crime. William Cok departed from Pinner at great speed in 1457 having apparently committed a felony, and his house at West End was seized.

The most detailed case was that of John Morgan, who lived on the site of 18-24 Pinner High Street, and was accused of robbing John Edrop in 1468. Roger Estend arrested him but Morgan escaped. Morgan was rearrested, and while in the custody of the Pinner constable Henry Estend, was pressured against his will to make his house over to Edrop. The lord's steward confiscated the property on the grounds of Henry Estend's deception, and fined Roger Estend for bungling the arrest. Morgan was hanged – probably at Newgate. His sister Christian claimed the cottage as the next heir but never came to court to receive it, so in 1473 it was granted to John Edrop. The matter was ended.

The fruits of crime were forfeit to the lord as deodand. So was any object which caused death, though the proceeds of this were applied to charity. In 1423 Roger Webbe's daughter Joan drowned in a large bowl of mead, so the bailiff took the offending vessel as deodand. Roger Webbe lived somewhere on the north side of the High Street; shortly after the tragedy he acquired Copped Hall (site of 25-7). In 1518 the young son of Thomas Rede died in an accident with a cart pulled by four horses, all of which became deodand. If fully exacted, that must have been a heavy financial blow to whomsoever was the owner. The Redes probably lived on the site of 46-52 High Street.

The Church of St John the Baptist

A CHAPEL FOR PINNER

The church played an important part in people's lives. First and foremost it provided the hope of salvation for a Christian population, so attendance would have been pretty regular despite backsliding. The most significant rites of passage took place there – baptism, marriage and burial. It also provided many occasions for relaxation or celebration, whether at the great feasts of Christmas and Easter, with Lent, and Whitsun, or the day of its patron saint.

St Mary's on Harrow Hill was the parish church for the whole of Harrow Manor. St John the Baptist was a chapel of ease to the parish church, a privilege and convenience for the parishioners of Pinner. The vicar of Harrow was responsible for providing clergy, whether resident or visiting we do not know. It was called the chapel of Pinner, or the chapel of St John at Pinner. The first mention was in 1234-40, when the income of the vicar of Harrow included all oblations and offerings of the chapel of Pinner. It was chosen in 1245 as neutral ground for a legal hearing between the abbot of Bec, who owned nearby Ruislip, and the rector of Great Wratting in Suffolk, and the locals must have watched the comings and goings of the ecclesiastical lawyers with interest.[9]

The first chapel was almost certainly wooden, but even so it would have been the largest, most solid, most impressive building in Pinner. It was rebuilt in stone and on 27 October 1321 the new church was rededicated on behalf of Archbishop Walter Reynolds by Peter, Bishop of Corbavia in Dalmatia, temporarily excluded from his own see because of civil strife.[10] On that day the whole population of Pinner would have been there and much of the rest of Harrow also. All would have gone three times round the church in procession, and watched the bishop strike the west door thrice with his crozier for admittance with the other clergy to perform the rites of consecration. Then the congregation would be welcomed in, bells would be rung and a great mass celebrated; St John the Baptist would be invoked to protect the church and all who worshipped in it. The rest of the day was probably a holiday with social festivities.

THE BUILDING

The church was rebuilt in flint with dressings of ironstone and Reigate stone, and had a long chancel, an aisled nave of four bays, and transepts. Pinner, and its mother church of Harrow, are the only Middlesex churches known to have had this cruciform plan in medieval times. The practice of beginning construction at the east end seems to have been followed at Pinner, for architecturally the chancel and transepts appear to be the oldest parts. The transepts are in the Early English style of the late 13th century, and in 1849 J. Sperling described an Early English triple-lancet window in the south wall of the chancel. The style of the subsequently lengthened chancel and the nave, whose octagonal columns support arches with an inner double-chamfered order, was common in 14th-century parish churches. The broad, battlemented west tower with projecting stair turret and the south porch are typical of the 15th century in Middlesex. The aisle roofs are of late 15th- or early 16th-century date, and the windows were enlarged in the same centuries except for those in the transepts and at the west end of the aisles, though all the glass is 19th-century or later. The octagonal font is 15th-century. The south chancel chapel was added in 1859, and the 20th-century vestry is the latest in a long line of vestries.

BEQUESTS

Such apparently continuous rebuilding could only have been financed by the lord of the manor. Once built, it was the rector's responsibility to maintain the chancel and the congregation's to maintain the rest. Many must have helped with the expenses but we know the names of only a few.

Thomas Neele, a head tenant in West End Lane, died in 1443 leaving £2 7s.8d. 'for the making of a new window in the north of the chancel'. His window could be the west window in the north wall of the chancel, which is 15th-century in style. In 1455 William Marsh, freeholder of land at the corner of Marsh Road and Eastcote Road where The Grove was built, left £1 6s. 8d. for general repair.[11] Avice Clerk of Pinnerwood House left money to repair the books belonging to the chapel in 1472.

Like many a medieval church St John's had altars subsidiary to the high altar, used especially for prayers for the dead – there was one each to the patron saint and to St Christopher. Neele left money for prayers at both Pinner and Harrow, and Marsh left £13 6s. 8d., more than most could afford, enough to last for two years at Pinner.

Some inhabitants bequeathed their property, should they die without heirs, to the chapel wardens to sell and apply the proceeds to the church's work or fabric. Thomas and Petronella Gardiner did this with Gardiners in 1468; similar arrangements by Richard Lane the smith operated after the death of his wife Margaret in 1475; and the head tenement called Alveryches, now West House, also passed through the chapel warden's hands when Joan, the widow of Hugh Dok, died in 1517.

THE CHANTRY

There was no chantry at Hatch End. The vision of a little chantry chapel by the entrance to Pinner Park is based on the ordnance survey map of 1865, which marked The Chantry as a site of antiquity just there. The truth is this. In 1324 William de Bosco, rector of Harrow, set up a chantry in the church of St Mary and endowed it with property to provide rent to pay a priest to sing masses for his soul. It included a freehold tenement at Hatch End. In 1538 the tenement was called The Chantry House. In 1764 it was 'Turners, alias the Chantry House' which can be placed in Uxbridge Road near 151-3, though it had collapsed by 1768. By some error the site of a copyhold sub-tenancy of Woleyes head tenement was marked as The Chantry in 1865 (no.87 on fig.2), and by now several nearby streets commemorate a phantom chantry chapel.

THE TITHE BARN AND CHURCH HOUSE

A large part of the church's income came from tithes, the great majority going to the rector, a few to the vicar. The rector of Harrow had three tithe barns at least, in Wembley, Harrow Weald and Pinner. The Pinner barn, variously called the Tithe, Rectory, Church or Parsonage Barn, stood in Church Lane about opposite the vicarage or Chestnut Cottage. There was also a church house there, available as accommodation for any clergy officiating in the chapel, or for activities such as church ales (a fund-raising activity) or festivals or weddings.

THE CLERGY

Only two of the medieval priests who served Pinner church are known by name. Thomas Neele mentioned 'Sir William, the priest of Pinner' and 'John Whash the clerk', in his will. 'Sir' was a courtesy title for a clergyman or a learned man. William Marsh referred to William Come or Comer, 'chaplain of Pinner'. These two Williams may have been one and the same person.

THE CHURCHYARD

Pinner had its own cemetery, a privilege seldom granted to chapels of ease. Thomas Neele and William Marsh both asked to be buried in it and so would their neighbours have wished for themselves. There, in the soil around St John's church, they all remain.

Medieval Houses

THE 15TH-CENTURY HOUSE

Most of the medieval timber-framed houses which stand today were built by yeomen, that is, substantial farmers, but they are seldom earlier than 1400 because it was only about then that they could afford sufficiently good and lasting materials. The yeoman's house had to provide shelter for one family or household, with space for storage of his produce, while outside there must be out-housing for livestock. In south-east England three rooms was the normal minimum, that is a hall, which was the main living and eating room, and might also be used for cooking, sleeping, and work: a chamber or solar, which offered some privacy for the family, and was normally used for sleeping and storage: and a service room, perhaps partitioned, usable for dairying or storing food and drink. More rooms could be added later.

The hall was the only heated room. In the time before chimneys were built the fire was placed centrally in a room with an opening in the roof to let out the smoke; no upper storey could be placed over this one so the hall was left open to the roof, and this type of house is called the open-hall house. The unheated rooms could be arranged in two storeys, commonly placed at one or both ends of the hall and the house was crossed by a passage between the hall and an end part, giving access back and front and to either side. If there was only one two-storeyed end it normally contained an upper chamber or solar over two service rooms. Kitchens were sometimes built as separate outside structures because cooking over the open fire was dangerous.

THE OLDEST HOUSES IN PINNER

The oldest house in Pinner is Headstone Manor, an early 14th-century house of high status, dealt with more fully in the chapter on The Lord and the Outside World. The next four are more than a century younger. Like Headstone they are open-hall houses with crown-post roofs, though smaller and with fewer rooms as befitted their lesser status. They are East End Farm Cottage, 35 High Street, 4 High Street and 25-7 High Street, all built by yeomen or their near equivalent in the period 1450 to 1520.

Originally each had only one end-wing of two storeys, except for 25-7, which had two and was the most capacious. The walls were of timber and plaster, set on a flint base for dryness, and their roofs were more likely to have been tiled than thatched. All those in the High Street had overhanging upper floors.

East End Farm Cottage, with its cross-passage, staircase, and two service rooms, is the least altered of Pinner's old houses. The most likely builder of 35 High Street was William Stokker, baker, owner 1456-95, when his son of the same name took over. A storeyed cross wing (a wing whose roof is at a right angle to the main roof) containing four more rooms was added in the 17th century and now forms 33 High Street. Henry Whitberd owned 4 High Street from 1459-1504, and is just the sort of person to have rebuilt it – a man of substance – miller, aleseller, and owner of other cottages. Only one wing remains. Roger and then William Downer owned 25-7 High Street from 1475-94, and one or other probably built it. When Roger and

15 The *Victory* actually dates from about 1480. The side and back part, still visible in the snows of 1947, give a good idea of its original front view, facing Marsh Road. Henry Whitberd, miller, probably built it.

his wife Margaret bought it Roger was a butcher and already had the shop opposite the church from which he would have traded. William was not a butcher.

SANITATION

Medieval sanitation was rudimentary. Household rubbish was buried or composted, or, as we have seen, parked at the front. John Whash's customers were not vexed by the whiff of his heap at the front – no doubt they had heaps of their own – but by the obstruction. Higher class houses had internal privies, like Headstone Manor, though the external privy was more usual, placed, it is to be hoped, at the end of the garden. But not in the case of Thomas Downer, accused in 1475 of erecting a stinking latrine by the highway and ordered to take it down before midsummer. As Downer – alehouse keeper, victualler and miller – adjoined Roger Downer's shop and slaughterhouse at 58 High Street, the double stench must have been a knockout.

16TH-CENTURY DEVELOPMENTS

During the 16th century crown-post roofs went out of fashion in favour of clasped-purlin roofs, and improvements were gradually adopted, principal among them the brick chimney. This allowed the hearth to be moved from the centre of the hall to one of its sides and it could be used for cooking with greater safety, while the whole room would be much less smoky. New houses could be built of two storeys throughout with as many fireplaces as means and local expertise could manage.

An intermediate stage between the open-hall and the chimneyed house was the smoke bay house. This was a variation of the open hall in that part of the hall was

16 Bee Cottage was built with two floors and chimneys from the start, probably by John or Richard Ferne in the late 16th century. This picture of 1924 shows it divided into two dwellings. The sliding sash window, top left, was of a type fitted into many cottages about 1800, including the dormer at East End Farm.

floored over, leaving a smaller space at one end open to the roof for the escape of smoke – the smoke bay – with the open hearth placed near that end. It would have resembled an inglenook fireplace, with the smoke bay above working like a huge chimney. An open-hall house could be adapted in this way.

It could also be updated with chimneys. They could be added to an outside wall, but the most popular option was to cut into the roof and insert a brick stack in the hall. The hall could then be divided by a floor into two storeys, which increased the number of rooms. Two hearths set back-to-back in the stack could heat two rooms, and it was not long before one or more hearths were being built into the stack at the upper level as well, offering up to four heated rooms if wished. Most open halls were modified in this way. In Pinner the only hall still open is at Headstone Manor, probably following the fashion of the grand house in keeping its open hall as a gracious entrance or reception room.

No. 9-11 High Street was a 16th-century version of 25-7 High Street, probably rebuilt by William Dodd and his wife Agnes, grand-daughter of Henry Whitberd, when they re-registered it at court in 1523. The Dodds were alehouse keepers.

Church Farm at the top of the High Street is a modified version of 9-11. Here a room was formed in the space above half of the hall, leaving the other half open as a smoke bay. The person most likely to have begun the house was yeoman John Bird, who owned it 1506-36, and it was perhaps his grandson Edmund who added the eastern wing around 1600. Orchard Cottage and 18a/22a Waxwell Lane are smoke-bay houses built about the middle of the 16th century.

Of all these East End Farm Cottage, Church Farm and 18a/22a Waxwell Lane were yeomen's houses, and Orchard Cottage was for a sub-tenant. The building of the others by tradesmen proves that business, allied to some agriculture, could be profitable at the end of the 15th century.

III

The Later Sixteenth and Seventeenth Centuries

Major changes in church and manor

THE REFORMATION

Henry VIII made himself Supreme Head of the Church in England in 1534. With this act he abolished papal control of the church in this country and ushered in the Reformation. Henceforward support of the pope, or any dissent from doctrine approved by the king, became acts of political disobedience. Under Henry, Edward VI and Mary I Catholicism became identified with foreign power, particularly with France and Spain, and remained so for the next few centuries.

Henry VIII interfered very little with doctrine, services or the appearance of churches. However, after his death in 1547 the Privy Council forbade ceremonies such as the Palm Sunday procession, or the use of the Easter Sepulchre, and urged the destruction of images. Chantries and guilds were to be abolished and their assets transferred to the new boy king Edward VI, and in 1551 it was decided to confiscate church plate. Commissioners were sent to each church to organise the seizures.

THE EFFECTS IN THE PARISH

These changes made little noticeable difference in villages like Pinner, and nothing tells us what Pinner people thought about them. They had not spent much in recent years on prayers for their souls because the commissioners found no chantry or guild funds to confiscate. But there were 'two tenements in Pinner churchyard, now in the tenure of William Tompson and Isabell [blank]' which the commissioners could only describe as being 'of unknown purpose'. The tenement rents would originally have been intended to pay for prayers for the donor, quite forgotten by 1547. The cottages stood on William Newman's freeholding, called Paynes, which abutted the churchyard on the north, and were probably the predecessors of either 64 High Street or Chestnut Cottage.

There was no church plate in Pinner when the commissioners visited in August 1552 to list it, not even communion vessels. This was unusual. It probably means that the churchwardens had sold the plate and put the proceeds to parish benefit before it could be confiscated. There were plenty of less valuable items. There were two crosses and one censer of a brass alloy called latten, six bells, including the sanctus bell, and two hand bells. There was an organ, a much smaller instrument in those days than now, and maybe portable. Eleven vestments were listed, half of them old, the others of velvet or silk; six surplices; one satin altar cloth and ten others; three altar cushions and one cross cover, all of silk; two sacrament cloths; six banner cloths and some towels. Two books had survived the Reformation – a bible (by this time in English) and the Paraphrases of Erasmus (a commentary in English on the gospels) which from 1547 every church had to have available for any parishioner to read. There were three old chests to contain everything.

17 This small plank chest at St John's, if original to the church, may have been one of those listed in the inventory of 1552.

Mary I restored Catholicism in England, and at Uxbridge in August 1555 three Protestants were burnt as heretics. People from Pinner may have gone to watch. Though the sufferers did not come from the area the town was chosen as a general warning. In Elizabeth I's reign Catholics were demonised, so the unfolding tragedy of the Bellamy family of Uxendon in Harrow must have fed local fear. The Bellamys were Catholic recusants involved in the Babington plot of 1586 against Queen Elizabeth; some were executed as traitors, some imprisoned.

In Pinner a clergyman's name surfaced for the first time since William Comer's in 1455. Henry Meredith (died 1586) described himself as curate of Pinner when he witnessed the wills of Robert Crowle of Pinner Park in 1564, and James Hukin in 1579. Meredith married, as Elizabethan clergy were allowed to do, and a Pinner widow named Amy Bird became his second wife in 1567. Henry had probably lived in the church house before this, but upon marriage we find the pair jointly owning 25-7 and 33-5 High Street. In 1615 Robert Chamberlayne called himself minister of Pinner when witnessing the wills of John Edlin in 1615 and Allen Nichols in 1617. Chamberlayne had no property and probably lived in the church house.

John Dey, who died in 1622, is commemorated by a tablet in the chancel of St John's church. He had studied at university, which was not always the case with clergymen in those days, and owned some property in Norfolk, which must have helped maintain him in Pinner. Dey did not live in the church house, but lodged with Margaret, widow of Richard Edlin, in her house at Pinner Green called Antoneys.[12]

A NEW LORD OF THE MANOR

The biggest effect the king's changes had upon Pinner was to wrench control of the manor from the archbishops of Canterbury after more than 700 years. Henry VIII's expropriation of monastic property had resulted in the greatest change among land owners since the Norman conquest. When he looked for more spoils, he saw the large ecclesiastical estate of Harrow and Archbishop Cranmer, under pressure, surrendered Harrow and Harrow Rectory Manors to the king on 30 December 1545. Six days later they were bought by Sir Edward North for £7,670. North was Chancellor of the Court of Augmentations, the office which took charge of confiscated lands, and was well placed to assess what was coming in – he had already bought the confiscated Charterhouse in London. Unlike many, he prospered throughout those difficult times. Queen Mary created him Lord North of Kirtling in 1554, and he died twenty years later, still in good standing, in Queen Elizabeth's reign.

The change of ownership should have had little direct affect upon the people of Pinner, apart from providing an absorbing subject for gossip in the alehouses. The manorial organisation remained in place. Harrow was an investment for Edward North just as it had been for the archbishops, and there is no evidence that he ever paid it a visit. He lived at Charterhouse, and at Kirtling Hall in Cambridge.

LORD NORTH'S SURVEY

The chief value of Harrow lay in its rents and in 1547 North commissioned a survey of his new manor. Rather like Domesday Book, it listed the demesne farms and woodlands, with their farmers and rents due, and all the tenants holding directly of him, by freehold, copyhold or wastehold, with the amounts of land and rents due, grouped in the 10 hamlets. The information given about boundaries or neighbours allows the location of some places to be worked out today.

Only 41 people in Pinner held property directly from Lord North in 1547, and they were the only Pinner individuals named in the survey. Twenty had freeholds, 14 had copyholds and seven had both. The majority of householders were not mentioned in the survey, either because their property was rented or bought from the direct tenants – most of the High Street property fell into this category – or because they had no land at all.

Four freeholders had large estates. Roger Edlin had 76 acres along the northern boundary and at Hatch End. Roger Bowerman had the southern part of the former manor of Pynnors or Females, some 56 acres including West End Farm and a house called Females. The rest of Pynnors or Females north to Pinner Green, with a house called Pynnors, plus the Pinnerwood House estate, about 52 acres in all, belonged to John Clerk. Hugh Wright of London had 48 acres, north of Pinner Park and also in the marsh.

Fifteen copyholders held the 20 head tenements. Richard Reading, the farmer of Headstone, had four (Redings, Downers, Canons, Sweetmans) plus another large copyhold called Rawlyns south of Pinner Park, and Francis Bird, the adolescent grandson of Robert, had three (Leonards, Blakes and Estends – usually called Ponders). The accumulation of holdings like this was usually the result of the death of heirs in the wider family. At this time a head tenement consisted of one, two or three closes (or fields) totalling an average of seven acres, with the addition of a variable number of sellions in the open fields.

SIR EDWARD EXPLOITS THE MANOR

North exploited the woodland first. In Pinner he began with Pinner Wood, which covered 120 acres, bounded west and south-west by the later lines of Potter Street Hill, Potter Street and Pinner Hill Road, and south by Latimer Gardens or Jubilee Close. Only 80 acres had trees, mostly 'beech and some oak of forty and sixty years growth', nicely within the age range – 25 to 70 years – at which trees were felled in medieval times. It was leased to Richard Taverner of London in 1550 for 99 years at £10 a year and £66 13s. 8d. down for the value of the timber. Taverner must maintain the supply of timber trees, and probably had to allow common pasture beneath them as in medieval times – beech and oak mast was a favourite with pigs.

Woodriding was leased in perpetuity – in effect sold – in 1552 to William Gerard, probably of Flambards in Harrow, and Bernard Dewhurste. Already it was almost denuded of timber, consisting of 158 acres of land and pasture enclosed by ditches lying between Woodhall and Weald Common. The new owners disposed of it steadily in smaller parcels by similar leases.

The demesne farms took longer to exploit because they all had tenants with long leases, and North let them run their terms.

THE DECLINE OF THE MANOR

The currents of economic change outgrew manorial control. The control of unemployment and the movement of population needed governmental direction and the authority of the Justices of the Peace for enforcement, and only the government could authorise fund-raising to relieve poverty. The Tudor administration chose the parish to carry out legislation, equipped as it was with a designated area and churchwardens, and with a constable of its own or else in the associated manor.

As is to be expected, the manor grew increasingly irrelevant. The court leet, usually called the View of Frankpledge by now, was still held annually, to deal with highways, nuisances, field regulations, assizes of bread and ale and so on, but after 1600 these functions gradually fell into disuse, leaving the manor court as little more than a land registry, of no significance to the increasing numbers of inhabitants who owned no land.

Lord North's descendants neglected even land registration in the 17th century, for they were players on the national scene. Dudley, who became the 3rd Lord North in 1600 at the age of 19, was accounted a man of engaging personality, an ardent participator in court life, and personal friend of Henry Prince of Wales. But he failed to keep as close an eye on the manor as had the archbishop's secretariat and its administrative affairs fell into arrears. No court baron was held for more than ten years from 1618, so that some tenants were without proper title and the lord lost fees. One or two persistent tenants took the trouble to travel to North's London home, Charterhouse, to have a conveyance registered. Eventually Dudley granted the stewardship of the courts of Harrow and Harrow Rectory Manors to Simon Rewse of Headstone for life in October 1629 for a lump sum (unstated) and

40 shillings a year, allowing him to keep the proceeds. At Rewse's first court on 22 October the huge backlog of cases was cleared and his pocket filled with fees. For Pinner alone there were some 72 registrations, with receipts exceeding £90, compared with totals of about £5, £13 and £14 at each of the three succeeding courts.

In granting the fat year to Rewse North was readying the manor for sale. He sold Harrow and Rectory Manors to Edmund Phillips and George Pitt for £13,000 in December 1630. Rewse, having cleaned up, lost no time in selling his lease of the stewardship to them the following month – he needed the money to buy Headstone.

For the former lordship estates were for sale at the same time and the year 1630 would bring new owners to them all. Rewse bought Headstone for what seems an advantageous price, £1,800 2s. 6d.; Woodhall went to William Pennefather of St Martin Orgar parish in the City for £3,443 17s. 6d.; and Pinner Park, together with Roxeth Manor or Place to Thomas Hutchinson and his son John, of London and Canons in Pinner, for £3,156. The manor which Edward North had bought for £7,670 in 1547 fetched a total of £21,400 in 1630, helped by late 16th-century inflation.[13]

None of the long-established families of Pinner could afford to buy but the local men holding leases saw out their term. Richard Nicholas stayed at Woodhall under his 20-year lease dated 1626, while at Pinner Park the old Crowle lease of 1560 still had ten years to run in the hands of the current holder Obadiah Ewer, whom the owner Thomas Hutchinson retained as manager after 1640. Headstone, in contrast, continued to be run by its owners until about 1670.

Pinner Society

THE TOP LAYER

The men at the top of Pinner society had been those who controlled large amounts of land – the demesne farmers, responsible for larger areas than anyone else, the larger freeholders, and the multiple copyholders. Most were resident.

With the ending of ecclesiastical ownership there was greater scope for outsiders to invest in Pinner. In this part of England they had usually been London businessmen or lawyers. At the top of the scale was the city merchant who had held office in his company, maybe as Master, or had served the city as a sheriff, or even as Lord Mayor. This office, with its reward of a knighthood, lifted its holder into the lower ranks of the nobility. Lesser city tradesmen, not aspiring to power or office, sometimes had enough to invest in a smaller way. Land was by far the most popular investment, solidly based and independent of trade, providing an income for the investor's old age or for his widow, and perhaps a springboard into the gentry for his posterity.

The increased interest of outsiders after 1547, and the sale of the demesnes, introduced a new top layer of society to Pinner, its members bringing with them their greater wealth, their wider experience of the world, and their contacts with the high and mighty. Several of the large freeholds changed hands and a new estate was created on Pinner Hill.

HEADSTONE MANOR

At Headstone Richard Reading had a 34-year lease dated 16 June 1535, which in 1553 North extended to 1602. There were 340 oaks and elms of 80 and 100 years' growth on the estate. The west front of the house was extended during the time of Richard (died 1555), or his son Thomas (died 1585), and by the close of the 16th century Headstone was a highly developed house, with ten or more private rooms, offering plenty of accommodation for tenants who were used to town houses. Thomas Malbie from London was the tenant living there in 1598 and at the time of his death in 1599. His father was Arthur Malbie, a city merchant sufficiently well-to-do to be expected to contribute to Lord Leicester's expedition to the Netherlands in 1585. Thomas's occupation is unknown, but he owned many properties in London, including a fine house in Fleet Street, and also in Essex. He was not buried in the family church of St Mary at Hill in the city, so he probably lies in Pinner churchyard, in the parish of his death, where all the registers prior to 1654 are missing. In his will he remembered the poor of Pinner as well as those of St Mary at Hill.

Henry Reding, the younger son of Thomas, was living at Headstone in November 1609, and had probably been running the estate since his father's death, minus the house while Malbie was there, under the lease to 1602.

A new lease of the whole, to run for 21 years from Lady day 1613 was granted in May 1612, this time to Simon Rewse, a member of Lord North's own household. Headstone was the seat of the Rewse family for two generations. In 1621 it consisted of 200 acres of land, 40 acres of meadow, 50 acres of pasture – the second largest property in Pinner, after Woodhall.

Simon Rewse served the North family for many years, as a steward to judge from the tenor of his correspondence with Lord North in 1604, which deals with North's Brocket Hall estate in Hertfordshire – audit, debts (including rents at Harrow), sale of woodland etc. At Christmas he wrote 'there hath been little company but the neighbours and tenants, which could not be avoided' – alas for such tedium! In an undated letter he reported the purchase of (?)two pounds of tobacco for North, 'the best that I could get with the help of those that have skill in it ... It cost me 32 shillings'. This must have been a London errand to include such a fashionable luxury. Whether he continued in this position while at Headstone is not known. The grant of the Stewardship of Harrow in 1629 was a separate matter.

This was probably the Simon Rewse who married Alicia Penifather in 1598 at Bayford, Herts., some seven miles from Brocket Hall.

18 Simon Rewse probably provided this early 17th-century settle, built into the panelled wall of the great hall at Headstone Manor. This picture was taken in 1980.

Dudley and Frances North were honoured in the name of their first two sons Dudley and Francis, the latter baptised at St Mary's Church, Harrow, in 1612. Once at Headstone the children were probably baptised in Pinner, not at Harrow, and Simon chose to be buried in Pinner. In 1622 he gave the Pinner churchwardens a new account book, which still survives.

Rewse had managed to extend his lease to 1651. On 1 December 1630 he bought the estate outright for £1,800 2s. 6d., then described as the manor and manor house and farm of Headstone with outhouses, dovehouse, barns, stables, gardens, orchards, plus a field called Cockhills field. The unexpired term of 21 years perhaps accounted for the low price he paid.

When he died in June 1638 Rewse had three adult sons, Dudley, Francis and Simon, and a late fourth, whom he called 'my poor little Tom', by his second wife Ann. She had been the widow of John Burnell of Great Stanmore. Ann was to have the use of the whole house for three months, and then exclusive use of one wing and common use of the hall with the sons. Ann could have the use of any goods in or about the house during her life, and 'all my scarlet and blue velvet chairs and stools' plus, very importantly, 'my carriage with the horses and furniture thereto belonging'. She should have an annuity of £100, plus another £20 if she chose to live elsewhere. Francis and Simon were to receive £400 each, Thomas was to have £1,000 at his majority, and Dudley inherited the manor on condition that he fulfilled the terms of the will. 'To that truly noble man, the Lord North', Rewse left £20, lamenting that he could not afford more. Dropping another big name, he appointed 'my noble friend Thomas Coventry esquire, son and heir apparent of the Right Honorable Thomas Lord Coventry Lord Keeper of the Great Seal of England' as overseer of the will.

Ann soon repaired with her two Burnell daughters and young Tom Rewse to live in Great Stanmore where she had property from her first husband. There Tom stayed, married Mary Norwood in 1666, perhaps a daughter of John Norwood of Tindalls, and died in 1690. Both he and his mother were buried there.

Tom had great difficulty in getting his £1,000 legacy, for his father had placed heavy burdens upon Headstone. Its annual value, or income, was stated – or understated? – in 1646 as £200, yet £120 of it was to be paid to his widow. The legacies, exceeding £1,800, would have to come from sales of land. Dudley Rewse failed in his duties, so the estate devolved upon Francis about 1642.

With Francis came disaster. His involvement with the losing royal side in the Civil War risked his share of Headstone, worth £400, being confiscated. Francis petitioned for the option of paying a fine instead – this was called compounding – and one of £300 was imposed at Goldsmiths' Hall in September 1646. He let it lapse, and in March 1647 the Committee for Middlesex ordered the confiscation of Headstone to recover the £400. They negotiated with the third son, Simon, agreeing to let him take the property on payment of £50 plus another £50 to be paid later, deemed the £400 to be satisfied, and discharged the confiscation order.

Two years later the three brothers sold Headstone to William Williams, a London merchant, for £4,200. Then, suddenly, in 1652 the Committee for Compounding stirred itself, apparently unaware that the sequestration had been settled. It noticed non-payment of the compounded £300 fine, and ordered the seizure of Headstone in December 1652. Williams, aghast, protested, claiming he had paid the full purchase money to the Rewses, and knew of no outstanding fine.

Williams must have won his point because he continued as owner, perhaps enjoying a few years of peace, until the summer of 1661 when Thomas Rewse lodged a claim for his £1,000 against him as owner of the house on which it was secured. Thomas was successful, and in default of full payment by November, had the right to enter the estate to get it. But he did not get his hands on his money until 1670. Williams sold Headstone in 1669 to two London merchants, who sold it on to George Kellum of London, and Rewse, who must now have been in his mid-thirties, sold Kellum his claim and right to enter in return for the equivalent of the unpaid sum.

Certain changes to the oldest part of Headstone, which are still visible – the raising of the hall ceiling and insertion of its surviving great window, panelling and settle, plus the porch at the rear – could have been made by either the Rewses or Williams. It was more likely that Williams added the extensive 17th-century wing.

On 31 May 1671 Margaret Chitt of London bought all the interests in Headstone for £7,000, and bequeathed it to her daughter Sarah, wife of Sir William Bucknall. Their heirs by one name or another had it until the 19th century.

PINNER PARK

The last reference to deer at Pinner Park was in 1504, and in 1543-4 it was called the late park. The change to a farm had begun properly when in February 1539 Cranmer gave a 50-year lease jointly to former deputy parker John Bird and Richard Reading of Headstone. The annual rent was £20, but far more important was the £66 18s. 4d. they paid 'for all woods and underwoods growing within the park', meaning they had the right to fell and sell. This they did with all speed. By 1547 the value of the wood and underwood, including 240 timber trees about 40 years old, was reduced by almost £50, and 80 acres had been converted to arable, 125 to pasture. They left the roots in the ground, which meant that the so-called pasture was useless until their removal, which Lord North's surveyor complained 'will be very costly'.

John Bird's daughter Anne or Amy continued the lease after his death. In 1560 North granted an 80-year lease of park, grounds and dwelling house at the old rent of £20 to Robert Crowle and his wife Amy, who was almost certainly Bird's daughter. Crowle died in 1564 and Amy married William Burbage who, in the way of husbands those days, made the lease over to his brother Robert in 1565, and after Amy's death in 1574 it passed through several hands. Anthony Bacon of Gray's Inn, brother of Sir Francis, the great lawyer, statesman and philosopher, acquired it in 1579, and kept Burbage as a tenant at £80 p.a.

Then, in 1592 William Crowle of Pinner, elder son of Robert and Amy, claimed in the Court of Chancery that the lease was his, saying that before her remarriage his mother had entrusted the document itself to William Gerrard of Harrow for safe-keeping with the promise that it should go to her son. Though the result is not known it was a lengthy case. Burbage was still tenant in 1593, Anthony Bacon left the lease to his brother in 1601, but in 1609-10 Robert Crowle, younger brother of William, was the lessee.

Thomas and John Hutchinson bought Pinner Park in 1630, the third highest rated property in Pinner after Headstone and Woodhall. Thomas commissioned a map of the park in 1634, drawn by A. Bowen, which is the first map of any part of Pinner. It shows a moated house at the centre, on a site different from the present house, the first indication of a moat. The map sets out each field with its name, area and use, revealing how little they have changed since, and shows that the path crossing from East End to Hatch End was already there. Thomas Hutchinson, a Londoner and member of the Vintners' Company, was already living at Canons, and for him and John the park was an investment, not a home. It was run for them by the Ewers, who continued after Sir Edward Waldo bought all Hutchinson's property, and only departed when St Thomas's Hospital bought the park in 1731.

WOODHALL

When lessee Henry Edlin died young in 1541 an 80-year lease was granted to Thomas Smyth of Harrow Hill and his wife Anne, but Henry's son Richard reacquired it when he came of age sometime between 1546 and 1553. He, and then his son, both called Richard Edlin of Woodhall, remained there until 1617. Richard Nicholas obtained a 20-year lease in 1626 at £160 a year. There were 220 acres of arable land, 100 of pasture, and 10 of meadow.

19 Woodhall Manor, and its barns, as drawn on a map of 1638 – north is at the right. Part survives as the north wing of the existing building.

Disappointingly little is known about the people at Woodhall. William Pennefather, the first purchaser, may have been related to Simon Rewse's wife Alice Penifather. In 1637 he sold Woodhall to William Wilkinson who had a map of his new place made straightaway, like the Hutchinsons. It shows very clearly how the fields had been cut into the woodland in medieval times, leaving bands of trees around their edges, some still there, and lists the field names and areas.

William Wilkinson moved in after Richard Nicholas, the lessee, died in 1644. When Wilkinson died in 1658 the estate went to grandchildren named Nevill, and thereafter, like Headstone Manor, Woodhall was usually let. The first tenant was John Crych, a newcomer, while in 1690 it was Matthew Fearne from Ruislip.

TINDALLS

Bowen's map of Pinner Park in 1634 reveals a dovecote on the freehold property in Uxbridge Road once known as Wapses, a touch of class which means that someone of pretension lived there; in previous centuries a dovecote was the privilege of the lord of the manor. Long ago there was in Pinner church on the chancel floor a brass inscribed (in Latin) 'Here lies Richard Ledsam gentleman sometime Steward of the Inner Temple London who died the ninth day of January in the year 1585'. The former steward was the resident owner of Wapses and his widow Joan lived there for another twenty years or so. Richard and Joan were shown praying in a standing position and beneath them was another brass plate showing four daughters, the other, depicting their son William, having vanished even earlier. The brasses were recorded in 1718 and disappeared later that century.[14]

20 Bowen included Tindalls on his map of 1634. For us the important thing is its dove house on the other side of Uxbridge Road. North is at the right.

In April 1612 William sold the house to Dean Tindall, whose name attached to the house. All we know about the family is Francis Tindall's bequest to the church in 1630 of land called Will at Streets or Howlis, which was at the corner of Headstone Lane and George V Avenue, and became part of the glebe.

John Norwood of Great Stanmore bought Tindalls about 1648 and Richard Hatch ran the place for him, from 1665 at least. It was one of the bigger houses, having six fireplaces in 1672. By the beginning of the 19th century it had come to be called Dove House Farm.

CANONS

Canons belonged to Thomas Reading in Elizabethan times, the first local man to approach the status of gentry, distinguished from his fellows by the huge amount of land he held personally – four head tenements – combined with the undoubted advantage of farming Headstone Manor.

Spotting the trends, Thomas developed his house at Canons head tenement into one suitable for a tenant of quality, and obtained a licence to add the socially significant dovecote. His son George planted a long walk of elm trees before the house – probably alongside the Pinn from about 28-38 Cannon Lane, and in return for extra land there he agreed in May 1594 that the estate would maintain for ever the bridge over the Pinn in Cannon Lane just outside the house.

The house was good enough in 1606 to attract a buyer from London, Nicholas Faunt, Clerk to the Signet (keeper of the monarch's private seal, as opposed to the state seal). He had died by 1610. Thomas Hutchinson bought Canons from his widow Abigail Faunt in 1622, and took up residence. An impressive memorial to him and his wife Margaret was placed on the north chancel wall of Pinner church after his death in 1658, but it was damaged and lost during 20th-century repairs and nothing but the achievement at its top remains to be seen today. Hutchinson's black marble grave slab has been shifted from the chancel to just outside the porch. Only Pinner Hill House was more luxurious than Canons, having just one more than Canons' 13 fireplaces of one sort or another.

Edward Waldo (1632-1706) who bought the mansion at Canons from John Hutchinson as his country home in May 1682, was a member of the Mercers' Company whose Huguenot great-grandfather had fled the Low Countries a century before. In 1671 Charles II knighted Edward in his own Cheapside house. Like several other members of his family Edward became a Governor of Harrow School, and a churchwarden of St Mary's. The Lady Hunsdon who repaired the bridge over the Pinn in 1728 was his daughter. Canons had passed out of the family within a decade.

PINNER HILL HOUSE

Pinner Hill House was a new foundation in the 17th century, the home of Sir Christopher Clitherow (1570-1641), a man with an impressive history of company and city office. He was Master of the Ironmongers' Company in 1618 and 1624, Sheriff of London and Middlesex 1625-6, M.P. for London 1628-9, President of Christ's Hospital from 1637 and Governor of the East India Company 1638-41. His apogee was as Lord Mayor in 1635, which brought a knighthood. Thereafter he retired to his new property at Pinner Hill. He had two wives, four sons and five daughters.

21 Sir Christopher Clitherow of Pinner Hill is wearing the Lord Mayor's chain of office.

22 Dame Mary, his wife, parades the latest fashion, a mill-wheel ruff.

Clitherow had bought a few score acres of freehold at the top of Pinner Hill, the highest spot in Pinner, from Samuel Edlin about 1617. They were called Spinnells and on them he built his country house, the largest and grandest in 17th-century Pinner. There is no description or illustration to give an idea of what it looked like, nor whether it was built of timber or, like the contemporary mansion of Swakeleys at Hillingdon, of brick.

Christopher was far too busy in the city to come often to Pinner or to attend the manor court, as fines for absence show. His town house was in Fenchurch Street, and he owned several properties in that area and in Essex. He was buried in St Andrew Undershaft where you may still see the tablet commemorating him and his wives Katherine and Mary, as well as Mary, second wife of his son James, and their infant daughter.

The Clitherows entered the local network of influential families. Sir Christopher's niece Katherine Offley married Philip Edlin, son of Richard Edlin of Pinner Marsh and older brother to Richard Edlin, later Master of the Tallowchandlers' Company.

Alliances were made with the most important family in Ruislip, the Hawtreys, through the marriages of his second son James and his grandson Christopher III. Jane, the widow of Sir Christopher's eldest son, Christopher II, took John Hawtrey as a second husband.

James Clitherow was successful enough to buy Boston Manor at Hanwell, where he founded the longest-lasting branch of the family. Christopher II, the eldest, inherited Pinner Hill. In 1646 he enlarged his domain by a huge 120 acres in taking up and renewing the residue of Richard Taverner's 99-year lease of Pinner Wood, granted in 1550. He established a home farm, possibly the first Pinnerwood Cottage, which was usually let. Thomas Wright was there during the 1640s, and Thomas Mare or Mears later in the century.

Christopher II (1612-54) died leaving his testamentary papers unsigned, so on his death-bed he wrote anxious directions for locating them, giving the tiniest vignette of his house – his handwritten draft of his will would be found 'lying amongst other writings in a little long wainscoate box which standeth on my Study Table in my house att Pinner the key whereof lyeth in my Wines Cabinett', and William Wilkinson of Woodhall and Francis Hamond of Pinnerwood House found it there on 5 July 1654. The draft of his wife's marriage settlement was 'lying in my Countore [i.e. office] in my lodging in Colemanstreete London', and on 28 July there it too was found.

The merchant connection ended with this death because his two sons Thomas and Christopher were babies. Christopher III, perhaps Thomas too, followed their stepfather John Hawtrey into the law at Gray's Inn – a suitable education for a gentleman, whether he practised or not. Both died young, Thomas aged 30 and unmarried in 1681, Christopher III at the age of 31 in 1685, married but childless. Christopher's widow Mary engaged one of the foremost monumental sculptors of the day, William Stanton, to create a memorial in black and white marble. It still delights the eye, the most beautiful monument in Pinner church. The grave slabs of the brothers lie outside the church near the porch, removed from the chancel during floor improvement.

So ended the Clitherow line in Pinner. Mary inherited all the property absolutely and married Sir Thomas Franklyn of Hayden Hall, Ruislip. They had a bowling alley alongside the house. Mary never had children, and was laid beside Christopher when she died in 1728.

Mary had sold Pinner Hill House long before, sometime during the 1690s, to Sir Bartholomew Shower. Shower had been called to the bar in 1680 at the age of 21 and did well. He might have rivalled Judge Jeffreys in the favour of James II, who knighted him in 1687, but for the debacle of the trial of the Archbishop of Canterbury and six other bishops for opposing the king's policy of allowing Catholic worship. Their acquittal caused public rejoicing while Shower's part in the trial drew public hatred upon him. After James fled Shower's rancour towards the new regime ensured that his own star waned. He withdrew from court and bought Pinner Hill House. On 2 December 1701 he died quite suddenly of pleurisy at his house in Temple Lane, aged about forty. He was buried in Pinner church where his slab is now outside the porch, beside those of the Clitherow brothers.

WIDER ASSOCIATIONS

The people of Pinner had circles of contact in neighbouring villages and further afield. There were family connections in Hertfordshire particularly, where the Readings, Edlins, Streets, and Bodimeads had relatives. The Readings were also connected with Writtle in Essex, and eventually removed themselves to Huntingdonshire. The Edlins also had relatives in Buckinghamshire, and at Acton and Uxbridge, the Birds at Loughton in Essex, the Ewers at South Mimms.

Some descendants travelled to the Americas, usually those who had left Pinner some time before. William, son of Philip Edlin of Pinner, founded a dynasty there; and the Reading descendants in Writtle (named Pyncheon) did likewise. Despite the perils these people recrossed the Atlantic several times.[15] Many younger sons went to work and live in London, and daughters were married to London businessmen, so family contacts with the metropolis multiplied, especially in the families just named.

Pinner Businesses

SHOPS

The picture of trade in Tudor and Stuart Pinner is incomplete because in the 16th century the manor court only fined traders concerned with ale or bread, and that spasmodically. After 1600 manorial control faded and we have to rely on chance references to traders. Agriculture was still the major occupation.

Retailing progressed after 1552 when purchase in one place for resale elsewhere was allowed by statute to persons, called badgers or kidders, licensed by the county court. Even so, Roger Edlin of Pinner was charged in October 1575 with buying and reselling ten quarters of beans 'against the statute' – probably because he was unlicensed. The Middlesex Sessions list of licences for 1613-17 is useful. In towns the trend to indoor shopping was already well advanced by the time the Royal Exchange was built by Thomas Gresham in 1568, with its shops enclosed in rows and tiers. The word shop initially meant a place where the work of a craftsman was done, and in later times, when he sold from his premises, it was extended to mean a place of retail sale.

The rise of the retailer hastened the decline of the open-air market. Harrow market had gone by 1600 but a couple of shops there had been noted as early as 1462. Pinner's market vanished too, though when (and whether it ever flourished) is a mystery. The first shop mentioned in Pinner stood on the site of 58 High Street. John Downer owned it in May 1463 but it could have been erected by his forbear Roger, who had bought the plot in 1391. The Downers were butchers so the shop would have been primarily a slaughter-house and cutting-room. William Hall bequeathed it to his son Robert in 1576 calling it a 'shop or dwelling house' without saying what the business was. When Robert sold it in April 1613 it was a cottage, 'previously called a shop'. In 1652 it was again a butcher's shop and so remained for nearly 300 years more, with one break from 1696-1702. The presence of specialised facilities or plant made it likely that a particular business would continue on the premises, and applied especially to the baker, butcher and smith.

From July 1547 to April 1561 William Winter, an aleseller in 1540 and 1544, had a shop roughly on the site of 13 High Street. It was an adjoining outhouse or lock-up rather than part of a house – London shops were often of this type. John Curtis used it as an alehouse from 1561-87.

There may not have been enough demand in Pinner to provide a living just from a business. Wayland and Dodds (see below) had more than one source of income, and others might have the buffer of a small amount of land to cultivate.

BAKERS

William Winter, who owned 4 High Street from 1544-89, was called a baker in 1548. In 1618 one Widow Andrew, possibly connected with bread seller Stephen Andrew of a few years earlier, lived there. Much later, in April 1739, there was 'an old accustomed bakehouse' on the premises, meaning a baker's oven, not a housewife's, which was by then defunct. No.4 was probably a bakery throughout the period, the existence of expensive plant being crucially significant. There is no clue to other bakeries at this time.

PROVISIONS

In the 17th century the victualler became primarily an innkeeper, and his place as the village grocer was taken by the badger. The badger retailed anything he thought would sell, but the most common goods were groceries and provisions.

In the four years for which records are available, 1613-17, 14 people from Pinner were licensed, most of them from yeoman families; Edlin, Street, Bird, Ferne, Elis, perhaps because some basic capital was needed and their fathers could finance them. One of the others was Robert Wayland (1614) who was also a shoemaker at 25-7 High Street. Another was Henry Dodds (1615), who probably lived at 7 High Street and owned several properties nearby.

By the end of the 17th century the word badger had been superseded by grocer, or tallow chandler, who was originally a candlestick maker and seller but now dealt also in groceries and provisions, together perhaps with meal, and hardware such as twine, rope, soap and small metal and wooden goods. John Cook, living at John Edrops old site 18-24 High Street from 1669 until his death in 1681, was the first named tallow chandler in Pinner. His widow Bridget and son Thomas probably continued the business until Thomas set up on his own at the old butcher shop, 58 High Street, in 1696. He was called a grocer when he died unmarried six years later, leaving a shop with grocer's goods in it. The inventory with his will lists cheeses, sugar plums (dried fruit), candles, haberdashers' items, 'divers other things' and, in a store room, a flitch of bacon.[16] The total value of the goods amounted only to £24 10s. od., not a great sum even then. Maybe it was only a part-time living.

MEALMEN AND MILLERS

A mealman was a middleman selling meal and flour. As the number of people with little or no land rose, so did the demand for the mealman's goods. John Edlin at 26-30 High Street from 1544-75 is the only identifiable one in 16th-century Pinner (1557), but there were several in the 17th, at least from the time of John Downer who died in 1631. Obadiah Ewer's out-building to the rear of 29 High Street was described as a mealhouse in 1689 and as a millhouse in 1691 and subsequently, but it was probably a storehouse for meal in reality. Ewer is not on record as a mealman.

There was still plenty of work for the miller, some of it perhaps done for the mealmen. In May 1617 the lord granted a site on Pinner Common to William Crane to build 'one good, strong and substantial windmill'. William, who came from Stanmore, may have been a son of John Crane, miller at the Harrow mill a generation before. William's mill lasted until it was brought down by wind in 1721.

CLOTHING

A handful of people provided apparel, chiefly the cobbler and the tailor. The longest-serving cobblers were Robert Wayland and his son Henry, shoemakers from 1607-72, at the present 25-7 High Street. The homes of several tailors can be located. There was Valentine Baily, who lived at the site of The Lawn in Elm Park Road in 1622, and his descendant William, tenant from 1657 at the one-time house of mealman John Edlin. John Bird, tailor, was at 42 High Street in 1658, and in the house he built next door at 44 lived tailor Peter May from 1678-1701. Meanwhile another tailor called William Read had bought 7 High Street in 1669, and died there in 1701, succeeded by his tailor son John. There were two glovers, who must have had to take their goods to other markets or fairs for a living. One was John Norbury, lodging at 5-7 High Street, threatened with eviction in April 1570 for soaking his leather in the Pinn round the back of his dwelling, and again in April 1571 for dumping his waste pieces in it – the smell was unbearable. Glover Henry Ward died in 1670, having lived in Bridge Street just south of the present Post Office.

The weavers of 16th- and 17th-century Pinner may have woven the wool of local people, or bought yarn elsewhere and sold the resulting lengths of cloth. There is no evidence of an out-working system in this area like that in East Anglia and the West Country. John Nicholas was a weaver for a long period, from 1525 when he was the tithing man for Pinner, until his death in 1551. His residence was probably in Love Lane, near the site of St Luke's church. Henry Smith, a weaver in 1573, lived at the site of Mayfield Drive. A century later weaver John Hollingworth was sharing the tenancy of a new house in Uxbridge Road, but the parish had to pay for his funeral in 1670. Henry Dearing, who owned 9-13 High Street, had his loom in a lower room or workshop at no.13 in September 1678, once John Curtis's alehouse. Daniel Shippey, living in 1699 at what became East End House, had learnt the trade of weaver through an apprenticeship paid from John Lyon's charity by the Governors of Harrow School in 1686.

GARDENERS

Henry Goldstone, who lived at Moss Cottage from 1652-66, was a gardener – a master, since he took an apprentice in 1657. Rather than being a jobbing gardener he was more likely a market gardener producing vegetables, salads and fruit on a small scale for sale in markets or to local people who had no garden of their own. He had just over an acre of his own land at Moss Lane, and could have rented more, or been allowed to enclose his common field land, which was becoming easier. Two others were described as gardeners in the burial register, John Nicholas of Love

Lane in 1687, and William East in 1703. Nicholas had about the same amount of land as Goldstone, but East has not been linked with any property so was probably a jobber.

CONSTRUCTION

The repair and maintenance of the church provided intermittent work for workers in the building trades – carpenters, smiths, bricklayers, plumbers, painters and glaziers – and the churchwardens' accounts are the best source of information about them. Most of those named were resident in Pinner or Harrow. In the earlier years the churchwardens had to look further afield for plumbers and glaziers.

Rising standards of accommodation and home comfort added to the demand. John Bryan, a Pinner bricklayer who made his will in 1577, would have built some of the chimneys inserted into older houses.[17] The wholly internal stacks at East End Farm Cottage and Orchard Cottage are of a date to be his work. Brick became the standard building material in the second half of the 17th century and then more Pinner bricklayers are known, primarily those of the Lee dynasty. William first worked at the church in 1668, and his descendants after him. They lived at Pinner Green (site of Abbey Close) until the early 18th century and then moved to Bee Cottage. In Pinner church-

23 These foundations (marked by the ranging rod) were uncovered at the rear of the *Victory* in 1985. The building has not been identified but could have belonged to Thomas Priest, a smith from about 1553-74, or his successor, Thomas Francis. The view is looking uphill.

yard stands the headstone of William's great-great grandson John Lee who died in 1819 aged 80 'a well respected man. He was bricklayer in this town 66 years and the last of his family of the male kind'.

The rapid adoption of glazed windows provided the chief opportunities for the glazier and plumber. The former did not make the glass himself but bought it, cut it with hot rods, and installed it. The plumber made the lead framework for windows; the demand for guttering and pipe work lay in the 18th century. The plumbers were not Pinner men, though glazier Thomas Jermyn of Uxbridge owned 34-6 High Street between 1671 and 1690.

SMITHS AND WHEELWRIGHTS

The smithy moved little because of its special equipment. The 15th-century one in Marsh Road near the foot of the High Street lasted until at least 1715, when blacksmith Richard Francis' widow was still organising work there for the churchwardens – with a gap for a while at the start of the 17th century when Thomas Francis set up around 8-16 Bridge Street. Thomas Bailey and Adam Bickerton practised at the rear of 33-5 High Street at different times.

There were wheelwrights to meet the requirements of the carriage folk who bought the demesnes or created new estates, in addition to the existing yeoman demand. Simon Downer was opposite the church from about 1650 until he died in 1691, and William Lawrence was at the Bay House in Church Lane in December 1666. He was involved as owner or tenant with several other properties in the last part of the century – the nearby Pinner House among them, and it is not clear where he carried on his business. He invested in two acres of wood at Waxwell in May 1674, which probably had to do with his trade. There was enough work to sustain harness maker Israel Larimore, and his colleague Edward Bird, who called himself a collar maker – the collars were for horses. Larimore was busy from the 1680s, took an apprentice in 1690, and could afford to acquire a 21-year lease of 21-3 High Street in April 1700. Bird, who died 1703, was at the same address.

TAVERNS AND ALEHOUSES

During Elizabeth's reign the terms aleseller, tippler and victualler were used interchangeably. Some Pinner alesellers were in business for many years, among them John Curtis, Robert Jordan and Robert Street. The last two were each fined in April 1591 for selling ale 'mixed with things not fit for the human body'.

Margery Bateman's tavern in Pinner was listed in John Taylor's *A Catalogue of Taverns in Ten Shires about London* of 1636. It was the present *Queen's Head*, though it did not then have that name, owned by the Bateman family from April 1633 until April 1684. After 1663, when their son Thomas died leaving infant sons, it either lapsed or was run by someone else. It was called the *Crown* when it was sold in November 1692 by absentee owner Philip Street, a butcher of Great Stanmore.

What we call a public house might have been an alehouse, selling ale or beer, a tavern, providing other drinks and probably food, or an inn, which could cater for the traveller and his horse, providing bed and board. Except for the *Queen's Head*, we have no idea of the category of Pinner's drinking places.

The oldest drinking place name in Pinner was the *Bird in Hand*, its existence assumed from a trade token which has on one side the design of a bird in a hand encircled by the legend RALPH PAGE OF PINER and on the other the initials PRI encircled by the legend HIS HALF PENNY 1667. PRI stands for Page Ralph (and) Jane. They were probably the Ralph Page and Jane Battman who married at St Peter, Pauls Wharf in London on 15 October 1657, she perhaps a daughter of Margery Bateman and her husband Thomas. It is not known where the tavern was, though the Page house was at the northern end of West End Lane, site of Hamilton Court, and when Ralph died in 1673 he had brewing paraphernalia there worth £72, a huge amount but appropriate to a tavern keeper. When Jane died in 1683 she had brewing vessels worth £10 6s. 8d. Nothing more is known about the tavern. Trade tokens were issued by individual traders for use in their premises at this time because small denominations of legal currency were in short supply, so Ralph must have been soundly based. His is the only known Pinner token.

At the foot of the High Street victualler John Bird bought nos.1-5 in May 1674, and then in 1676 some nearby outbuildings, later called a cellar and brewhouse. It is a wonder he did not call his place the *Bird in Hand*. When his son John, a butcher, sold the premises to John Street in April 1703 Gideon Lott was there, and was still there when Street sold to William Aldwin in April 1714 under the name of the *Queens Head*. Then Lott moved up to *The Crown* and decided to call that the *Queens Head*.

The last alehouse name we know of in Pinner,

24 This is Ralph Page's token. The top view contains the hand holding a bird.

prior to the many used in the 18th century, was the *Harrow*, which in 1696 was in a cottage occupied by Andrew Gowlett, standing on the site of Myrtown, opposite St John's in Church Lane. It was a popular name, but meant the agricultural implement, not Pinner's near neighbour.

Troublemakers

BAD BEHAVIOUR

There was dislocation in the 16th-century English countryside as land was accumulated into fewer hands, and the towns suffered from the resulting pressure of immigrants from the countryside. Some areas were affected by the booms and depressions in the cloth industry and all places were affected by inflation.

Society considered that suspicious behaviour or a bad reputation was a virtual prelude to crime and tried to banish the offender. Reports in the manor court rolls imply that concern went in waves.

The late 1520s provide examples. Widow Elizabeth Elis of Hatch End was ordered to clear named people of suspect behaviour from her house in May 1528. An unusually large number of cases in May 1530 included John and Margaret Downer, probably of Pinner, fined for harbouring persons of evil conduct, one of whom, Joan Colyer, was singled out and made the subject of a separate order. John Smith, the son of Richard Smith of either Weald or Pinner, but living with a relative named Henry, was said to lead a suspect life and be both a privy pyker and a vagabond, so he and his wife were to be thrown out. A pyker was a thief, especially of small things. In 1529 John Aylward of Pinner was fined for playing bowls.

Two cases concerned tenants' wives. The wife of Hugh Elis of Hatch End was a common gossip who often stirred up strife among her neighbours, so in May 1531 Hugh was told to remove her from the manor, or amend matters, or pay 20s. if he did not. This is curious. How could Hugh have removed her from the manor, other than by leaving with her, or by setting her up in a home elsewhere, if he could afford it – a husband was responsible for maintaining his wife. Hugh and his descendants continued at Hatch End, so he must have amended matters. One wonders how. A similar case in December 1530 concerned William Aylward of Weald and his wife Tybbe. No ducking stool or scold's bridle for dealing with such matters is ever mentioned in Harrow records.

Playing bowls continued to be thought an encouragement to idleness or worse. William Loveday (residence unknown), was fined 4d. in 1564 for laying out a bowling alley and ordered to get rid of it. Robert Bird, probably living at Crowchers with his father Thomas, was fined 12d. in spring 1566 for indulging in illegal games – bowls perhaps?

ASSAULTS AND AFFRAYS

In the early 17th century more offences concerning poaching or physical assault came to the manor court. The Pinner people cannot always be picked out. Four men were fined 33s. 4d. between them in May 1593 for using guns, powder and bullets to shoot birds, because the use of firearms was illegal. John Hoy, a leather worker with a workshop on the site of the later *Red Lion*, was fined 10s. for killing hares on the lord's warren at Sudbury Green in April 1633, and just over four years later he was fined again for killing partridges with a firearm.

Assault seldom got as far as court more than once a year in Pinner, but the perpetrators represented all walks of Pinner society. Gentlemen and yeomen, who might have been expected to set the tone, were sometimes guilty of very rough behaviour indeed. Two families featured more often than most, the Birds and the Clerks – there had been an affray between Henry Bird and John Clerk long ago in 1504 – and it is not always possible to distinguish the head of the family from the brothers or sons. Thomas Bird, 'a rowdy man' who assaulted Richard Hope in April 1564, may have been the head tenant of Crowchers whose son Robert had played illegal games in 1566. Edmund, his kinsman of Church Farm, attacked Mr Burbage, the lessee of Pinner Park in 1566. Burbage had married Amy Crowle, who was born a Bird and it was Edmund who was later granted letters of administration for her estate in 1574. A different Edmund Bird, of Barrow Point, was accused in October 1593 of letting his children despoil the common hedges and take away wood.

Hugh Bird, Thomas's great-grandson and successor at Crowchers, was a notable malcontent. In April 1614 he was charged with armed assault on Thomas Bird, exact relationship unknown. The same year he accused fellow yeoman Henry Edlin of snatching up money at play. This amounted to theft, potentially a capital offence, and so was heard at the Middlesex Sessions which met at the Sessions House in St John Street, Smithfield. Hugh admitted he had made wrongful charges while drunk and was fined 3s. 4d. The atmosphere back in Pinner cannot have been good. He was at the Sessions again on 5 October 1615, described as a gentleman, where both John Edlin and Robert Sheppard of Pinner swore that he was 'a most disordered person, a common quarreller and drunkard'. He also had to ask John Edlin's forgiveness publicly for having called him a rogue and villain in open court, and was arraigned for unspecified bother with Thomas Fulmer of Ruislip. He took his civic duties very lightly. On 3 October 1616 he was charged with contempt in letting go a vagrant whom he was charged with by a constable, 'with a pass to be conveyed from constable to constable according to the law', and again in April 1618 for refusing to pay his share of the assessed contribution towards maimed soldiers.

The other chief troublemaker of the time was John Clerk, causing problems almost every year from 1612 to 1617. Violent, abusive, provocative and uncontrolled, John was a very young man, born in 1594 or 1596, who had come into his inheritance when his father Richard died in 1609 – the property was Pynnors, the house at Pinner Green. At the manor court of 16 April 1612 he was charged with two assaults, in one of which he stabbed his victim in the arm. At the Middlesex Sessions the next July a Pinner tailor called William Ryland was bound over to keep the peace towards John Clerk, and so was William Garrald, a turner from Pinner, on 8 December 1615. On 15 June following, Thomas Edlin of Pinner, a joiner, was at the Sessions to answer for his wife Helen's abuse of John Clerk's wife. John was summoned on 5 October for using foul language to the magistrate – perhaps at the Edlin hearing – but was discharged later. He was described as a gentleman. The magistrate was Mr Hawtrey of Ruislip, whose relative Ralph was an executor of John's father Richard's estate. Finally, on 14 July 1617 both John Clerk and Hugh Bird, the champion scoundrels of Pinner, were bailed at the Sessions – on each other's recognizance! – to appear at the next Sessions, when they were discharged. The matter was not stated.

Other Birds were unsubdued. The most spectacular defiance of authority came from Thomas Bird of the Well who, with the help of Thomas, Henry and John Nicholas, rescued his relative Thomas of the Marsh from the hands of the bailiff of Middlesex, who had taken and detained him upon a charge by a William Leversage, gentleman, in February 1628. This startling deed was first reported to the manor court of 31 March 1630 but no official retribution can be traced there or in the sessions records. Imagination conjures much talk about the event in Pinner alehouses. Thomas Bird of the Well cannot be identified, though the well was probably one half-way up Bridge Street, but Thomas Bird of the Marsh almost certainly lived in the cottage once known as Muggs, carved out of the family holding Crowchers. One of the Thomas Birds was summoned to the Sessions in 1616 for failing to pay ten days' wages to John Pett of Northolt, whom he had hired as a carpenter.

THEFT

Theft was the most serious type of case referred to the Sessions and, if the value of the goods stolen was worth one shilling or more, attracted the death penalty. Hugh Bird's allegation against Henry Edlin in 1614 might have had very serious consequences if it had been genuine.

On 23 January 1613 John Havergill of Hatch End was charged with stealing a ewe and his neighbour Richard Downer was summoned to give evidence against him. The outcome of this case is not known. Juries sometimes deemed the value of the goods stolen to be less than one shilling so as to reduce the penalty. This was so for John Collins of Pinner, accused on 3 December 1616 of stealing a coverlet worth 30s., a pair of curtains worth 30s., a pair of sheets worth 13s. 4d. and a blanket worth 5s., all belonging to James Defrane, a joiner who was temporarily in Pinner. The jury stated the value of the goods to be only 11d. and Collins was ordered to be whipped, the punishment presumably inflicted in London. Collins' goods were forfeit but he had none, a good indication that he had stolen through want. He was a relative newcomer to Pinner and his case no doubt fuelled the widespread fear of strangers.

It was still possible for a man to escape capital punishment and be sent to an ecclesiastical court as though he were a clergyman, if he could prove in open court that he could read, at one time a skill possessed only by the clergy. Ecclesiastical courts did not impose the death penalty. There were at least three cases in Pinner. Reginald Gurney, previously of London, stole two white sheep worth 13s. from John Edlin of Pinner on 13 March 1595. Gurney confessed but claimed 'benefit of clergy'. When the Bible was brought he read 'like a clerk' and instead of being hanged was branded with the letter 'T' for thief (usually upon the thumb). On 20 May 1622 Christopher Woods, William Hurlock and John Sharpe, all labourers previously of Pinner, stole a ram worth 20s. from Thomas Randall, using force. Woods and Hurlock were found guilty on 5 June, claimed benefit of clergy, read, and were delivered to the Bishop of London, who probably had them whipped or branded and sent on their way. How had these two labourers come by such life-saving education, and had their fathers appreciated just how valuable it was going to be? Both men came from established Pinner families, though not yeomen. Randall was a butcher at the site of 2 High Street in 1630. One wonders if a woman who could read might claim the same benefit, since there was no question of her being a clergyman.

In the meantime Richard Allen had not been so lucky. On 11 October 1614 he was charged with breaking into the house of William Tripps, labourer, at ten in the morning and stealing a pair of sheets worth 10s., two pairs of breeches worth 10s., a jerkin worth 2s., a pair of stockings worth 12d., a hat worth 2s., a sack worth 8d., a bottle worth 4d., a girdle worth 4d., and £4 in money belonging to the said William. Allen was found not guilty of house-breaking, but guilty of felony. He asked for benefit of clergy but when the book was brought he could not read, and was sentenced to be hanged. Though described as a yeoman he had no goods himself, as indeed the range of items he stole implies. His residence is unknown, but Tripps house was in West End Lane on the site of 1-3 West House Cottages.

WITCHES

Witchcraft was frightening, and according to E.M. Ware there was a case of this usually female offence in Pinner during the reign of Elizabeth I. On 19 February 1585 a grand jury found that Joan, wife of James Barringer of Harrow Weald, labourer, 'practised the detestable arts of Witchcraft on and against Rose Edlyn, daughter of Richard Edlyn, of the said parish, with the intention of murdering the same Rose, who languished from the effects of the said diabolical practice till she died thereof on the 17th March then next following'. On 28 March 1585 Richard Edlyn of Parkgate, Hatch End gave his bond that he would appear at the next Gaol Delivery of Newgate (31 March) to give evidence against Joan Barringer regarding

25 Parkgate, from Bowen's map, was the home of Rose Edlin, believed to have died of witchcraft. The single house was Elis's.

the felony. His daughter, being unmarried, had probably been young.

Here was something that would have thrilled everyone in the manor, and beyond. The wood of Weald had sheltered a witch! They were real and close at hand! Joan would surely have been friendless then, if not before, because everyone would have wanted to be rid of her. Her fate is not known, whether she was tormented for a confession, whether she was hanged, or whether – which did sometimes happen – she was acquitted.

Unwanted People, Unwanted Responsibilities

THE UNEMPLOYED

The problem of the poor during the 16th and 17th centuries became a more obvious public problem than ever before and the government began to concern itself. People were fearful that landless or masterless people would resort to begging or crime, especially if moving in groups. An act of 1495 ordered that vagabonds – wandering unemployed – be put in the stocks. In Harrow residents were heavily discouraged from harbouring them – even John Aylward, from a local family, was ordered to be thrown out of his lodging for being a vagabond, that is, unemployed, and playing bowls.

In the first inkling that unemployment was not always the wilful desire of the unemployed, the parishes were made responsible in 1536 for relieving those incapable of working, though no funds were given them for the purpose. In 1552 residents who could afford to contribute to poor relief were to be pressed to do so, but not compelled. In 1572 justices of the peace were ordered to raise taxes for poor relief and imprison non-contributors.

Prohibitions at Harrow manor court were renewed. In April 1559 all lodgers were ordered to be removed by September, and no unmarried stranger was to remain here for more than forty days. Lodgers were forbidden again in May 1578. John Elis of Hatch End was fined 12d. in May 1587 for failing in his duty to apprehend vagabonds. Richard Dodd of 7 High Street was fined 10s. in May 1590 for having had a lodger for more than one month.

By the end of the century, in the great statutes of 1598 and 1601, the law recognised three categories of poor and provided three solutions. The churchwardens were to give relief to those unable to work through age or infirmity; they must set to work those fit but unable to find any, or send them to school or apprentice them if they were children; the rest, able-bodied but unwilling to work, were to be whipped and returned to the parish of their birth or legal residence (or 'settlement'). The churchwardens must appoint overseers of the poor, together with four other householders, and must levy a rate to provide for the first two categories of poor. Owners of property worth £10 or more a year could be assessed.

We do not know how the churchwardens of Pinner reacted prior to 1622, when their first accounts survive. In the meantime the manor court used its own powers, threatening Francis Hawkins with a fine of £10 in April 1614 unless he could prove his sub-tenant Richard Weedon would not need parish support, and Widow Emma Finch with one of 20s. regarding her lodger. These were large sums.

THE POOR

The parish was the first provider of relief for the poor. Only two Pinner Overseers of the Poor are known by name, William Tripp, who lived next to West House, and John Bird. All the official expenditure in this field in 17th-century Pinner is contained in churchwardens' accounts, there being no separate overseers accounts.

A poor box was listed in the church inventories, but whatever was put in it and how it was paid out was not written down. Individuals, usually yeomen, occasionally left a few pounds, seldom more than three, to the poor of Pinner, to be distributed at the discretion of executors or churchwardens, but no official record was kept. One private record does survive, a list of recipients made in 1610 by Richard Clerk's executors Thomas and George Reading. It shows how far a bequest of 20s. could be spread, because 30 people received 8d. each. All were from virtually landless families, except perhaps for a Widow Edlin. Eighteen were female. The old or widowed included six widows, plus three 'mothers' and two 'fathers', usually a description of the old or bereaved. The gentry were more munificent. William Hamond of Pinnerwood left 200s. in 1617, Sir Christopher Clitherow of Pinner Hill the same in 1640. Clitherow's sons Anthony and Christopher left 200s. and 132s. respectively in 1650 and 1654, but William Wilkinson of Woodhall topped them all with 400s. in 1657. Bequests came irregularly, and were distributed at one go, except in the case of John Bird who in 1630 left 20s. a year for three years.

Apart from Richard Clerk's bequest the names of few poor people come to light in Pinner. There were three burials at parish expense, Widow Symonds and Old Harley in 1639, and John Hollingworth, once a weaver, in 1672. Five other acts of individual relief were noted. Garret's son was bound apprentice in 1626 and provided with a hat; four shillings and sixpence was spent in charges about Harris's children in 1635, the year their father John died; Goody Snape was given 6s. in 1666 to relieve old Snape, probably her husband and maker of the bell-frame (see page 68), in his last illness; William Bocket, who lived in the house once used by John Harris on the site of 42 High Street, was given 3s. 9d. for victuals for himself and his children in 1669; in the same year a Mr Pares was paid £2 10s. 0d. towards the cure of William Aylward's boy, but in vain, for young Richard was buried the next February.

These widely-spaced instances amount to nothing near the average of one seventh of the population that scholars reckon might have needed relief at some time during a year. The people mentioned above were from families which had only come to Pinner in the 17th century, except for Richard Aylward, and the people buried were the last of their family. Yet most people in Pinner managed the problems of old age, sickness or orphans. Perhaps there really were few poor people in Pinner, or perhaps they had to be destitute to qualify for relief. Otherwise we can only assume the poor box sufficed.

But Pinner money was spent on poor people and it went on shifting the problem elsewhere, and to a few outside causes. Parishioners were reluctant to pay for non-parishioners. The 1662 Poor Law allowed overseers to prevent people not 'settled' in the parish from taking up residence. Settlement meant either: to have been born in the parish; to have been resident 40 days after notifying the overseers of intention to stay (so as to give the opportunity to eject); to be apprenticed to a parishioner; to have had one year's service to someone in the parish (if unmarried); to be the owner of property worth £10 a year and therefore to be paying the parish rate. Otherwise, especially if it was feared the newcomer might become a burden to the parish, he or she could be removed to the proper parish of settlement. Residents wanting to move away could get a certificate of settlement from their own overseer which simplified their return should they be unwanted elsewhere. From 1664 to the end of the century annual sums ranging from 1s. 6d. to £3 14s. 10d. were spent on poor people with passes, that is, on transporting or passing along such individuals from Pinner to their parish of settlement, but there are no details of the individual cases. And there is no information about anyone being returned to Pinner from elsewhere.

The largest charitable contributions were made to causes quite unassociated with Pinner. The most recurrent were payments to maimed soldiers licensed to apply for relief in parishes they passed through on their way home, and these totals far exceeded those for other poor. The first was in 1662, the last in 1684, and in the decade from 1669 the annual sum usually exceeded five or six pounds.

From time to time the bishop or the Privy Council asked for special collections. The special sums raised in Pinner included:

1689	for the use of the Irish Protestants	£28 6s. 2d.
1691	to ransom slaves in Algiers	£3 1s. 8d.
1699	for the poor Vaudois (*Swiss Protestant refugees*) to be settled in Germany (Sir Edward Waldo of Canons in Pinner Marsh gave £10)	£15 16s. 1d.
no date	for captives in Fez and Morocco	£3 16s. 7d.
1702	for Bromley Church, Staffordshire	8s. 10d.
1702	for Chester Cathedral	£1 0s. 0d.
1704	for the Orange Protestants	£7 9s. 2d.

It is easy to see which causes aroused most sympathy!

HIGHWAYS

The only information about Pinner's highways comes from a review in 1686 of the responsibility for maintaining bridges, provoked by the lord dragging his feet over repairs, and made by the overseers of the highways, parish officials appointed by government regulation.[18]

Anyone else carrying out a repair risked setting a precedent for lumbering himself with the responsibility. The bridge in the marsh, approximately where West End Avenue begins, was in poor condition in 1574. It was outside John Edlin's Pinner Place, and when he repaired it at the lord's request about 1650 he was merely recompensed with a bottle of wine. After that dispiriting outcome he took to patching it up at his own cost. It was a footbridge in 1686. William Wilkinson was said to have once repaired one of the Uxbridge Road bridges near Woodhall.

In 1686 the town bridge was big enough to carry vehicles, the only such reference before the 19th century. However, describing it as a danger to the lives and goods of users, the overseers alleged it was the lord's responsibility to repair it, and under the leadership of John Street the lawyer they sought legal opinion. Subsequently it was repaired by John Pond, a Pinner carpenter and wheelwright, almost certainly at the lord's expense.

The bridge in Cannon Lane by Hereford Gardens was the special responsibility of the adjoining Canons. In 1728 it was rebuilt by the owner, Lady Grace Hunsdon, who placed a tablet anouncing this fact to the world on the bridge, where it still remains.

There was a bridge in the road 'from Pinner to Brentford ... beyond William Edlins (i.e. The Grove) towards the common field'. As both Eastcote Road and Rayners Lane flank the Grove, it could have been in the former by Lyncroft Avenue or in the latter by Whittington Way.

Further improvement to bridges had to wait for almost a century.

Seventeenth-Century Upheavals in Church and State

THE CIVIL WAR

The 16th-century religious upsets had caused many people to think deeply about politics and religion, and their parliamentary representatives even more so, just when James I and Charles I were trying to extend royal powers. The Civil War made the people's representatives in Parliament the masters of the Crown, and by the end of the century Parliament was able to depose a king who did not suit its religious and political preferences.

Armed conflict came no closer to Pinner than Brentford, where the Royalists repulsed two Parliamentary regiments and looted the town on 12 November 1642. The next day there was a stand-off at Turnham Green, which ended when the king turned away to Kingston. Uxbridge was chosen as the venue for an abortive attempt at a conference early in 1645. In May 1646 the king's hurried ride through Middlesex with a few followers took him through Harrow itself en route to Newark. It was intended to be unnoticed, and few residents could have been aware that he was passing. Middlesex in general favoured Parliament during the contest, taking its colour from the capital which dominated it. In Harrow the animosity between lord of the manor George Pitt and landowner Sir Gilbert Gerrard of Harrow on the Hill was exacerbated by Pitt's allegiance to the royalist cause and Gerrard's to the Parliamentarian – Gerrard was distantly related to Oliver Cromwell by marriage. At Uxendon two members of the one-time Roman Catholic Page family supported the king.

In Pinner the king had one known adherent in Francis Rewse, son of Simon of Headstone. Francis took up arms and followed the king to Oxford in 1642, where he was knighted. Though he had to pay a hefty financial penalty after Parliament's triumph, Sir John Wolstenholme at Great Stanmore suffered much greater pecuniary sanctions. Sir Christopher Clitherow of Pinner Hill was used to making forced loans to the king in his capacity as a city magnate, but has never been accounted either a royalist or a parliamentarian.

When the king levied the ship money tax upon inland towns as well as coastal ones, forty people from Harrow refused to pay it in 1638, but we do not know if any came from Pinner. We do know that every man in Pinner, 186 in all, signed the Protestation Oath – in 1641 members of Parliament had sworn an oath to uphold its own rights and privileges and the rights and liberties of subjects, and urged every male aged 18 or above to do likewise. Oaths were signed in every parish and few people refused.

What was the general attitude of the people of Pinner during this conflict? Did they approve of Francis Rewse, or of Pitt or of Gerrard? The only recorded individual observation comes from yeoman John Clerk of Pinner Green, probably the son of the lout, who in his will of 1644 lamented 'the punishments wherewith for our sins we are now afflicted throughout this Kingdom'.

THE GREAT PLAGUE

Plague was a frequent visitor in the 17th century, more so in London and its environs than in outer Middlesex. There were major outbreaks in 1603, 1609-10, 1625, 1636-7 and, famously, in 1665. The churchwardens paid for the burial of five plague victims in Pinner in 1639. The burial registers, lost prior to 1654, do not show the cause of death, but the 55 deaths from 1656-9, and the 40 from 1668-70, way above the annual average of eight, arouse suspicion of plague. By contrast the single burial in the Great Plague year of 1665 is astonishing – Henry Wood's wife Mary was buried in October. The churchwardens had spent 1s. 6d. on a 'declaration and a book with it for a monthly fast during the visitation of the plague' – perhaps it had done the trick! It may be that the registers are incomplete.

THE GREAT FIRE OF LONDON

There could hardly have been anyone in Pinner who did not climb to the top of Pinner Hill to see the Great Fire from afar. One person was particularly involved, Richard Edlin, third son of William of the Marsh, and brother of Philip, who had grown up at The Grove. Richard had been apprenticed to a tallowchandler (William Greenhill, probably of Harrow) in 1622. When the fire broke out he was Master of the Tallowchandlers' Company, living in Golden Lane at Cripplegate. He rushed to Tallowchandlers' Hall in Dowgate Hill, snatched up the charter, records and plate, and dispatched them forthwith to his family in Pinner for safekeeping, probaby to his brother William at The Grove. The Tallowchandlers' accounts show £3 reimbursed to Richard for 'carrying the plate, writing and other things belonging to this Company (in the time of the late Dreadful Fire) unto Pinner and bringing them back from thence unto the Master's house in Golden Lane'.

OTHER MAJOR EVENTS

Some political events were commemorated officially. Every 5 November the church bells rang in thanksgiving for the failure of the Gunpowder Plot, and again on the anniversary of the sovereign's accession. The churchwardens paid for these and others besides. They had to buy specially printed versions of prayers for special occasions, such as for the queen's safe delivery in 1631, the king's health in 1636, or a day of thanksgiving for the victory over the Dutch and the plague fast in

1665. Prayers for the queen being with child in 1687 foreshadowed the Glorious Revolution of 1688, for the birth of this prince, who became the Old Pretender, was swiftly followed by the deposition of his Roman Catholic father James II. Pinner supported the new king, William of Orange, as the monies raised in church for the Irish Protestants during 1689 and 1704 showed.

The Congregation Divides

MURMURINGS OF DISSENT

Prior to 1640 only clergymen of safe opinion were licensed to preach and if they wished they need only recite the service from the Book of Common Prayer and read one of the officially approved homilies. However, many parishioners wanted proper sermons, and in some places paid an extra preacher or lecturer to preach in the church on Sunday afternoons in addition to the incumbent.

We can see the beginnings of this in Pinner. In 1622 Richard Street left £2 a year 'towards the maintenance of a preaching minister ... at Pinner'. The 'preaching minister' suggests he had a lecturer in mind, though he may only have wanted to subsidise the curate supplied by the vicar of Harrow, who paid him but £10 a year out of the tithes of Pinner. Francis Tyndall of Tyndalls (Dove House) in Uxbridge Road, did not consider £10 to be sufficient provision and means of livelihood, so in 1630 he gave a field to be let at a profit 'for the benefit of John Willis and his successors [who] serve the said cure, being a preaching minister'.

John Willis had been minister in Pinner since 1622 and Tyndall's description of him suggests he had started well. As time went by Willis gave less satisfaction. Maybe he grew neglectful of preaching, or nonconformism in Pinner had increased, because in 1642 some parishioners complained to the Parliamentary Grand Committee of Religion in London that Willis 'seldom preaches or procures any other to perform that duty for him'. They petitioned for a lecturer, offering to maintain him if they could choose him themselves, and Philip Goodwin, M.A., was appointed to provide sermons in addition to the normal services.

But they had underestimated John Willis. Galvanised by the prospect of competition in his pulpit, on the day of Goodwin's arrival he went into St John's church and preached all Sunday afternoon until six o'clock in order to deny Goodwin the opportunity. This happened several times, and eventually the Parliamentary Committee ordered him to allow Goodwin to preach. In 1645 Goodwin became vicar of Watford.

John Willis continued as curate, perhaps preaching more satisfactorily, until his death about 1649. He must have had income of his own to support his family – his wife Joan, two sons, who both became clergymen in the Church of England, and three daughters – and to buy Moss Cottage as a home in 1634.

William Rowles followed Willis. A man in his early twenties, he had been born in Devon, where he had a little property, and was educated at Exeter College, Oxford. In 1649 Parliament authorised an augmentation of £60 to the official £10 which seems good, but these augmentations were not always paid. Rowles had married Martha Edlin, daughter of William and Mary of Pinner Marsh, whose house used to stand on the site of Pinner Grove and Grove Avenue. They would have been able

26 This was the original front of Moss Cottage, the home of John Willis, minister of Pinner, though much of what you see was added in the 19th century. The 17th-century pargetting is on the front of the little porch and the sketch shows the different designs. It is likely to be later than Willis's time.

to see that he did not go short. Rowles had a lecturer for a while, William Adderley, who left in 1651 to become a minister to the Navy at Chatham with a promised salary of £100 a year – dazzling in comparison with Rowles' money. After the Restoration of 1660 Rowles refused to take the Oath of Uniformity and was ejected from his position. The vicar of Harrow resumed control.

THE ESTABLISHED CHURCH

The average parishioner, chiefly wanting only to keep on the right side of God, was content with the established church. In 1676 the vicar of Harrow stated that there were no papists or nonconformists in the parish, patently untrue as far as Pinner was concerned. But there is no evidence of animosity between the sects in Pinner. In practice Dissenters had little alternative to using the parish church for baptisms and burials. Those very Dissenters who financed Rowles, or made their houses available for meetings, probably attended ordinary parish worship between times. They bore their share of church responsibilities, taking their turn as churchwardens or as trustees for Francis Tyndall's gift of land and other parish investments.

It has never been clear how well or ill the vicar of Harrow met Pinner's need for a minister but after the Restoration he seems to have provided curates regularly, and their names are known. Not so where they lived. The church house opposite St John's was still available; in 1663 and 1664 the churchwardens paid Mr Lane the curate £3 house rent because the church house was out of repair; he rented part of Simon Downer's house next door. Curates with Harrow School connections may have lived on or near the hill. In 1703 William Norrington, a city man who had grown up at Barrow Point in a cottage on the site of The Hall which he sold when he moved away in 1685, bequeathed £100 to buy a house for the minister of Pinner, and the predecessor of the present vicarage was acquired. The eventual fate of the church house is not known.

PARISH ORGANISATION

The new account book which Simon Rewse gave the churchwardens shows clearly how they looked after the church fabric and other matters, and how they raised the money. It also reflects the stresses of the times. The accounts for 1640-43, years of disturbance in the parish, are missing, though space was left in Rewse's book to write them in later, which was never done. There are no accounts for Rowles' period, and no space was left to put them in later, which may have been due to a change of, or breakdown in, practice. Yet the earliest extant parish registers to survive actually date from Rowles' period.

Church rates provided the chief source of income, based on the value of property. Just under half the householders paid them, specifically 63 people in 1665 and 1669, but rising later, to which were added another thirty or so non-residents who owned or rented substantial areas of land in Pinner. The total raised averaged five or six pounds a year, with greater sums for years when heavy expenditure on repair was planned. It exceeded £39 in 1637 and approached £50 in 1663.

Other sources of income were more erratic. A grave inside the church usually cost a parishioner 6s. 8d., or 10s. for the chancel, double in both cases for a stranger. Interior burials averaged one or two a year. As it became more fashionable to have memorials inside the church, parishioners at the front of the congregation could rest their eyes upon the large memorials in the chancel to Thomas Hutchinson of Canons, 1658, and Christopher Clitherow of Pinner Hill, 1685, should the sermon grow tedious.

The hire of church utensils provided occasional funds, and gives some clues about leisure pursuits. The equipment included three roasting spits which were sold by general agreement in 1627 for 17s. 9d. They had not been hired out since 1622 and were perhaps relics of communal activities no longer pursued. The hire of the church pewter – 30 dishes – which might have been used for community or private celebrations, brought in between 4d. and 4s. in some years. There were no receipts after 1662 though the church still had the pewter in 1689.

Games at Shrovetide – throwing at cocks – brought regular though variable sums. Edwin Ware explained it well: 'The birds were trained beforehand to avoid a stick thrown at them. Then, on Shrove Tuesday, the cock was held by a string nine or ten yards long tied to its leg. The competitors stood 22 yards away and were charged 2d. for three throws. It was won by the competitor who threw a stick and knocked it over and then ran up and caught it before it could recover its legs.' There must have been several limping cockerels in Pinner at the start of Lent. The highest amount was 20s. 4d. in 1627, far above the average of 8s. The game took place annually before the Civil War, but was only occasional after the Restoration, never reaching the earlier average. There were no entries after 1679, when it brought in the smallest sum ever, one shilling.

The parish outgoings covered running costs like communion wine, cleaning, keeping dogs out, repair of the fabric, some poor relief, and less frequent things like special prayers and bell ringing.

A new bell-frame inside the tower, made of vast timbers, shows how much repairs might cost. In 1631 £7 17s. 6d. was spent on timber and William Snape was paid £3 8s. 8d. to hew it. It must have been left to season until 1635 when Snape was paid a further £15 5s. 0d. to make the frame itself, Thomas Bayly was paid £2 12s. 0d. for ironwork, and £1 18s. 2d. went on additional items. The distinctively tall cross on the little cap-steeple was put up in 1637, possibly the first one. It was an enormous thing to haul up, and when it was in place the plumber covered it in lead, getting an extra ten shillings for doing it there rather than on the ground. Much was spent to quench everyone's thirst; wine for the plumber but beer for his workmen and the muscle men. A further £3 4s. 0d. was spent on a weather vane for the top of the cross. The vane lasted until blown down about 1880, but the cross did not require renewal until 1937. The roof was releaded in whole or part in 1663 for about £43, while the old lead was sold for £8. A fourth bell was commissioned in 1673, costing £27 – £15 for the metal, £12 for the casting, at Chertsey, plus more for carriage and attachments. There was already a clock in 1623, very likely in the tower, as now, which required attention every few years. It had two dials which were repainted in 1691. The clock-work was replaced in 1845, though in 1956 the local historian Edwin Ware considered that the dial itself was old, possibly the 17th-century one. The interior of the church was whitewashed every thirty or so years, and hassocks – a new comfort? – were provided in 1663. Local people were engaged for most of the work about the church, whether carpentry, ironwork, painting, laundry, transportation, ringing the bells, keeping dogs out of the building, or grave digging.

LICENSED DISSENTERS

William Rowles stayed in Pinner and the Edlins rallied round, giving, or selling, him one of their houses, Antoneys. In 1671 William Street of Love Lane left him £10 p.a. for life, and he was left small sums by two of the Stanbroughs of East End Farm Cottage.

Rowles was the first person in Pinner to be licensed as an Independent minister, which happened in 1672. The Independents opposed all forms of superior church government in favour of independent self-governing local congregations, and gradually after about 1662 became known as Congregationalists. Rowles' house, Antoneys, was licensed for religious meetings, and so were those of four local yeomen. They were Richard Stanbrough, who owned East End Farm Cottage; John Finch, who owned Waxwell Farm; John Winchester, who was probably renting the later West End Farm; and William Edlin – there is a choice of these, but the one concerned was probably William Edlin of The Grove, brother of Mrs Rowles. The first two of these houses still stand today, houses where the earliest nonconformist meetings in Pinner were held, and the second, the home of The Grail, is once again a place of religious activity and worship, this time by Roman Catholics. Rowles died in August 1684, having spent all his working life in Pinner. His assistant Joseph Heywood called him 'a very faithful, laborious ancient minister, whose strength is decayed, [so] that he cannot preach'.

Thomas Goodwin, a man of much wider experience and no apparent relation of Philip Goodwin, was the next known nonconformist minister. His father Thomas (1600-80) had been a leader among the Independents in London and an author too, with a large library which he left to his son. Thomas the younger (c.1650-1708) was educated partly abroad, and well travelled. He had published a history of Henry V and several religious pieces. By 1690 he had settled in Pinner, renting Pinner Place from William Edlin of the Grove.

Here Goodwin kept a school, not for children, as is usually assumed, but for students of divinity, an activity recently legalised by the Toleration Act of 1689. It was one of the early academies maintained by the Congregational Church to train its ministers. They were held in the master's home, like Goodwin's, and the students boarded. The school disappeared with Goodwin's death in 1708.

His successor was Stephen Crisp, possibly the son of a notable Quaker of the same name who died in 1692. An unnamed meeting house in Pinner was licensed for 'Protestant Dissenters called Quakers' in 1700, but nothing more is heard of it. Crisp's congregation was Independent and probably worshipped in Henry Street's house in Bridge Street, later called Dears Farm, which had been licensed in 1711, and subsequently in a barn licensed in 1714. Fairly soon afterwards John Street of

27 Dears Farm was a yeoman's house of the 16th century to which the right-hand part was added c.1684. The Independents met here for a few years from 1711. It ended its life as three dwellings, with the yard occupied by Pendry's cartage business.

West House financed a purpose-built meeting-house adjoining the barn. It stood just behind the site of the present shops adjoining St Luke's church. Crisp lived at Antoneys, which had reverted to the Edlin family, and was buried in Pinner churchyard in 1729.

With Crisp our knowledge of dissenting ministers in Pinner comes to an end. Most of the early dissenters came from the Edlin, Stanbrough and Street families, among whom there was a good deal of intermarriage. Thomas Hunt and John Bell, who are mentioned in the 1711 licence, are no more than names.

Getting an Education

UNIVERSITY

At least eleven young men of Pinner had a grammar school education in the 16th and 17th centuries and nine of them proceeded to university. All the university boys came from three yeomen families – Reading, Edlin, Clerk – with the exception of Francis Rewse, son of the lord's steward, then resident at Headstone Manor. They were these:

Name	College	Entered	School
John Reading of Middlesex	New College, Oxford	c.1572	
Richard Reading of Middlesex	Hart Hall (Hertford), Oxford	c.1572	
Thomas Reading of Pinner	King's, Cambridge	c.1573	Eton
Philip Edlin of Pinner	Emmanuel, Cambridge	c.1617	
Richard Reading of Middlesex	Emmanuel, Cambridge	c.1635	
Francis Rewse son of Simon	Oriel, Cambridge	c.1637	
Christopher Edlin son of Philip	Trinity, Cambridge	c.1656	Denham
Samuel Edlin son of Samuel of Pinner	Magdalene, Cambridge	c.1660	Watford

John Clerk of Pinner, described himself as an M.A. in his will 1644, but no further details known.

THE SYSTEM

The most usual subjects taught in village schools were the principles of Christian religion, morals, reading, writing and the casting of accounts with counters. Some pupils then went on to grammar schools. Girls were sometimes accepted at village schools but not at the grammars. The grammar school curriculum consisted of Latin grammar and literature, with such history and geography as might come through a study of the classical authors; perhaps some Greek after the 15th century; more Scripture; written arithmetic and manners. Exercise was thought important, so games and sports were played. Boys attended school six days of the week and church on Sundays. So shadowy is the history of many schools that it is not easy to distinguish village from grammar schools.

The people who valued the ability to read, write and reckon were those who could afford to do without the child's earnings or work for as long as necessary – tradesmen or skilled artisans, yeomen farmers and even some of the gentry. The 'poor', for whose benefit free grammar or other schools were established, meant this sort of person, unable to afford the individual tuition used by those higher up the social scale, who did not use schools.

OTHER EVIDENCE OF EDUCATION IN PINNER

The free grammar school which John Lyon founded in the manor of Harrow in 1572 has become famous far beyond its boundaries. There was an earlier school at Harrow, which Lyon's foundation may have invigorated or replaced. The first pupil from Pinner who can be identified, in 1637 or 1640, was John, son of Thomas Mathews, who owned three cottages on the site of 26-32 High Street and was resident in 1641.

Some boys were educated much further away as the list of graduates shows. There were two other grammar school boys at least, John and Simon Ewer, father and son, both yeomen, neither of whom went further. John recorded the births of his ten children and the deaths of his father and father-in-law in a book of hours (a medieval prayer book which went out of favour after the Reformation), and his own death was entered on 8 June 1589, presumably by his eldest son Simon.[19] The significant point is that the entries were in Latin, proof that the writers had been to grammar school. John Ewer, who bought Nowermans head tenement in Nower Hill about 1572, was new to the district and might have attended school in Watford, where his father Ralph died in September 1575. They had a great bible which Simon's widow Joan bequeathed to their son John in 1644.

It would not be surprising if Joan could read the bible too, even though she was unable to write her name on her will, for reading was a skill more frequently taught, and used, than writing. Neither needed a grammar school education. Even labourers sometimes learned to read, as the two Pinner men who used their ability to save themselves from the gallows in 1622 proved.

Signatures are the only other obvious evidence of educated people in Pinner. They were needed on wills, from testator and witnesses, and on churchwardens' accounts, from the wardens and parishioners' representatives. Those who could not write made their mark. Signatures may not represent all the educated people of Pinner, but they do give an idea of the minimum number who had the rudiments of learning. There are some 67 signatures, excluding those of the clergy; some are shaky, some accomplished. In the two years 1647 and 1648 15 different people signed wills or accounts and, in the four years from 1665 to 1669, 18 did so. The number of adult males listed in the Protestation Oath in 1641 was 186, so one might say that at the very least about one in ten adult men had some sort of education. The sample is a small one overall. The signatories included yeomen, tradesmen, husbandmen, and five women.

Very little is known of the writers' personal circumstances. It is a surprise to find Obadiah Ewer, son of Simon, and manager of Pinner Park Farm, making his mark in 1664, though he signed his name in 1666. Robert Stanbrough of East End Farm could write but only marked his will in 1660, which perhaps meant he was too ill or old to do more. His sons Richard and Joseph wrote, and so did his granddaughter Mary, Richard's daughter. Most women's wills were witnessed by men, literate or not, but in 1635 Katherine Street found two literate women to witness her will – Rose Burton, daughter of Robert Lawrence, a husbandman of Paines

Lane, and Elizabeth Randall, wife of Thomas the butcher, living close to the river beside the later *Red Lion*. In 1688 Mary Robins' will was signed by herself and two female witnesses, Mary Street of West End (Richard Stanbrough's daughter) and Emma Hobson, of whom nothing else is known.

THE SCHOOL IN PINNER

There was a village school in 17th-century Pinner, held in parish premises and repaired at the parish expense. The churchwardens spent £1 19s. 6d. on 'ripping' the school loft in 1634; an unstated sum on timber, boards and iron work for the school loft in 1675; and 5s. 7d. on mending the windows in 1681. The school seems to have been on the top floor, attic or loft of the church house opposite St John's. Its beginning and end are undiscovered, but it carried on throughout the upheavals of the Civil War and religious dissensions. There is but one other reference to the school – by William Norrington, when endowing the parsonage in Pinner 'where I once went to schoole'. His father Thomas had been unable to sign his name.

House and Home

From the later 16th century new houses in Pinner were built with two storeys throughout. The favourite form, L-shaped, had a main range with two rooms and a cross wing at one end with four rooms – as at 34-6 and 26 High Street, 3 and 125 Waxwell Lane, Bay House in Church Lane, Letchford House at Hatch End and Pinnerwood House. A linear plan with three rooms down and three up, all in a row, came second. This sort included Sweetmans Hall and the *Queen's Head* – as first built the *Queen's Head* was the uphill part of the present hostelry, with an adjoining house incorporated later. The houses had internal stacks with one or more hearths at either side, though Letchford House had external stacks along the back walls. A house could be improved by adding a wing, or by completely replacing a wing, so that whole parts are sometimes of different dates.

Window-glass was another major improvement. The windows of village houses had hitherto been small and unglazed, keeping out wet and chill by wooden shutters, or oiled cloth, which also excluded daylight. When first used, window-glass was regarded as a fitting which could be taken away when moving to another house – the lattice, or small sheet of glass pieces, was merely placed against the mullions and tied to them with wire. By *c.*1600 glass had become much cheaper and began to make its appearance in the better houses of a village. Window frames of the period are still in use at East End Farm, 34 High Street, Waxwell Farm – where one of the lattices may be the original leading and glass, and at Headstone, where two lattices may be original.

People in Pinner were as ready in those days as they are now to make their homes as comfortable as they could afford. It is easy to imagine the woman of the house arguing for an inside hearth to cook on – much more convenient and safe, so little smoke – while her husband might enjoy getting ahead of his neighbours and be proud of his brick chimney. And window-glass would keep the heat in, illuminate the hall and look good. The 17th century was the time when most open halls were converted – people were so eager to install chimneys that from 1662

28 The three distinct phases of 58 High Street are clear in this photo of 1923, when Peircey's butcher shop was still there. Odell's timber yard at the right would soon make way for Grange Gardens. The 17th-century white house half-hidden at the left was once the *Harrow*.

to 1689 the government seized upon them as a new object of taxation, called the hearth tax.

VARIATIONS

The timber-framed dwellings of Pinner are varied, and several remain only in part, particularly in the High Street. The chief distinction is between those in the High Street and those in the hamlets. The yeoman's house nearly always lay back from the road behind a yard formed by the barns, stables and other outhousing – East End Farm Cottage and Sweetmans Hall are the best examples today. One or two, like Gardiners, Waxwell Farm and Sharpes were set end-on to the road at one side of the yard. The small-holder's house was set end-on to the street, as at Bee Cottage and East End House, or at the front in line with the roadway, like Orchard Cottage and Bay House. They needed fewer ancillary buildings and their small yards were at the side or rear.

Unlike in towns, where competition for street frontage caused most houses to be built end-on to the street, those in Pinner Street abutted the street frontage and were parallel to it, though with room left at the side for access to the rear. Over time these spaces too were gradually filled by new houses or by simple enlargement of the old ones. The *Hand-in-Hand* (36-8), the *Queen's Head* and 29, 27 and 26 still have their side access from the street. At the *Victory* (no.4) access remains from Marsh Road. At 33 access was made by pushing a side wall of the house back about three feet at ground-floor level. Some houses were built quite late, like Bay House in Church Lane, about 1664, whose first tenant seems to have been wheelwright William Lawrence.

Some houses had few rooms. No. 58 High Street is a complicated house; the front part belongs to the late 16th century, the middle part the 17th, and the rear brick wing the 18th, the two last being in Church Lane. The front part of 58 is the oldest surviving purpose-built shop in Pinner, dating from the first half of Queen Elizabeth I's reign, and seems to have had two units on each floor. The other examples are 17th-century additions to High Street houses, on spare street frontage, usually used separately. No. 33, which was a wing added to 35, and the middle part of 58, each had two rooms to each floor, one on each floor heated, plus the possibility that the unheated lower room was partitioned. Smaller than these is 6 High Street with only one room to each floor, heated and perhaps partitioned. It was added to no.4, but faced the High Street, not Marsh Road, like that did. No. 7 High Street can be interpreted as a small house of one room per floor built onto no. 9-11, or as the remnant of a larger house, as is 26 High Street.

There was no extravagant ornamentation in Pinner houses. With occasional exceptions this moderation was a Middlesex characteristic rather than the result of poverty. The most widespread form of ostentation was close studding at the front, but as that is the part most liable to alteration or replacement it is easily lost. (In close studding the spaces between the vertical timbers is little wider than the timbers themselves, and is expensive in material and labour.) The only known example in Pinner was on the 16th-century cross wing at Dears Farm.

The overhanging upper storey or jetty was a very popular feature throughout the land until about 1620. Outside towns it was usually used at the front of a cross-wing which is where they were to be seen in Pinner. Eleven were in Pinner Street. The jetties at nos.31, 4, 6, 26, 36, 58 are still apparent but those at nos.7, 9, 25-7, and 33-5 have been lost in alterations. There were jetties also at Church Farm and Dears Farm.

Other current features were adopted in Pinner: gables on the facade at Waxwell Farm; diamond-set chimneys on several houses, the best at East End Farm Cottage; small windows set high in the wall abutting a larger one, at Waxwell Farm (removed); a staircase placed in its own wing, at the *Queen's Head*, Letchford House, Sweetmans Hall and 34 High Street; an arched tie-beam as a feature of the chief upper chamber, at Sweetmans Hall and Letchford House. At East End Farm Cottage a hunting scene, which experts date to the early 17th century, was painted on a wall of the downstairs room served by the new stack. Perhaps the new and young owner of 1610, Robert Stanbrough, was improving his house for a bride. Another individual touch was the pargetting on the porch gable of Moss Cottage, attributable to a later part of the century. A few old houses contain 17th-century panelling. The pieces at the *Queen's Head*, Church Farm and 25-7 High Street may be original to those places, but as it is easily movable it could have been put in later. In the half century up to 1930 it was very fashionable to introduce genuine panelling from elsewhere into an old house, which is probably the origin of the panelling in the dining room of Pinner House. Several 17th-century doors of planks with decorative moulding are still to be found. Though fairly standard they would have been the best doors, and being easily movable are often no longer in their intended position.

The timber-framed houses are Pinner's great treasure. They give a strong character and great charm to the High Street and lone specimens still identify several of the old original hamlets. Above all they are pieces of our past, the very places where our forebears lived, worked, drank, went home to, worried about, improved. They trudged up to them, looked at them across the street, passed them by – just as we do now.

THE HOUSEHOLDERS

Generally, houses with more than seven fireplaces were occupied by gentry or above; with four to seven by prosperous yeomen, craftsmen, and tradesmen; with two to three by lesser yeomen, craftsmen and tradesmen; and with one by husbandmen, labourers, or the poor. From the chimney (or hearth) tax list for 1664 we know that there were 141 households in Pinner. Twenty-eight of these had four or more hearths, about half had two or three, and a quarter had one. Compared with other places Pinner was right in the middle range.

Pinner Hill House had 15 fireplaces, Canons had 14, Headstone Manor had 12, and Woodhall Manor had ten. Seventeen of the 28 with at least four hearths belonged to yeomen, one to the ejected minister William Rowles, one to a mealman, while another was probably the tavern later called the *Queen's Head*. Weavers, gardeners, labourers, smiths, cobblers, husbandmen, servants all varied from one to three hearths. Only the mealmen stand out – John Street of Dears Farm with four, and John Lawrence of East End House with three, perhaps a result of the affluence which might accrue to a middleman who sold ground wheat or other grain.

As there were about 112 dwellings in Pinner some of the 141 householders lived in divided houses. A timber-framed house is easily partitioned and in the late 17th century some cottages were being described as 'now in two parts' or 'two houses formerly one'. The parts would have had one or two fireplaces in each. A few identifiable ones remain in the High Street – Thomas Read the tailor at no.7, William Bignall, labourer, in the gabled part of 34-38, and at 33-35 Robert Jacket had 33 and Thomas Bailey, a smith, had 35. Henry Dearing occupied part of 9-11 with one fireplace, but which part is unknown.

Houses worth less than 20s. per annum were exempt, provided no other property over that value was owned, and so were people already exempt from paying church rates, and paupers. Predictably, 13 of the 17 widows on the list were exempt, having places with one or two hearths – five at least in the High Street.

About 55 per cent of Pinner households were exempted from charge, which did not mean that they were poor. This compares with 62 per cent at Harrow on the Hill and 48 per cent at Ruislip. Ten people with three hearths and two with four qualified for exemption, none of whom paid church rates either, though it stretches the imagination to understand why. One of those with four, Humphrey Bishop, actually compiled the Hearth Tax list, but his residence has not been identified.

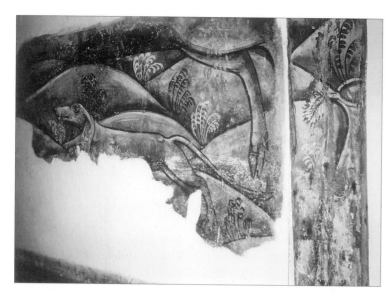

29 The wall painting at East End Farm Cottage was carried across both timber and plaster surfaces. Here we see the belly and shanks of a deer savaged by the hound chasing below it.

STANDARDS OF LIVING

A few shafts of light fall upon the yeoman's standard of living during this period.

Richard Clerk may be taken as a fair example. Clerk had about 40 acres of freehold land adjoining his house plus land at Pinner Wood, and this formed his real wealth. He died in 1609 and the following information comes from his will and inventory of property.[20]

The Clerk house at Pinner Green, called Pynnors, was a converted open-hall house in which both the hall and the new room created over it were heated. In the hall were two tables, a chair, seven stools, a long form, six cushions, and cooking utensils beside the fire. The parlour's contents show that it was both a withdrawing room and bedroom, characteristic of the time. It was hung with painted cloths (wall hangings), and contained a table, a chair, six stools, a panelled cupboard, a court cupboard – which was a two- or three-tier sideboard with some open and some closed shelves, a trunk, a bedstead with two feather mattresses, bolster, pillow and covers. In the new chamber was a similarly furnished bed, plus a round table and a stool, a trunk and a little chest, and two chairs, one of them wicker. In the bedroom over the parlour stood a canopied bed and an old bed, with insufficient coverings for both, and an old trunk. Clothing and Mistress Clerk's store of linen – eight pairs of sheets, 18 table napkins and spare pillow cases, were kept in the trunks or cupboards.

Mistress Clerk had a kitchen full of pots and pans, deep brass ones, shallower cooking pans with side grips, a couple of posnets – small cauldrons which could be placed inside a larger one to simmer in its hot contents, dripping pans, pestle and mortar, knives, hooks, tongs, ladles, washing-up bowl and a dresser – whether this was a table or cupboard is not clear. The buttery was also a dairy, full of tubs, casks, milk bowls, and pewter of all sorts – platters, saucers, basins, spoons, even fruit dishes and flower pots; a frying pan and a box holding 12 round trenchers (wooden plates) and 15 square ones. There was a boulting house (shed) for bread making, and a cheese house containing cheese-making equipment and a pickling tub with two flitches or sides of bacon inside. Feathers were stored in one loft, apples, pears and wool in another. Somewhere there was a men's chamber for workmen, with only one bed.

Richard Clerk had winter wheat in the ground, threshed wheat and beans in the barn, hay, oats, straw and chaff to feed the stock. He had a dozen horses, for work and perhaps for sale. His nine cows gave work for the dairy, his 14 sheep produced the wool, the seven swine were destined to follow their former companion into the pickling tub, while the geese, ducks and hens, 21 in total, provided eggs, meat and feathers.

But although this was obviously a rural family, the painted cloths show an awareness of, and desire for, some of the finer things of life. Other wills and inventories give similar hints: Henry Street of Dear's Farm had a clock (1683); Richard Stanbrough of East End Farm left books to son and daughters, and many auriculas in pots – rarities at the time, to his servant Henry Barber (1683); Elizabeth Street of 18a/22a Waxwell Lane had silver cups (1687); John Todd of The Elms had a silver tankard (1709). The painted wall at East End Farm cottage (c.1610) was especially aspirational for a yeoman, even more so given its very high quality.

The embroidery skill of Martha Edlin of The Grove (1658-1735) shows the type and quality of home furnishings. Between the ages of eight and 13 Martha worked samplers, work-box, jewel-box, and furnishing accessories like mirror

30 Made in Pinner in 1671 – Martha Edlin's casket embroidered with silk and metal threads, seed pearls and applied motifs, with her initials at the top. It had internal compartments for keeping small personal possessions.

frames, in tiny stitches using very fine thread and beads. This type of work, going beyond clothes making, characterised families with pretensions to sophistication. Martha's embroidery, accomplished and delicate, is amongst the best surviving in England and is on display at the Victoria and Albert Museum. Her parents were William and Abigail Edlin, who owned The Grove and soon inherited Pinner Place too. Martha was niece or great-niece to Richard the Tallowchandler and to Martha, wife of William Rowles. She inherited Pinner Place while younger sister Hannah – there were no brothers – inherited The Grove. Martha married Richard Richmond, an apothecary practising in Charterhouse Street, and in her widowhood returned to live at Pinner Place. She lies in Pinner church and is commemorated on the black and white tablet of her son-in-law and chief heir, Edmund Aubrey.

The Land

THE BEGINNINGS OF CHANGE

The common-field system continued in Pinner through the 16th and 17th centuries with the crops still grown according to the three-field system. Timetables for fencing were still being made in November 1676. General regulations about ploughing-up balks or greenways, picking other people's crops, gleaning too soon, pig-ringing, excluding animals, overstocking the common and so on were periodically promulgated, but fining for these offences dwindled until it had ceased by the middle of the 17th century. In the 18th century the manor court occasionally reiterated the rules about fences and overstocking and only threatened fines.

There was no enclosure of common or open-field land for pasture on a scale such as to bring about the dispossession of villagers. In a manor with few owners, they were more easily united to press for enclosure than in one like Harrow where most land was held in smaller quantities by yeomen and smallholders. Piecemeal enclosure of strips here and there did happen, however. The method is plainly stated in a court entry of April 1615 where John Greenhill of Roxeth was allowed to enclose, that is fence off, one common-field acre, 'the customs of the manor notwithstanding', and was charged 2s. 6d. for the licence. On this piece, therefore, the villagers lost the right to pasture their animals after harvest and the holder's yearly timetable of cultivation was his own. Other small pieces were enclosed from time to time as the Harrow Enclosure map of 1817 shows – portions of the common fields, particularly around their edges, and virtually all of Newlands – most of them in the 18th century, and seldom larger than a couple of acres.

THE PASSING OF THE YEOMEN

By the second half of the 17th century some yeomen were letting their houses to outsiders. This is the last century where we see many Pinner yeomen, especially the head tenants, clearly farming their own sizable holding themselves, be it copyhold or freehold. By virtue of their particular holdings they had had automatic responsibilities, pronounced on local matters, run the lord's farms, and been the virtual leaders of Pinner society. Now more and more they were being replaced by outsiders, even selling to them, while at the same time their old arena of influence, the manor court, was waning.

The medieval system of landholding, with its emphasis on residence and inheritance, was rapidly losing ground because most new owners regarded land purely as an investment and were not interested in manorial responsibilities. And as the holdings became fragmented, the tenants of the parts did not share the heritable rights of the tenant of the whole. During the century we can observe yeomen families dying out, that is, having heirs who already lived elsewhere or moved away, whether those heirs were sons or sons-in-law.

FOUR YEOMAN FAMILIES

A few yeoman families had been more than usually successful through some advantage of luck, aptitude or health. Each of the Reading, Bird, Street and Edlin families was in the manor in 1315, and at some time controlled a lordship estate, which was always beneficial. And each conformed to the usual pattern in the 17th and 18th centuries – the propertied heirs sold up, died out, or were females marrying elsewhere, while the remaining descendants of younger sons made do with smaller holdings or went into trade.

The Readings were associated with Headstone Manor from the end of the 14th century, and by 1550 the five family head tenements were concentrated in the hands of Thomas Reading of Headstone. Thomas Reading was thus a man of considerable status, surely one of the most influential people in Pinner, and maybe in Harrow, and began to share the gentlemanly aspirations of many ambitious yeomen in the fluid social climate of the 16th century. His children were wet-nursed, two sons went to university, and he obtained a licence for a dovecote at one of his houses, like the lord's dovecote he enjoyed at Headstone. Thomas and his son Robert were governors of Harrow School. But his large family moved away or dwindled. Great-grandson Simon, of Readings at East End, was the last of his line to live in Pinner, dying in 1703. Four of their houses still exist, Headstone, East End Farm Cottage, Tudor Cottage and Sweetmans Hall.

John Bird took over Crowchers from Henry Sewale in 1430 and almost exactly three hundred years later, in 1731, his direct descendant William Bird died there, without heirs, the last yeoman in the family. John's son Thomas ran Woodhall Manor for a while from 1456, and Thomas's son Hugh seized a fresh opportunity in 1479 by securing appointment as deputy keeper of Pinner Park. The last family member there was Robert Crowle, son of Amy Bird, in 1610. The branch at Crowchers became quite disreputable after 1560 while the branch at Barrow Point virtually founded the hamlet there, having created four of the five dwellings which straggled along Barrow Point Lane. The last member in Pinner was Mary, who ran the *White Hart* during the 1750s with her husband William Bellamy.

By 1409 John Street had the head tenancy in Bridge Street which became known as Streets and his descendants in the female line kept the house until Daniel Hill sold it in 1889 (rear of 53-7). John's great-grandson William became farmer of Woodhall in 1478. West End was the heartland of the Streets in the 17th and 18th centuries. They began with Aldryches (West House) and then bought much of the land west of the old lane, where they added West Lodge, and soon they were gentlemen. Henry Street of West Lodge (died 1750) was one of the Gentlemen Yeomen who formed the personal bodyguard of the king. During the 18th century the other branches left Pinner for business in other places while those remaining were the chief support of the Dissenters. William, the last member of the West End branch, emigrated to New York in 1796 and disposed of his many properties in Pinner. Both 18a/22a Waxwell Lane and East End Farm Cottage were owned by Streets at one time.

The Edlin name lasted longest, by a whisker. Farmers of Woodhall for long stretches, there were also periods when they dominated Hatch End and the Marsh. During the 17th century they had many London connections – Richard of the Tallowchandlers' Company, Philip, rector of St John Zachary, and marriage into the city families of Offley and Clitherow, both of which supplied Lord Mayors. Some of Philip's sons went to America where great numbers today count him as their ancestor. Martha Edlin's embroidery belongs to the nation. In Pinner they had died out in name by 1700, except at Oxhey Lane Farm, where they never lived, owned by Edward Edlin, a Baron of the Exchequer. His last daughter sold it in 1806.

IV

The Eighteenth Century

The rise of landlords

The 18th century is one of the lesser known periods in Pinner, lying as it does between the centuries of the highly informative manor rolls and the 19th, when more activities were recorded, and their survival rate is greater.

The tentacles of landlordism nevertheless continued to reach into the village and affect its society. London and other towns did not merely draw people away to work, they were attractive places of residence, as the proliferation of fashionable houses and shops in London's new and expanding West End demonstrated so well. The momentum of opportunity in the capital enabled more men to practise a trade or profession there, and have their land bring in rent, instead of having to work it for a livelihood as had been the case for their forebears.

In Pinner the result was a decided increase in both the number of absentee landlords and of resident gentlemen paying rent. The three former demesne farms had long been examples of this, and the practice travelled down the scale as the old yeoman families of Pinner moved to London, or elsewhere, or had non-resident heirs, or died out. By 1800 most of the one-time yeoman holdings in Pinner, copyhold or freehold, were either managed for absentee landlords, or their houses were let to gentlemen, and the fields let separately. Some were let whole – Canons, Dove House, Parkgate, Letchford House, Pinnerwood, Waxwell, and possibly West End Farms. Two new farms of substance were let from the start – Oxhey Lane Farm created about the end of the 17th century by the Edlins, and Woodridings Farm (end of Woodridings Close) created by Lord Hunsdon early in the 18th.

Renting land was popular at all levels, even by those who only had a paddock, and makes it difficult to assess how much land was worked by a particular individual at a given date. By way of example Edmund Aubrey of Pinner Place let his land to five people in 1727. Gideon Lott the victualler, who bought Sweetmans in 1719, still needed to rent from four or five other people between 1727 and 1743. William Reeve the butcher rented fields from three people between 1739 and 1741, and his successor Thomas Hodsdon rented from five in 1755 – they probably used the fields for keeping stock prior to slaughter.

In the High Street between nine and 15 of the two dozen or so properties were owner-occupied in 1700, but only between two and seven in 1800. William Bodimeade, the brickmaker of Weald, exemplified one trend by investing profits

31 This row of three humble cottages on the site of 53-7 Bridge Street may have been built by John Ward, died 1742, his daughter Mary, or Thomas Trevethan, who purchased the property in 1773. Farmer William Hedges bought them in 1852 and added the row of about four brick buildings behind, all known as Hedges Cottages. At the right is The Cottage, late 19th-century, on the site of 59.

32 Cottages at West End. In the early 1800s John Ewer squeezed three plastered cottages against the back of three weather-boarded ones built in the 18th century, and a seventh was later added across the further end. They look like the work of Thomas Trevethan. All seven fitted into the house and garden space of the present 16-17 Dickson Fold. The gable at the extreme left belongs to 65 West End Lane.

from his expanding business in property, including 15-27 and 26-32 High Street. Several High Street properties were refronted – nos. 1-9, 13-19, 25-27, 48-52.

Humbler dwellings for rent arose also, with ground floors of brick and upper storeys of timber and plaster, not very solid. A row of three cottages for letting went up at the site of 53-7 Bridge Street and a similar one at West End (site of 16-17 Dickson Fold). For owner-occupation a cottage was built by John Tame, a carpenter, opposite West Lodge in 1727, and another by bricklayer Daniel Lee on waste at Wood Lane End (site of 56-8 Bridge Street).

At the same time flourishing Londoners wanted country residences, and houses in the environs of the capital were refurbished or rebuilt. Timber framing would not do – brick was by now the preferred building material, even if the changes made were only cosmetic. Six houses in Pinner were rebuilt and made suitable for gentlemen – Pinner House, Pinner Place, Pinner Hill House, The Lodge, possibly The Grove, and 32 High Street. Three cottages came down to make way for a new mansion later called The Hall. The smaller West Lodge, whose name was taken by the school which stands on the site, was built shortly before 1749 for William Street, gentleman, third son of John of West End, and two new houses in Headstone Lane at Hatch End were probably for gentlemen. Some houses were remodelled – the parsonage, East End House and Nower Hill House.

People and Places

JOHN GIBSON

John Gibson, who built The Hall, is a nice example of social improvement. He was a businessman who married a genteel lady with property of her own, invested heavily in more property, sent his eldest son John to grammar school and university in order to enter the gentlemanly priesthood of the Church of England, set his other two sons up in businesses of their own, and provided good dowries or legacies for his four daughters.

John was a jeweller with a shop in Bow Street, London, somewhere between the present opera house and Russell Street, which he inherited from his uncle Martin Darden (died 1711). Darden had owned a cottage at Barrow Point in Pinner since 1696, and with his attention thus attracted here Gibson bought an adjoining one in 1715. Or perhaps the attraction of a potential wife had prompted the purchase, for in Pinner Hill House lived Dorcas Shower with her aunt Lady Anne, widow of Sir Bartholomew Shower. Dorcas would inherit Islips Manor in Northolt when her aunt died, which happened in 1723. John and Dorcas were married in Pinner church in 1716.

John was soon buying more houses in Pinner – The Bay House in Church Lane in 1720, Elmdene, a few yards away, in 1722, Barrow Point House (then a cottage) and land near his first two Barrow Point houses in 1724, and Church Cottage at the western end of Church Lane in 1727, which he may have rebuilt, though it is not the one now standing. He bought two big properties in Harrow Weald which in general were let. Gibson replaced his uncle's and his own first cottage at Barrow Point with The Hall, a mansion in extensive grounds at the eastern corner of Uxbridge Road and Paines Lane. In 1731 he was allowed to enclose two rows of trees in front of

33 The Hall, originally built by John Gibson, was much altered by George Bird in Victorian times. In this 20th-century picture St Thomas' Drive is in the background.

it. The Gibson descendants gradually moved away, and the last Gibson property in Pinner, Elmdene, was sold in 1859.

A notebook survives which was used by various members of this family between 1724 to 1746. The entries are irregular. There are wages paid to nurses, probably children's nurses, and it is a surprise to find that they were only paid at six- or twelve-month intervals; one was Sarah Elkin, probably a resident of Pinner. Dorcas listed 21 pieces of green and white satin, pieces of new sheeting, and 37 flaxen sheets. Only one entry mentions the business – a receipt by Richard Stanton (a relative) of £96 14s. od. for diamonds and an annuity. There are repairs, refurbishment, even rebuilding, sales of timber, agricultural expenses at Islips Manor, and some details of lettings.

THE HILL FAMILY

Joseph Hill of Harrow took over the butcher's shop at 58 High Street in 1702 and died in 1741, having founded a Pinner dynasty of successful businessmen. In this family it was the practice to leave the trade to the youngest son, and Joseph's younger son Thomas inherited it and prospered. Successful butchers bought stock, sometimes from individuals, sometimes from drovers on their way to the capital, and kept them for short periods while awaiting slaughter or for longer-term fattening. Thomas rented many pieces of land, which he probably used in this way, or rented temporarily to passing drovers to graze their flocks or herds – his son Daniel, who inherited the business, called himself a grazier in 1809. In the course of his long life (1718-97) Thomas bought many properties; a cottage near the *Red Lion*, Church Cottage in Church Lane and the divided cottage adjoining, two cottages at Barrow Point Hill, and Church Farm. He was living at Church Cottage when he died, having let the residential part of Church Farm to John Procter, one of the churchwardens.

His sons added more properties. Joseph, the oldest, whose livelihood came from his tenancy of Sudbury Court Farm in Harrow, bought Bee Cottage, and inherited Marsh Farm, 34-8 High Street and cottages at Barrow Point from his wife's brother, John Carter. Thomas junior bought Coldharbour (Gulls) and 41

High Street. Daniel the youngest (1761-1823), the grazier, who inherited most of his father's properties as well as the business, added Nowermans and a cottage between the *Red Lion* and the Hills' existing cottage.

The Hills acquired much land from the Enclosure Award at the beginning of the 19th century and they invested in more, most of it concentrated along Rayners Lane where they built a couple of farmworkers' cottages (erroneously called Rayners Lane Farm). The family spread beyond Pinner. Daniel the grazier let the butcher's shop and went to farm in Hertfordshire, where his wife had connections, though his son Daniel returned to Pinner. During the 19th century the Pinner branch contracted. Daniel's grandson Daniel III (1835-1906) is said to have loved the eldest daughter of William Burrows, the vicar, who forbade the marriage. Daniel died unmarried and his lands, still including the original butcher shop, went to the children of his sister, Patty Cox. In the churchyard of Pinner stands a row of tombstones, marking the resting places, just yards from their houses round the top of the High Street, of the Josephs, Thomases and Daniels of this once dominant family.

THE BLISSARDS

In the burial register of Pinner Parish are written these two entries; '3rd March 1781 – Jeremiah Blissard, a negro; 23rd October 1781 – Phillis Blissard, a negro woman.' This is all we know about them.

Most of the several thousand people of African origin estimated to have been in England in the latter part of the 18th century originated as slaves brought from the West Indies by their former masters. In 1772 the Lord Chancellor, Lord Mansfield, gave his renowned judgment in the case of James Somersett that, in England, slavery was illegal. The majority of black people were probably servants, especially outside London, because few other employments would have been available to them. Indeed it had long been fashionable for the aristocracy to keep a black servant as an exotic accoutrement of the household, to be shown off to visitors. Often they were children and are sometimes seen in portraits, as part of the decor along with horses, dogs, drapes and works of art.

Jeremiah and Phillis Blissard may have been like that, for they are hardly likely to have been able come to England independently. There were two places in Pinner where minor aristocrats lived who might have had the inclination to keep and show off black servants, Pinner Hill House, home of James and Lady Jane Brydges, and The Hall, home of Lady Beauclerc. Neither family is known to have had direct connection with the West Indies but their relatives may have had. Jeremiah and Phillis probably began as slaves, entering the household of either the Brydges or the Beauclercs as fashionable treasures and staying there after becoming legally free. They may have been brother and sister, mother and son, or a married couple. A Jeremiah Blizzard married Mary Gunthorpe at St James Church Piccadilly on 17 July 1759, but no connection has been established.

The Blissards are the first Africans so far found in Pinner – indeed the first people of non-European origin known to have been resident in the parish, and would have been curiosities whenever they ventured into public places. Though free when they died, what meaning did this have for them at that time? Perhaps it was significant that they died within a few months of each other.

PINNER HILL HOUSE

The best society in Pinner was to be found at Pinner Hill House, which, after a succession of lawyer owners, was bought for Lady Jane Brydges in 1755 by the Marquis of Caernarvon. They were cousins, grandchildren of the 1st Duke of

Chandos, whose seat was Cannons in Little Stanmore. Jane's father had been the heir, but died before he could inherit, so the title went to the nearest male in line, her uncle Henry, father of the marquis. The widow, who would never now be a duchess, hated Henry. Jane married another cousin, plain Mr James Brydges in 1755 – hence the need for the house – and in Pinner they lived a very quiet life indeed, though Jane had once ruffled the waters of Mayfair before her marriage. Coming home late one night in a sedan chair after attending a function against her mother's wishes, her mother shut her out. Jane went to her brother-in-law. Next morning the dowager marchioness, seriously drunk, raved and screamed outside the house of Duke Henry in Cavendish Square, accusing him, falsely, of giving her daughter refuge. It was fine entertainment for the hoi-polloi and delighted the malicious letter-writers in society, from whom comes the information.[21]

34 Lady Jane Brydges and her husband, who lived at Pinner Hill House from 1755-89, were probably the owners who rebuilt it. The portrait is by Alan Ramsey.

It was most likely James and Lady Jane Brydges, owners 1755-89, who rebuilt Pinner Hill House towards the end of the century, though it could have been James Forbes of the East India Company, who bought it from Catherine, Janes sister and heir, in 1790. Forbes was a collector of far eastern antiquities, and owned a couple of houses in Great Stanmore, including one bought from the Duke of Chandos.

35 The eastern wing of Pinner Hill House, which was rebuilt in the 18th century.

THE HALL

The Hall had been built for letting to townsfolk. A Lady Scott rented it from 1737-42 or so; in 1746 the high rent of £50 a year was being paid by a Mrs Ruston; and James and Lady Jane Brydges rented it while the purchase of Pinner Hill was going through. It reached its social apogee during the 1770s when rented by Martha Beauclerc, herself the daughter of the Earl of Lovelace, and widow of the impecunious Lord Henry Beauclerc, grandson of Charles II through Nell Gwynne. In Pinner churchyard lies William Skenelsby (1657-1775), who spent the last 29 of his 118 years as a retainer of the Beauclercs; he claimed to have pushed a loaded barrow up the High Street in his hundredth year. In 1779 Francis Legge, of the family of the Earl of Dartmouth, and called Governor Legge, bought The Hall and lived there until he died four years later, leaving it to William, Earl of Dartmouth, who also let it. John Spranger, an important lawyer, bought it from the earl in 1795 for his residence.

PINNER HOUSE

Pinner House could only boast 'honourables', the style accorded to daughters and younger sons of lords, but which did at least make them feel superior to gentlemen. In the middle of the 17th century the name of the place was Brickwall House, which implied a house, or at least a boundary wall, of brick, but the present Queen Anne house is a rebuilding or radical improvement of about 1720, probably by Robert Stanbrough, local man, prior to selling it to London bookseller Gavin Stokoe in 1721. It still has its fine early 18th-century staircase, panelled parlour and panelled chamber above. Owned since 1742 by a gentleman named Charles Palmer, Pinner House passed into the ownership of Col. the Hon. Samuel Townsend, of the 34th Regiment of Foot in 1780, and was let to Lady Jane Hamilton, legally separated from her husband, a man perhaps related to the Hamiltons of Great Stanmore. Townsend was a general when in 1788 he sold Pinner House to the vicar of Pinner, Walter Williams, and his wife, the Hon. Mary Williams.

THE LODGE

The Lodge at Pinner Green, replaced by Elm Park Court, was occupied by lesser-ranked people of quality. It was handsomely rebuilt about 1750-80, either by John Dewsall, a wealthy landowner who acquired it in 1753, or by Allen Wall, a townsman who had made his money in the expanding furniture-japanning business and invested some of it in this place in 1780.

John Zephaniah Holwell, who bought the house about 1794, was probably more renowned in his own day, and now, than his contemporary residents in Pinner. Holwell had been the acting Governor of Bengal when the Indian Mutiny erupted in 1756. His tale of how he and 165 English soldiers and others had been forsaken by the British forces at Calcutta, and crammed into one small room called the Black Hole by the rebel leader Suraj ud Dowlah on the evening of 20 June, of how only 16 had survived till morning, to be marched off and further imprisoned in the baking heat for another couple of weeks, had resounded around the country and made Holwell very famous.[22] A few years later he erected a monument over the common grave of the victims at his own expense. Holwell did not come to Pinner until his

36 The very elegant Lodge at Pinner Green, where John Zephania Holwell ended his days, was pulled down about 1934.

eighties. He rented Pinner Place, where his second wife died in 1794 – he placed a tablet to her memory in St John's Church – and then bought The Lodge, where his daughter Sarah looked after him until his own death in 1798. The burial place of Governor Holwell is a mystery. Long after his death his figures were disputed by some historians of British India.

PINNER PLACE

The home of Martha Edlin, nee Richmond, Pinner Place was given a baroque facade in the first or middle part of the century, presumably by Edmund Aubrey, her son-in-law. He was a coach maker in Long Acre, the centre of this booming business, but his sons left the trade and entered the gentlemanly callings of the church and the law. After the death of Stephen Crisp, Pinner Place had been let to William Charles, curate of St John's, and then to his successor William Saunders.

THE GROVE

Montjoy Kirton, husband of Martha Edlin's sister Hannah, let The Grove to gentlemen. Sir Michael Foster (1689-1763), a judge of the Kings Bench, is said to have lived there and several military men followed him – Francis Bolton, an officer of the Welsh Fusiliers in the time of Queen Anne who died there in 1746 and had a fine marble monument in St John's church, Colonel Miles, an owner, and General Jones, his tenant. Pictures of The Grove suggest 18th-century alterations.

Only Pinner Hill House and Pinner House have survived.

OTHER GENTLEMEN'S HOUSES

Three smaller 18th-century gentlemen's houses still stand in Pinner. No.20 Waxwell Lane was newly-built between 1732 and 1739 by Mr Burr or Mr Shepherd. It is a small, gentleman's house added to the old timber-framed farmhouse behind, which

37   Giant pilasters give Pinner Place a baroque air. It could be seen looking towards Marsh Road from across the Pinn until nos. 137-183 Marsh Road interrupted its view.

continued to be let to the tenant farmer, an arrangement producing an odd juxta-position of residents when towards the end of the 19th century the farmhouse was divided into five tiny tenements. The bay windows are early 20th-century additions.

The elegant and neat facade of 32 High Street is emphasised by its central position in the street, despite its small size. This was one of William Bodimeade's speculations, built in 1773 and insured with the Sun Fire Office the same year. It still has traces of its original interior decoration downstairs. James Madgwick, nonconformist minister and father-in-law to William Street of West End, rented it for a few years, followed by Richard Bickham, surgeon, who bought East End House a little later.

East End House had been improved by his time, from the look of its symmetrical five-bay facade, though the improver is not known. Bickham sold it to Henry Horne and in 1811 it was bought by its most famous resident, Henry James Pye, the Poet Laureate (died 1814).

Church Farm is worth a mention although it was not new. The present entrance hall and staircase were remodelled – about mid-century to judge by their style – so they would probably have been installed by Samuel Clark, who bought the place in 1733 and resided there until he acquired The Hall in 1751. He placed a memorial in the church to his wife Rebecca, who died at Church Farm in 1737. Clark became a J.P. and was himself buried in Pinner in 1760.

A CURIOUS RELIC

An enigmatic picture is still to be seen on the wall of Bee Cottage, painted in the naive style but now dark and worn. Scratched across the top are the words J LEE 1757. What does it commemorate – could it be the fair? And who commissioned it – the Lees, who were bricklayers? This sort of painting is a rare survival, so they were probably never common. Pinner is lucky to have two wall paintings, this, and the one at East End Farm Cottage.

Commerce

SHOPS

Not many shops were yet needed in Pinner. The butcher's facilities at 58 High Street came back into use when Joseph Hill, a butcher from Harrow, took over after Thomas Cook's death, and the family carried on there into the 19th century. John Bird's butcher shop at 1-5 closed in 1703 with his sale of the property to John Street, who only kept the tavern going. William Reeves, whose family was devastated in the epidemic

38 In the wall painting at Bee Cottage men and women in 18th-century costume hold hands around what looks like a maypole in front of a cottage. In the damaged foreground there seems to be a melee involving an animal and men fighting with fists and swords.

of 1741, had a butcher's shop at 18-24 High Street from about 1724, continued by his widow Mary, and then his son-in-law Thomas Hodsdon, but by 1760 the premises were registered as a tavern, the *White Hart*, in the name of his son John Reeves.

The old bakery at 4 High Street had gone out of use by 1738. Samuel Tame had a bakery at no.13, where he lived, or perhaps at 15, which was John Ives's bakery by 1757. This one remained a bakery until about 1890. The bakery at 35 High Street came into use about 1800 and continued into the 20th century; its defunct 19th-century oven is still to be seen.

Thomas Cook's death provided the opening for William Aldwin, a tallow-chandler who arrived in Pinner about 1703 and rented 7 High Street. He bought it from John Read in 1706 and had bought the four adjoining properties (now 1-13) by 1720. One was the original *Queen's Head*, subsequently renamed the *Lower Queen's Head* and then the *Crown*, and another was Samuel Tame's baker's shop. These premises have been so much altered since 1700 that it is difficult to be sure where the lines of division were at any particular date. James Wilshin had a shop at 25 High Street in 1767, but by 1778 was renting no.11, calling himself a grocer and draper.[23] Cook, and later Wilshin, had quite a wide range of goods, which would make a shop viable, and they may have been general stores, very close to what was more recently called the village shop. Some others were called, simply, shopkeepers – William Seymour 1704-35, William Tiler 1707, George Howard 1767, Mr Ratcliffe 1773 (25 High Street), Daniel Wilshin 1773 (23 High Street). There were also mealmen in Pinner – Philip Aldwin, John Hill and Matthew Carter (4 High Street).

James Wilshin was the first person in Pinner to be called a draper when, in 1778, he insured his combined stock as draper and grocer to the value of £390, an enormous difference, even allowing for the lapse of years, from that of Thomas Cook some 76 years before. Once a maker of woollen cloth, by the 18th century a draper sold ready-made cloth and haberdashery – small items of clothing such as hats, caps and kerchiefs, plus accessories for dressmaking like needles, pins and thread, ribbons and tapes.

A shop of a different sort – John Evans' barber shop – was opened by 1783 at 25 High Street. Who would have thought there would be so much demand for this service in a rural village?

Some businesses needed workshops or yards, rather than shops. There were shoemakers or cobblers – William Ward, at the site of 57 Bridge Street in 1703, John Beck between the *Red Lion* and the stream from 1726-57, one Clayton in 1764 at Daniel Lee's cottage, 56-8 Bridge Street, and, unplaceable, Ingram Blanchett in 1753 and John Seymour in 1784. There were tailors – Philip Kirkham at what became the *George*, Daniel Whitlock at 23 High Street 1767, and James and John Murch at Daniel Lee's cottage. Wheelwrights were based at 27 High Street from 1763; first Joseph Lack, then John Putnam, and lastly, from about 1789 for over two centuries, the Beaumont family. There were carpenters for over a century on the south side of Chapel Lane where the railway embankment is. John Blake I (died 1742) had a covered yard there in 1712 and was followed by his son John II (died 1749). New carpenter Thomas Trevethan bought it from their heirs in 1767, and another new carpenter, Charles Woodbridge, who took over the business from Trevethan's heirs sixty years later, still had his timber yard there in 1842. The blacksmith's premises in the late 18th century have not been discovered.

TAVERNS

Two taverns survived from the 17th century; the *Crown*, called in 1722 the *Upper Queen's Head*, then in 1766 the *Queen's Head*, which continues; and the *Queen's Head* at 3-5 High Street, renamed in 1722 the *Lower Queen's Head*, and then in 1759 the *Crown*, which closed in 1896.

39 The *George* in the marsh, painted by Eleanor Rummens of The Grove, shortly before the Metropolitan Railway was built beside it in 1885. It was rebuilt in 1889.

In 1751 the authorities began to list the names of houses they licensed as taverns, which reveals a fuller picture. The newer ones, in order of approximate age, were as follows, though most of the names were first written down in 1751:

name	site	first and last presumed date	first licensee
Red Lion	Red Lion Parade, Bridge St	1727-1961	Francis Barrett
Chequer (no.1)	Myrtown, Church Lane	1722-55	Jeremiah Frayle
George	Marsh Road	1742-present	Jane Chapman
Bell	south end of Bell Close	1751-present	William Tyler/Taylor
White Hart	34-6 High Street	1731-72	William Bellamy
Crooked Billet	about corner of Barrow Point Lane and Oakhill Avenue	1751-81	John Langley
Chequer (no.2)	Chantry Place, south side	1747-63	James Nutt
Sun	Chantry Place, south side	1767-81	William Evans

There were always five establishments in business, three of them still with us – the *Queen's Head*, the *George*, and the *Bell* (now the *Orange Tree*). The short lives of the second *Chequer*, *Crooked Billet* and *Sun* may have been a measure of their peripheral and isolated situations. The first acquisitions by a brewery occurred when Stephen Salter of the Rickmansworth brewery bought the *Bell* in 1765 and the *George* in 1786 – whether all the publicans had brewed their own beer before this is a moot point. The name *White Hart* was revived for a beerhouse in the 19th century.

THE WINDMILL

The windmill blew down in 1721 and John Blake I or II, carpenter, bought the wreck and rebuilt it. Most of the millers were probably employees and none is named after William Mayne died in 1706. Samuel (1718-68) second son of John

40 This is probably John Blake's windmill of the 1720s, with the miller's house at far left, which originally stood isolated on the common. When this painting was made about 1870 the house had become three cottages and newer buildings between were used as Mill Farm. The view is from Pinner Hill Road.

Blake II, sold the mill about 1752 to absentee landlords. In 1775 Joseph Dell bought the mill – he too was a carpenter.

The last Pinner windmill was a tower mill with wooden walls upon a brick base, according to a painting made in 1870, two years before it burned down. It may have been Blake's, though if diagrams of a smock mill (which was a slightly different type), on two 18th-century maps can be trusted, it could be that Dell had had to remodel it. The miller's house, probably built by John Blake, survived until the early 1960s as 1, 2 and 3 Mill Farm Cottages.

Joseph Dell also had a small mill on the Pinn behind 27-35 Love Lane which burned down in 1787, causing damage worth £90 and destroying stock worth £20.[24] He seems to have rebuilt it between 3 January 1788, when he insured the utensils, stock and goods 'in his water corn mill and kiln for drying beans therein' with the Sun Insurance Company for £500, and 15 February when he reinsured for £200. A small dam or sluice-gate would have produced a sufficient height of water to turn a small wheel. The mill was out of use when Victor White redeveloped the site in 1828.

A Parish at Last

THE ESTABLISHED CHURCH

A most significant event occurred in 1766 when Pinner was at last made into a parish independent of and separate from Harrow. The vicar of Harrow was entitled to all the existing tithes, so the new living was endowed from other sources, primarily Queen Anne's Bounty. The new incumbent was styled perpetual curate, not assistant curate, because, although independent, with no tithes he could not be called vicar.

The living was made up of; £200 from the Bounty; the land Tindall had given in 1630; land in Downfield bought in 1732 with the proceeds of timber felled on Tindall's gift; an annual sum of £4 given by Sir Thomas Franklin in 1728; £8 a year from the vicar of Harrow in lieu of tithes – to be paid quarterly in the porch of St John's; and the parsonage. In 1772 another 22½ acres were bought for £400 (£325 collected by public subscription, £75 from the Harrow School Governors) and the perpetual curate bought an adjoining 12 acres on his own account. Together these 34 acres constituted the medieval virgate of Hugh Elis of Hatch End, later called Howells, still surviving as one entity. It lay at the corner of Pinner Road and Headstone Lane, and in the 20th century Southfield Park was formed across it. In 1811 the annual income from all these sources was considered to be £180, plus the house.

Before separation Pinner was served in the old way by clergy from Harrow, their names, but little else about them, usually known from their signatures on the registers. All had an academic education, of course, and counted as gentlemen. In the 18th century Pinner duty was often given to the assistant master, later called the under-master, of Harrow School. John Hooker was the assistant throughout the period, 1714-16, when he looked after Pinner; so too were James Cox, 1717-28, William Saunders, 1743-7, William Cox, 1747-8, and William Prior, 1748-58 (called a detestable tyrant by one of his pupils). James Cox not only married the headmaster's daughter but succeeded him in office in 1730. In that position he adopted drunken and irregular habits, and absconded, deeply in debt, in 1746. Before then, in 1736, he bought the new Woodridings Farm from William Hunsdon, which provided a fine dowry after his death for his daughter Margaret when in 1763 she married Samuel Parr, a surgeon and apothecary in Harrow. Samuel Parr, her stepson and her heir, was the Dr. Parr who left Harrow School to set up a rival institution at Great Stanmore in 1771.

The parsonage bought with William Norrington's bequest did not suit everyone. Both William Charles and William Saunders rented Pinner Place, and William Prior was said by Archbishop Secker (see below) to have resided in Harrow.

Walter Llewarch Williams (c.1735-1810) was sent to Pinner in 1764 and became the first perpetual curate in 1766. Ten years later he was appointed Vicar of Harrow. Now the old system might have re-emerged, with Williams attending to Harrow while an assistant curate took care of Pinner, but he did nothing of the kind. He performed most of the work in Pinner and used assistants – easily available from Harrow School – at St Mary's. A later incumbent of Pinner, Charles Grenside, liked to imagine Williams 'standing every quarter day in Pinner porch and solemnly taking money from one pocket as vicar of Harrow and transferring it to the other pocket as perpetual curate of Pinner'. In 1779 Williams was appointed rector of Throwley in Kent. He now had three incomes, and in 1781 he ventured upon matrimony. He was able to attract the Hon. Mary Beauclerc of The Hall, great-grand-daughter of Charles II through Nell Gwynne. She was the third of Henry and Martha Beauclerc's six daughters, all of them

41 Walter Llwarch Williams, the longest serving minister of Pinner, from a miniature, whereabouts now unknown, given by an anonymous lady to the Rev. Francis Joyce, vicar of Harrow, and photographed about 1907.

poor relations of the Drummonds of Great Stanmore. It was a late marriage – he was 45, she was 37 – and their first and only child, Mary, arrived in 1783. With two parsonages at his disposal Williams nevertheless decided to buy one of Pinner's grandest houses, Pinner House next to the parsonage, as a residence. It cost him £700 in 1788. Perhaps the Hon. Mrs Williams would not be satisfied with less, despite her straitened upbringing. They moved in a wide society, attending a ball at Moor Park and 'an illumination' at friends in Mayfair in 1802, but they were not very wealthy and such enjoyment may not have been typical. In 1810 they enlarged their front garden by having Church Lane realigned to produce the current big curve. Walter Williams holds the record as the longest-serving minister of Pinner – 1764 to 1810.

The churchwardens continued to have a dual responsibility, for the business of the church, and for local organisation. From 1727 rates were regularly raised in alternate years for church expenses and repairs. The total averaged £30, but sometimes reached more than £50 in the 1750s. Tradesmen's bills accounted for most of the expenditure, with scant detail showing purpose; repair to the church house in 1708, recasting a bell in 1713, 'a problem about the pillar' in 1718, new dials in 1725, and much leadwork in 1732. Archbishop Secker's *Speculum*, or review of parishes, 1758-68, found everything in bad condition – walls, windows, floors of pews, porch, altarpiece, bell frames, and parsonage – though there were plans afoot to repair the roof of the side aisles.

The most obvious-18th century relics are several tombstones in the churchyard, Samuel Tame's stone of 1727 being the oldest, and wall memorials to a few of the gentry who lie there or within the church. The best of these was Francis Bolton's, carved with trophies, but its broken remnants have disappeared. The others are an undistinguished set of grey, black or white tablets. Less apparent are the bells. In 1771 the five original ones were recast, and three new bells added. They still ring regularly from the belfry, though the tenor was recast in 1926.

Local organisation left little trace in the accounts. The firefighting equipment was kept in the church and it was the wardens who bought 18 leather buckets in 1702 and had them mended in 1718. In 1732 a man who threatened to fire the village caused them an expenditure of 5s. Very mystifying is the £5 spent in 1740 or 1741 on 'taking up the house where Bellamy lives'. This might have been the William Bellamy, who could not pay the church rate in 1739. What did 'taking up' mean?

NONCONFORMISTS

The history of the Meeting House mirrors that of nonconformity in Pinner during the 18th century, vigorous at the start, moribund at the end. The old Dissenter families – Edlin, Stanbrough and Street – gradually left Pinner during that time and we do not know the numbers or financial position of any nonconformists who remained. In 1750 John Street of West End left £3 a year to pay any dissenting minister 'as shall from time to time' preach to the dissenters in Pinner, his brother Henry of East End Farm Cottage left £4 4s. 0d. a year similarly just a few weeks later, and his widow Elizabeth left £2 a year for the meeting house in 1757.

The Streets and Stanbroughs maintained their positions as trustees of Tindall's bequest. Secker's *Speculum* complained that 'the chief dissenters put one another in ... as trustees and let it [the land] out under half the value'.

The *Speculum* says there was a meeting house in Pinner, with a 'teacher' named James Madgwick, but that attendance had lessened. Madgwick lived at West Lodge, owned by the Streets, and subsequently at 32 High Street. His daughter Martha married William Street, the last of that family in Pinner, in 1784. The Pinner congregation was included in a Dissenters' list of 1772, and Daniel Lysons mentioned a small Independent meeting house in his *Environs of London* of 1795.

Early in the 19th century two dissenters from Harrow, Joseph Freshwater and Henry Puddyfoot, were wont to walk over to Pinner, or even into Watford, to worship, there being no nearer place. In 1806 Mr Schofield 'of the ministry of Pinner' advised them to meet in Harrow, presumably because numbers there were increasing. In 1811 the Harrow Baptists bought the Pinner meeting house and re-erected it at Byron Hill, Harrow, at an overall cost of £421.

42 The 'Independent' Meeting House used to be in Love Lane *c.*1714-1810. It was dismantled and re-erected by the Harrow Baptists in Byron Hill, where one of them drew this sketch many years later.

Roman Catholics, the other nonconformists, find no reference, even in the *Speculum*. They had no general freedom of worship and their civil liberties were restricted; the Glorious Revolution of 1688, the Jacobite rebellions of the Old Pretender, 1715-16, and the Young Pretender, Bonnie Prince Charlie, 1745-6, had seen to that. The only Roman Catholic known to be connected with Pinner was the absentee owner of Woodhall, Cosmas Nevill, a descendant of William Wilkinson through his mother Mary. A law of 1700 debarred Roman Catholics from inheriting land, and about 1750 Thomas Laws, descended from Wilkinson's sister, used it to challenge Nevill's title on behalf of himself and the Protestant relatives, and Henry Nevill was ousted from Woodhall.

The next chapter in Pinner nonconformity belongs to the Methodists.

The Needy, the Young, the Wrong-doers – and an Epidemic

THE POOR

The churchwardens' accounts are the only source of information for this, and there are none for 1758-1810. Small sums were given to non-local poor before 1734 – hardly anything afterwards – a few shillings to travelling poor, including pregnant women, and about 30s. between 1727 and 1732 to more than 100 people, Christians freed from slavery in Algeria, who seem to have passed through Pinner in groups.

There were only two effective benefactions available for the poor of Pinner in the 18th century. The £50 left in 1737 by Dame Mary Franklin, widow of Christopher Clitherow, produced interest of about £2 a year for spending on bread for the poor who attended church, while the interest on Mrs Elizabeth Deering's £100 of 1781 was to provide 10s. worth of bread for the poor on Christmas Day, and some residue for paying to ten poor widows.

Relief for the local poor must otherwise have continued to come from the poor box, with no accounts preserved. Very few sums were paid by the churchwardens but they do show how help was given: a shilling to Widow Colsey on Widow Bird's account in 1720 seems like home help; in 1727 money for William Wakeman's wife is obscure, but 5s. for Moses Moreton's coat is simple relief; medical expenses were met when 'a surgeon for Hemins' was supplied in 1726; and again in 1752-3 when 19s. was spent on taking Susanna Garraway to hospital. At that time hospital care implied a long-term malady of mind or body, and we do not know the hospital nor Susanna's fate; she was probably the 17-year-old daughter of James Garraway of Readings, now Tudor Cottage at East End.

EDUCATION

There is only intermittent reference to education in 18th-century Pinner. The church school was not mentioned after 1710, though there was a Sunday School using the west gallery of the church in 1790. The Governors of Harrow School gave it £10 annually, which in 1790 was spent in providing 20 girls with a gown and shoes, and eight boys with a waistcoat and shoes. Probably more children than this attended.

In 1764 Mrs Goditha Martin bequeathed the annual interest on £100 – it averaged £3 – to be spent on teaching as many poor children of Pinner to read as the money would provide, but there are no records. Nothing else is known of this lady. Four men called themselves schoolmasters in various property transactions, probably teaching privately in Pinner itself: Joseph Baxter (from 1737-53), who lived in Chapel Lane opposite John Blake, William Street of West House, called a schoolmaster in 1777, Jeffs Inwood, who lived at Church Farm c.1783-1800, and Thomas Murch, who occupied Moss Cottage 1785-95. Writing master Thomas Shaw, who took an apprentice paid for by the Harrow School Governors in 1749, may have been associated in some way. Writing was still an accomplishment less easily acquired than reading, and one ignored in Goditha Martin's bequest.

CRIME

Pinner in the 18th century has an air of peacefulness and orderliness which may be quite deceptive. The ways in which the inhabitants plagued each other were no longer reported to the manorial court, and there is no other local record, such as newspapers, to fill the gap. The constable, still appointed at the manor court, was responsible for the custody of offenders until they could be taken to the Justices at Edgware.

Apart from two extremely brief references in the churchwardens' accounts – to a warrant to send Sarah Corby to prison in 1727 and taking her to London the next year, and to the man who threatened to fire the village in 1732, only the records of cases serious enough to reach the London courts give any idea of wrong-doing.

Four cases occurred, two of them in 1748. The first concerned the death of John White, 16-year-old son of Randolph White, who lived in a house later called Weatherleys Farm (site of 49-51 Paines Lane). On 16 May 1748 John had been fishing with a friend in a pond belonging to the lord of the manor and was chased off by the gamekeeper James Wood. In a later encounter that day John's insolence provoked Wood to hit him on the side of the head with the butt of his whip, and a few hours later he died. Two days afterwards an inquest was held somewhere in Pinner, whose jurors included Francis Randall the smith, James Murch the tailor, George Howard the shoemaker, and Thomas Mould a smallholder, with others from Harrow. At Wood's trial at the Old Bailey, reported by *The London Evening Post* of 26-28 May, he was found guilty of manslaughter, sentenced to be branded on the hand, and then discharged. On the same day, for stealing a watch worth £3, another man was sentenced to hang.

Some months later Pinner was a bystander, so to speak, in another tragedy. One Richard Coleman of Southwark, a family man charged with murder at Kennington on the evidence of the dying victim, fled arrest and took refuge in Pinner in September 1748. Two months later he was discovered, charged, found guilty and executed on Kennington Common. The tragedy was that three years later two other men confessed to the same crime, exonerated Coleman, and were executed in the same place. But why Coleman came to Pinner, where he stayed, and who was involved with him, remain to be discovered.

In July 1783 Edward Lee of Pinner survived an attempted robbery with violence.[25] He was a labourer, whose house has not been traced. On his way home from Harrow he was set upon in Pinner Road by a man demanding money. They struggled but Lee managed to get away before two companions could help the assailant. The first man, John Field, was caught and charged at the Old Bailey, but the others escaped.

An attempted murder of the early 19th century which involved a man of property and re-activated medieval customs is best noted here. Thomas Bowler of Alperton, who had bought West House and another property at Nower Hill from William and Martha Street after their emigration to New York, conceived a hatred of William Burrows, also of Alperton, who also owned a Pinner property, namely East End Farm Cottage. At Alperton in May 1812 the 70-year-old Bowler shot at Burrows with a blunderbuss outside a smithy where he had just had the piece repaired, hitting him in the neck but not killing him. Doctors at Cold Bath Fields Prison, Clerkenwell, found Bowler to have been insane ever since he had fallen from his horse in 1810, but nevertheless he was convicted of attempted murder on 12 July and hanged outside the Old Bailey on 8 August. The lord of the manor claimed all the property of this convicted felon according to ancient custom and it was regranted by grace and favour to Bowler's three heirs in September 1813 for fines of £70, £70, and £60 respectively. These were far larger than the usual inheritance fines, which was the purpose of the seizure. The heirs also signed an agreement in January 1816 to meet costs of £404 which the lord said he had incurred in the matter.

The village lock-up, or cage, had stood for more than fifty years on the west bank of the Pinn at the foot of the High Street, just where the river now passes beneath the embankment, and was reached by a pathway from Chapel Lane. Soon after 1827 the cage was transferred to the adjoining workhouse site, and Charles Woodbridge built three wooden cottages on the pathway, demolished in 1941-2. Though the cage's subsequent history is obscure, it probably lasted until the Police Station was built in 1899.

AN EPIDEMIC

In Pinner and nearby parishes burials exceeded baptisms in the first two-thirds of the 18th century, particularly between 1720-50. By 1800 however, the population in Pinner had risen by 50 per cent.

In 1741 an epidemic had broken out, thought now to have been a form of typhoid. The previous year had been abnormal countrywide – even the Thames froze. In Middlesex Pinner suffered worst, with a death rate of about 15 per cent. Harrow lost 10 per cent and Ruislip, Ickenham and Great Stanmore had heavy losses, yet Little Stanmore, Edgware and Harefield were scarcely affected.

At Pinner the pestilence gathered force in September but loosed its fullest fury in October. In that month alone there were 25 burials, exceeding the annual average of 20 since 1700. On three dates in September and October there had been three funerals each day. The worst week was 4-10 October with 10 funerals. Three families in particular were prostrated. William Reeves, the butcher at the site of 18-24 High Street, buried three daughters within one October fortnight, and died himself six days later, leaving his wife Mary with their three remaining infants. James Garraway, a smallholder at Tudor Cottage, lost three daughters and his wife Mary within one month. Elizabeth Boncey lost two daughters and her husband George in October. She lived somewhere opposite the Reeves and the two widows must have regarded each other across the street in mutual misery. Half the dead were children, and 31 families were affected, yeomen, tradesmen and labourers.

The Beginnings of Change on the Land

THE LARGER FARMS

The sometime demesne farms were still farmed by tenants. Woodhall Manor was quickly sold by Thomas Laws once he had got it away from Roman Catholic Henry Nevill and nothing is known of its progress until the 19th century.

Thomas Corbett was in charge of Headstone Manor for a quarter of a century until 1749. Daniel Wilshin rented the smaller farm there in 1726 and took over the big one as well from 1757, followed by his son of the same name. The Wilshins gradually increased the extent of pasture and hay farming at the expense of arable.

Pinner Park Farm was bought by St Thomas's Hospital of London in 1731. This place gives the one glimpse of farming practice in 18th-century Pinner, because a manager named Nathaniel Charles ran it for a 14-month gap between tenants, beginning in November 1746, and his account book survives. Calves and butter were the principal produce. Butter was sent to market almost every week, though the distance was too far for the sale of raw milk. Calves were the by-product of milk and 55 were sold in the year, in addition to surplus heifers and spent cows. Pigs were fattened on the buttermilk and sold as porkers or dead meat. The farm was almost self-sufficient in feed. Hay was grown on one quarter to one third of its area, plus beans and peas. A little wheat was grown, presumably for human consumption. Small surpluses were sold, but never the hay. The markets used were at London, especially for the butter, Uxbridge, Watford, Harrow and Brentford – Pinner market was defunct. Animals were sometimes sent off in single numbers, even to London. The butter provided just over a fifth (£101) of the sales of produce. There seems to have been only one regular male hand, Samuel Flower, probably a stockman, and related maybe to the out-going tenant John Flower. There were maidservants, who probably took care of the milking and butter-making. A wide range of casual workers was hired, often skilled – haymakers, threshers, day-labourers, hedgers, blacksmith, butcher, charwoman, sweep, glazier, cooper. A vet had to be called in when two cows suffered from 'the gargens' in September 1747.

Philip Aldwin took a lease at the beginning of 1748 and the manager was paid off at the rate of £1 per calendar month, less than the shilling a day paid to day-men, though of course he had bed and board. He had previously been the Hospital's porter, that is gate-keeper, but perhaps he had been raised in agriculture, as many town-dwellers had at that time. In 1751, the Hospital filled in the moat and rebuilt the farmhouse, the present one, a little to the north-east.

AGRICULTURAL IMPROVEMENTS

During the 18th century plenty of beneficial new practices were developed to improve farming; the Norfolk Four Course Rotation using clover, vetch and turnip as both ground nutrition and fodder, eliminating fallowing; Jethro Tull's invention of the seed drill, eliminating broadcast sowing; and Robert Blakewell's progress in the selective breeding of livestock.

In Middlesex methods were mostly old-fashioned. At the end of the century John Middleton was commissioned by the Board of Agriculture to survey farming in the county, both open-field and enclosed, or private, and in 1798 he published *A View of Agriculture in Middlesex*. It contains little specific information about Pinner or Harrow, except to characterise Harrow and westward as a district of strong land, that is, clay soil.

Middleton found that enclosed land was mostly under grass. In his opinion the art of haymaking in Middlesex had been brought to a degree of perfection unequalled elsewhere even in wet weather. It had the best formed haystacks, and several barns capable of holding 50 to 100 loads of hay – the great barn at Headstone Manor was one of them. A load contained 36 trusses weighing about 60lbs. each. Grassland was also used to rear livestock for the meat or dairy markets, and to fatten beasts on the way to market from elsewhere. Veal calves were sent off at ten weeks and hogs were sold for bacon.

Most of the arable land was still open-field. Middleton was not impressed by Middlesex farming practice apart from haymaking. 'The farmers in the neighbourhood of Pinner and Ryslip', he wrote, 'seldom if ever plough their fields more than once and for want of so doing they rarely obtain a good sweet tilth to sow their wheat in.' The failure to cross-plough was compounded by the use of the swing plough, which was going out of date. He blamed them for the poor drainage: 'they do not cut water furrows sufficiently across their heavy clay lands to take the water off.' He noted that a three-year rotation was still followed but periodic fallowing had gone out of use, except in Ruislip and Eastcote. Middleton was among those who considered open-field farming was out of date and hindered improvement. The strips themselves prevented proper drainage of individual pieces because cross-ploughing was difficult over a narrow strip. Their scatter entailed loss of time shifting people and equipment from one to the other, while their openness exposed them to everyone's weeds and pests. Rotation in common precluded the use of soil-improving crops, or even just growing the crops which most suited the soil.

CHANGE IN THE AIR

The price commanded by farm produce rose because of the demand from the increasing population. Improvement to raise production entered the minds of progressive or large-scale farmers everywhere, but open-field farming was an obstacle to a tenant or owner wishing to group his strips together and protect them by enclosure. The major farmers of Harrow and Pinner caught the wind and decided it was time to press Parliament for an Act permitting the enclosure of all the commons and open fields in the manor.

Physically and socially Pinner in 1790 was not so very different from the medieval settlement, but changes were already in progress – communications, rising population and a property revolution – which by 1830 had changed the place forever.

V

A Period of Change – Fifty Years to c.1830

Communications

ROADS AND BRIDGES

Communication by road had become easier during the 18th century as the system of funding the maintenance of major thoroughfares by charging road users at turnpikes for their journeys increased. Even so, heavy carriages made only five miles an hour over the major highways of the county in 1807, according to John Middleton, in his *View of the Agriculture of Middlesex*, and lighter ones six miles, whilst mail carriages raced ahead at seven, and that only because their stages were widely spaced. The road from Paddington Green to Harrow on the Hill was turnpiked in 1801, and thence to Rickmansworth in 1809. The route lay along Pinner Road, Church Lane, High Street, Bridge Street, Elm Park Road, and north-west along Rickmansworth Road. The only toll gate in Pinner was at Pinner Green just west of the present crossroads with the toll-house situated at the north-west corner. In the 1841 census the keepers were Ann Dewsell, widow, and her daughter Elizabeth, and in 1851 they were Emma Byer and her sister Margaret. The next turnpike town-wards was in Harrow, where Roxborough Bridge is now. The Rickmansworth Turnpike Trust was transferred to the Edgware Highways Board in 1872.

The other roads in the parish were the responsibility of the inhabitants. Middleton considered that parish highways in Middlesex were kept in much better condition than the turnpiked roads. For the first time in 1808 we can see the accounts of the Surveyors of Highways for Pinner, appointed by the vestry to organise the effort of collecting funds and getting the work done. According to the amount of land owned, people were expected to contribute one or more teams of horses, or a cart, or cash, and from 1808 to 1836 between 107 and 209 people were assessed in a year. Labourers were sometimes hired by the day at a rate of eight to twelve shillings per week. From 1829 a man named Steptoe was employed full time at a weekly rate of 7s. and after him Thomas Weedon. In 1827 the Pinner and Ruislip surveyors joined to make work for the unemployed by lowering the top of Cuckoo Hill – not much though – as is still in evidence today.

At Enclosure the Vestry arranged for landowners Spranger, Aubrey and Milman to maintain roadways, as will shortly be seen. Similar tactics were used in 1826 to

43 This anonymous lithograph must be of the two-arched town bridge of 1809 and reveals the great width of the river just here. The barns of the *Crown* loom up and the old Marsh Road facade of the *Victory* is apparent.

persuade Ralph Ellis and his son John to pay half the cost – almost £50 – of a bridge at West End which carried West End Lane across the Pinn and past the entrance to Emily Cottage, newly built by Ellis at today's Lloyd Court. In 1840 John, who then owned the land on both sides of the river, was permitted to divert the lane away from the cottage provided he built another bridge over the river, the one in Eastcote Road near Lyncroft Way. Thus was West End Lane rerouted from the south side of the Pinn to its present course along Ellis's northern property boundary.

The Edgware Highways Board took over the responsibility for Pinner roads in 1863 and three years later the Vestry complained that it used to manage the roads more cheaply than the board did.

The town bridge had deteriorated during the 18th century until it was just a footbridge. In 1809 the Trustees of the Rickmansworth Turnpike built a new bridge in brick with two arches. The arches were 3 feet 6 inches high, the total span was 16ft, and the width between the parapets was 19ft 6in. West of the bridge the stream spread 40 ft wide when in flood. By 1894 the bridge was too narrow for current transport and a new one was built in 1896, with a pavement for pedestrians, at the joint cost (just over £500) of Hendon Rural District and Middlesex County Council. Since that last major rebuilding there have been several alterations. During the latest work in May 1994 a small core of earlier brickwork, believed to relate to the 1809 bridge, was seen by archaeologists.

In August 1814 the Surveyors of the Highways disputed liability for Paines Bridge with the lord, pitting the testimony of Mr Lee the bricklayer and Mr Dell the carpenter that they had repaired it at his father's expense, against the lord's statement that his accounts showed no such cost. In April 1817 the surveyors accepted responsibility.

THE COACH

A carrier, which was a goods waggon on which people could also travel, went to London (*Oxford Arms* in Warwick Lane) and returned to Pinner on Mondays and Fridays in 1738. In 1768 a coach ran twice-weekly from Harrow on the Hill to Paddington along the Harrow Road, and perhaps the coach operated by Robert Turner of the *Crown* in Pinner was associated with it. Turner called himself a coach master in a Sun Fire Insurance policy of 1787, and in 1788 was paid 4s. by the churchwardens 'for carriage of Wealy's wife to and from town' – the circumstances requiring the parish to pay for Mrs Wealy have to be guessed.[26] If this was the usual return fare, nearly half a week's wages for a labourer, there is no doubt the ordinary man would have set out for London on his own two feet. Daniel Grey, living in one of Bodimeade's houses on the north of the High Street, and described as a coachman in 1773, may have been coachman at one of the big houses. Or perhaps it means that Joseph Turner of the *Crown*, father of Robert, was already running a coach and employing Grey.

The earliest documented route to pass through part of Pinner was the London to Rickmansworth coach listed in *Cary's New Itinerary* of 1798. This was a trunk route, using the Edgware Road, then turning west to pass through Great Stanmore, Harrow Weald, Hatch End, and Pinner Green, by-passing the centre, and so on to Northwood.

About 1800 Stephen Artaud advertised a daily coach from the *Crown* at Pinner to *The George and Blue Boar* in Holborn, via Stanmore and Edgware Road, leaving at 7.30 am. Apart from Harrow, Pinner was the only village in the area to have a coach service. Artaud had come from St Martin-in-the-Fields in the 1790s and quickly played a local part, becoming an overseer of the poor, only to be disqualified when he became bankrupt in 1801, and seems to have returned to his old haunts.

In 1813 the service was in the hands of Charles Turner, the son of Robert. Charles prospered. He bought the house next to the church in 1822 (64 High Street), which was called, maybe in his time, Equestrian Villa, rather suitable for a coach driver. In 1824 or 1825 he became licensee of the *Queen's Head*, though not the owner. The coach to London was already departing from this hostelry and he continued the service, leaving at 7.30 am and arriving back at 6.30 pm. In the 1830s it left at 3 pm on Saturdays and 4 pm on Sundays – the hour of return is not stated! Charles suffered sometimes from gout, but was otherwise said to have been genial and sociable, according to John Graham, who wrote a detailed account in 1894 of the coach journey to London as a schoolboy about 1835 (printed in the parish magazine 1894-5). In 1838 the coach was called the Comet, leaving at 8 am for the *Bull* in Holborn, returning by 7 pm. The last printed reference to the coach was in 1845, when it was called the Era, run by Frederick Meredith.

The coach journey took about three hours and the London termini were traditional galleried coaching inns. The *George and Blue Boar* was on the south side of Holborn opposite Red Lion Street and the *Bull*, once the *Black Bull*, stood between Leather Lane and Hatton Garden. In 1842 the London & Birmingham Railway had opened its Pinner station at Hatch End and, of those who could afford transport, only the most old-fashioned would have preferred a three-hour coach journey to a train ride. John Graham says the usual number of horses used was two, but occasionally more in bad weather. The inside seats were generally reserved for ladies, invalids, or young children, all others going outside, that is, on top, which could have been hazardous over bumpy ground. Graham adds,

> Our coachman would occasionally drive round to pick up a dowager ... or a family with luggage, for which of course he was handsomely compensated. If we got clear away by eight oclock we were lucky. [At] the turnpike gate at Roxborough ... you had to show your ticket as having passed the previous gate at Pinner Green, or pay the toll. At the foot of Harrow Hill ... it was the custom for the outside passengers to descend, and mount the hill on foot.

He remembered passing several inns, the *Crown and Anchor* and the *King's Head* in Harrow, the *Black Horse* at Sudbury, the *Coach and Horses* at Stonebridge – you can still see the second and third of these, as well as the starting point, the *Queen's Head*.

THE POST

The Royal Mail benefited from improved roads and Pinner joined the network in 1823 when William Davis opened a receiving office at 7 High Street, where he sold bread, groceries and drapery. Letters left at a receiving office were sent to the local post town for sorting and dispatch to the destination. At first the post town for Pinner was Southall, but was changed to Watford in 1824. Davies sent the letters off soon after 5pm and received incoming mail before 9am. Prior to the penny post of 1840 postage could be paid by either sender or recipient, the rate ranging from 4d. to 2s. 10d. outside London.

When Medieval Farming Ended

ENCLOSURE OF THE COMMON LAND

The enclosure of the open fields and commons of Harrow, including Pinner, revolutionised the appearance of the area. Enclosure was not just a matter of individuals putting fences around their strips in the common fields. It was the removal of everyone's rights in those fields and the reallocation of the land, as privately owned land, in proportion to their previous rights.

The 'Act of Parliament for the Inclosing of the Open and Common Fields, Commons and Waste Grounds within the Parish of Harrow and within the Manor of Harrow or Sudbury' was passed in 1803. It had been promoted by the leading landowners of Harrow, leading, that is, in terms of the amount of land they owned, namely Richard Page, owner of Wembley Park and more, George Harley Drummond of Kenton, Lord Abercorn of Bentley Priory, and the Lord of the Manor. There was vigorous opposition from some who owned less, mobilised by Joseph Sellon of Pinnerwood House, with the help of his brother John of Pinner Hill House, an experienced serjeant-at-law, or barrister as he would be termed today. Joseph had foiled two previous attempts in 1797 and 1802 with a campaign capitalising on the less-than-open methods used by the advocates. The real dispute was about conditions and terms of the reallocation rather than any principle, even though Sellon made much of his concern to protect those who only had the right to use the commons. It took 14 years for the appointed Enclosure Commissioners to gather the claims and allocate the land and the award with its accompanying map was published in 1817.

The tracks across commons were formalised into roads and all roads graded into public carriage roads for which the local authority was responsible, or private ones for which landowners were responsible but which the authority would maintain to the standard of bridle ways. Some of the land was sold to defray the costs of the scheme. The biggest complication was the extinction of tithes as part of the process, which were payable at this time to Christ Church, Oxford. Landowners were offered the option of giving up some of their land entitlement to cancel liability to tithes, or of making an annual payment, called a corn rent, to the college in lieu.

THE REALLOCATION

After adjusting for roads and the Grand Junction Canal, 4,560 acres of Harrow manor were available for distribution among about 270 persons. In Pinner there were 940 acres of open field and 250 acres of common to be shared among 82 successful claimants, plus whatever the small greens and roadside verges totalled. Pinner's was the largest amount of open field in the manor, the next being the 590 acres each of Harrow Weald and Roxeth, while the common compared with 685 acres at Harrow Weald and 285 at Sudbury. The lord of the manor received 22 acres of Pinner in return for the loss of his rights to allocate waste, the vicar of Harrow 25 acres for loss of vicar's tithe. For part of the rector's tithes due to them the Dean and Chapter of Christ Church Oxford were awarded a huge chunk of 241 acres covering south Pinner and west Roxeth. The northern outline of this – Rayners Lane, High Worple, and (roughly) Raynton Close – was preserved in the boundary of the Tithe Farm Estate which Thomas Nash Ltd. built during the 1930s on that same land, bought directly of the college. Aside from these the largest award in Pinner was Daniel Hill's 131 acres, and the smallest the 20 perches (or one eighth of an acre) allocated to the wealthy Ralph Dean of Eastcote.

There are lists of claims made and allotments awarded but no evidence now exists of how the Commissioners measured those rights, what weighting they gave to common field land, pasture rights, enclosed land and houses. Nor do we know how they arrived at the deduction of land for those who did not pay corn rent, nor whether they adjusted for the quality of land allotted – common land, for example, was generally agreed to be worth less than cultivated land. Attempts to correlate previous holdings with the amount awarded do not give consistent results.

The allocation could be be located anywhere within the manor though there was some attempt to suit claimants. Against Daniel Hill's claim was noted, 'requests his allot. in Longfield in Pinner' and for the most part the commissioners obliged him. John Stiles seemed unlucky, with a sliver of two acres at the furthest point of the former Down Field and no apparent access from Cannon Lane – but this was about the nearest to Eastcote, where he lived. Generally, small pieces adjoining a property were allocated to the owner, particularly enclosed road verges. The effect was best seen at West End where everyone was allocated the piece of green or verge outside their premises. Where this was impracticable the commissioners grouped most of the small entitlements of about an acre or less along the edges of Pinner Common, where they were accessible from the new roadway.

Beneficiaries sold and exchanged allotments. A small plot, inconveniently situated and requiring to be fenced – a disproportionate expense in relation to its size – might be better got rid of than kept, and that is probably what John Stiles did with his. Even without waiting for completion of the award John Babb had sold his tiny entitlement to Daniel Hill and Daniel Pritchard had sold his to Sir Francis Milman of The Grove.

When the commissioners were selling land to meet expenses a few gentlemen, like Sir Francis, were keen to buy pieces adjoining their houses so as to create large grounds or parks. John Sellon of Pinner Hill bought 24 acres of the former common from the commissioners, and then bought adjoining allocations of ten and eight acres from Robert Tubbs and Lord Northwick.

Others struck different bargains. William Spranger of The Hall had been negotiating since 1798 to enlarge his estate by buying half of Bury Pond Green, with part of the Pinn. During the course of the Enclosure he agreed with the Vestry to create and maintain for seven years from 1804 the newly marked out northern end of Paines Lane from Moss Lane to Uxbridge Road in exchange for the land at the east. Before this the track had passed diagonally north-eastward from the top of Moss Lane to about the north of the present Nugents Park, very close to his frontage. In Pinner Marsh, where the the new southward road was laid roughly along its centre, Sir Francis Milman of The Grove and Edward Aubrey of Pinner Place bought the relevant strips alongside to extend their grounds and incorporate stretches of river. In 1804 Aubrey agreed to pay for the new road southwards to the present Meadow Road and maintain it for seven years at his own expense, and Milman did likewise for the road from there to the Hunsdon bridge.

THE NEW LOOK OF PINNER

The visual impact was enormous in every direction. The once wide roads were narrowed and the irregular verges which had been available as common pasture were treated as land to be enclosed. Thus the little greens at the main junctions of the hamlets vanished, except for Nower Hill Green, now called Tookes Green. So, of course, did the wide expanse of Pinner Common and the meandering Pinner Marsh. All newly enclosed land was ordered to be fenced, certainly before any animals were put on it, and over the next decade fences and hedges arose or grew where there had been none before.

The old roads were designated as public carriage ways – Pinner Road and Marsh Road to the south; and to the north Rickmansworth Road, Pinner Hill Road, Oxhey Lane, and the northern parts of Headstone Lane, Paines Lane and Elm Park

Road. The ancient tracks were upgraded to private carriage-cum-public bridleways. Rayners Lane, Cannon Lane, Pinner Hill, and one approximately on the line of Kingsley Road, were all former field access ways. The line of Rayners Lane was altered in parts to take account of changes in land ownership. Barrow Point Lane was formalised, as well as the line of what is now Ashill Drive, and also what now remains only as the footpath from Pinner Green to the west end of Hazeldene Drive. A large pond in Elm Park Road south of the footpath to Antoneys was declared a public watering place. Filled in between the two world wars, it was remembered as a favourite place for horses to cool their feet. The spot still looks rather low.

Half a dozen houses which had stood in gardens isolated upon common now found themselves part of a street or lane. On Pinner Common there were Camden Cottage (later Northwold), Ashill Cottage and the windmill. Daniel Lee's house (58 Bridge Street) had been in the middle of Wood Lane Green until the space east and south was enclosed and awarded to the cottage owner. The *George*, solitary beside the stream, and equidistant from both sides of the marsh, was now part of the western side of Marsh Road. At the top of the High Street the old butcher's shop, a little island site since medieval times, was incorporated into the street frontage and ever since has half-choked traffic in Church Lane.

Allocation of verge left some houses further from the road. This was unwelcome to the *Bell* at Pinner Green and the problem was solved by rebuilding it at the new street edge (now junction of Bell Close). The long path which became necessary to reach West End Lane from Poplar Cottage (rear of no.83) is still marked by the row of oaks leading to no. 87.

OTHER EFFECTS

The enclosure affected farmers, gentlemen and the employed in different ways. For farmers the primary aim was achieved in that their land was now entirely under their own control, and generally more consolidated than before. Large and small holders had benefited. Over the next couple of decades there were more rationalisations and a new type of farm began to appear. And, as we have noted, some gentleman-landowners had been astute in securing the acres needed for the future aggrandisement of their houses.

But what about those people who had just a little land in the common fields, or only had rights of common pasture? In some parts of the country inhabitants were entitled to keep a beast or two on the common, be it sheep or cow, and to collect fuel and wild fruit there. These privileges, and the acre or two of common field, could mean the difference between subsistence and destitution.

In Harrow rights of common field and common pasture originally belonged to the old medieval holdings. People on later holdings, which included many cottages built for newcomers or the already landless, had never had such rights, and would get nothing from the award, nor would the tenant of an absentee, for the landlord benefited from the rights. In Pinner, people without any of these rights were in the majority. Only 82 landowners, just over half of them non-resident, received awards in Pinner, yet there were 151 families living here at the 1801 census, and 216 at that of 1811. More than two-thirds of the resident heads of families therefore were dependent on the labour market or business.

Only 34 people in Pinner claimed just in respect of land they held in the common fields and not for anything else. Every one of them was either non-resident, or the owner of other property in Pinner. So vanishes the vision of a body of humble, partly self-supporting cultivators harshly dispossessed.

The question about rights of common pasture is much more open. Nobody had claimed for it and the Harrow Enclosure Award is silent on the matter. There had been no reference to any agricultural matter in the court rolls for several decades before 1800. If any inhabitants were putting animals on the common illegally there is no reference other than Joseph Sellon's allegation that 'the poor' would get no recompense for 'those advantages from the commons which they have immemorially enjoyed, even though it may have been without any strict legal title'. His claim may have been rhetorical, because a hard-up villager would have found it costly to keep an animal in feed during winter. In Pinner the right to gather fuel on the common was probably the greatest benefit, but it would have been difficult to restrict the activity to those strictly entitled.

There was hardship and poverty in Pinner at this time but the enclosure of the common fields and pasture was not the cause. It must be sought elsewhere.

Even More Poor

THE GENERAL SITUATION

The outbreak of war with France in 1793 brought economic disturbance to England, and in addition the harvest failed four times in the next seven years. At the same time the army needed to be fed and extra supplies could not be brought in from abroad. Thomas Malthus, in his *Essay on Population* (1798) argued that the rising population would outstrip production and lead to the impoverishment of society as a whole. Everywhere the price of food rose but moves to legalise the fixing of minimum wages failed, even though there were laws to fix a maximum. As a consequence far more people needed help to survive, and landowners were presented with larger demands for rates.

THE SYSTEM

An amendment in 1697 to the Elizabethan Poor Law of 1601 had allowed a person's parish of origin to sign an undertaking that it would take him back if he needed poor relief. From 1722 overseers were given power to acquire a workhouse and oblige their own able-bodied poor to work there or else go without relief. Gilbert's Act of 1782 let them use the workhouse for the aged and infirm only, and find work outside it for the able-bodied, giving them a cash supplement if need be. After 1795 a sick pauper was not to be returned to his parish of origin until well, the cost being reclaimable from it. The pendulum of practice swung back and forth as vestries tried vainly to confine relief to the deserving unemployed or infirm, and deny it to the feckless or recalcitrant.

THE POOR IN PINNER

By the end of the 18th century provision for the poor presented a serious financial problem to the overseers of Pinner. In 1795 the overseers in one Berkshire village reckoned that a family with five young children could subsist on about a dozen loaves a week, plus one pound of bacon, greens, potatoes, half a pound of fat, and one ounce of tea, the greens and potatoes presumably being home-grown. John Middleton had written that on average a Middlesex labourer earned 10s. a week in winter and 12s. in summer, peaking at 15s. during harvest, and paid rent of one to four shillings a week. According to him the price of a quartern loaf in Middlesex – it weighed about two kilograms – rose from an average of 7d. or 8d. before the war to 12½d. in 1795, and 17½d. in 1800, settling to about 10d. thereafter. Even in good times there would be little left for drink, clothes or treats. The working man was still in the age-old trap; he could not earn enough to save, so any illness or unemployment threatened penury.

The Pinner Vestry Minutes are extant from 1787 and the account books of the Overseers of the Poor from 1782-1805 and 1814-31. The total of rates collected seldom exceeded £300 annually before 1785-6 but they then rose steadily until they reached £845 for 1800-1. For 1813-14 the total was £1,262, to which £62 was added from the earnings of paupers hired out. Thereafter it ranged from £665 to £957 (in 1829-30, the last year for which totals are available, a time when Harrow was raising over £3,000). There was difficulty in collection.

Removing the problem elsewhere could be expensive. It cost Pinner's overseers nearly £6 (about nine weeks' summer wages) to shift John Saxton and his wife Hannah back to Uxbridge in July 1789, and over £11 to remove the Sparks family to Exeter in 1837. In March 1831 they received £37 16s. 0d. from Hammersmith for a sick pauper named Hitchcock, and paid £26 5s. 0d. to Rickmansworth for a Pinner man called William Weedon.

THE WORKHOUSE IN PINNER

An almshouse had been built in Pinner in 1785, adorned with a foundation stone bearing the names of churchwardens James and John Wilshin. Four years later the vestry and parishioners' meeting at the *Crown* (23 attended) decided it was 'necessary to erect a Workhouse for the Reception of the Poor as the best method to reduce the Expences of the same' and Thomas Trevethan, the local carpenter and house-builder, was engaged to make it for an ultimate cost of £261 7s. 0d. An existing building was adapted and the almshouse is the obvious candidate, especially when we learn that Trevethan took away the foundation stone and reused it in one of his own houses in Bridge Street, later called Fir Cottage (site of 35-7), where it was found in 1869, according to E.M. Ware, for it has disappeared. The workhouse contained a working room, kitchen, wash house, bakehouse, storage rooms and an apartment for the governor or master. Sleeping rooms were not mentioned, but were surely there. The workhouse was situated on the west bank of the Pinn, just north of the *George* and almost adjoining Trevethan's builder's yard, and was reached by footbridge.

The vestry's policy for the workhouse fluctuated between contracting it to someone to support, maintain and employ the poor for an annual sum, or employing a master at a weekly rate, or managing it directly. No expedient was fully satisfactory. Over a period of 45 years there were 10 contractors or masters and two periods of direct control. But even the contractors always needed extra

44 The poor house or workhouse, with its bridge from Marsh Road crossing the Pinn, and the grounds of West House behind. From a drawing about 1884 by W. Henderson.

sums. Stephen Reddington was appointed in September 1790 at £200 a year but in January 1823 William Charles' contract was for £600. The only local contractor was William Murch junior, 1818-20, at £550 p.a. From June 1826 a Mr Bates was employed as master at 12s. a week and from March 1832 his wife was employed as mistress at £13 a year.

The workhouse was for the old, ill or young and they were fed, clothed, and given medical treatment. The food provided was basic; gruel or broth with bread for breakfast; hot meat for dinner on four days of the week and broth or cheese on the others; and bread and cheese or bread and butter for supper; the drink was small beer and tea. The number of inmates was never stated, but would have fluctuated with seasonal and economic conditions. On an arbitrary estimation of 2s. per head per week £200 would allow for about forty on a constant basis before 1800. Children received some education, and were apprenticed or sent into service where appropriate. A few were placed with people who received allowances for them – in 1786 Mr Roberts took Shuffle's boy, Mr Dean one of Shuffle's girls and Mr Priest another. The inmates did the work of the house and were set to other work where possible – for example a spinning wheel was bought in 1800 for spinning flax, and a lace pillow and bobbins in 1801, whilst oakum for picking was a frequent purchase.

The legal obligation to put the able-bodied to work was difficult to fulfil because the number of jobs in agriculture, the obvious solution, was diminishing as hay-farming spread in Middlesex. The Pinner census recorded that 143 of the 216 families (53 per cent) were engaged in agriculture in 1811, and 134 out of 203 (66 per cent) in 1821. It was one of the worst periods in the history of English agriculture. In Pinner the winter of 1819-20 was noted as severe; in January 1823 the vestry remarked on the great number of families thrown out of employment. Nevertheless the Pinner vestry persisted, trying to oblige farmers to take turns at providing work in 1812, and sending labourers 'round the parish to work' in 1827 and 1828. Some were sent further afield. In 1804 Ann Lilly was hired to a Mrs Reed of Wembley, and Joseph Gates and James Hitchcock were hired to a cow-keeper in Marylebone Lane named John Treble.

Though the cost of outdoor relief dropped a little after the workhouse opened, it was never stopped. Every year, except for a few years after 1800, regular allowances over lengthy periods were made to a number of individuals or families while others received occasional sums. In 1782-3, 20 persons received regular payments, ranging from six pence to 6s. weekly, and eight occasional payments, but by 1830-1 the numbers had zoomed to 33 and 55, fluctuating considerably in between. They included families as well as the widowed, aged and orphaned and are therefore difficult to quantify, but would have represented a minimum of five per cent of the population in 1783 and a minimum of eight per cent in 1830. Four family names appeared persistently throughout the 50 years of records – Cooper, Franklin, Evans and Richardson. The last two families, together with the Dells and Levys, who featured in the 1782-3 list, were still living in Pinner in the middle of the 19th century, labourers all.

During the winter of 1799-1800 a soup kitchen was organised on 21 days. On average 342 individuals a day, from 95 families, shared 253 quarts. It cost £42 8s. 4d., about 2d. a quart. If the figures are correct this meant that more than half the families were affected, the largest number of people ever assisted in any one year. In 1800 poor parishioners earning 10s. a week or less who had more than two children were allowed one quartern loaf a week for each extra child. The workhouse oven was used to bake bread for the outside poor in October 1822, and extra bread was given or sold cheaply in the winters of 1825 and 1826. Sometimes clothing was given.

Medical men were retained on behalf of the poor, at a rate rising from £10 to £42 a year, beginning with Richard Bickham, of 32 High Street and then East End House, and ending with Hubert Kelly of Chestnut Cottage. In addition to general care they were expected to provide midwifery in cases beyond the ability of the local midwife, which happened often, and, at least from 1825, to vaccinate the children in the workhouse.

Though it is impossible to gauge now the atmosphere of those days, there must have been some unpleasantness, directed more likely against the improvident fecund than the aged or infirm, though a refusal in 1826 to give relief to anyone keeping a dog must have affected the elderly. The fear that what had begun as charity was now demanded as a privilege was underlined in 1822 when some labourers complained to the Edgware magistrates that the overseers refused to relieve them. The clearest expression of ill-will came in the award of £5 to Mrs Bates, the workhouse mistress, when she left in 1832, partly in 'gratitude for her exertions in getting rid of Denchfields and Osborns families'.

But not all was gloom. When Mrs Walter Williams, the apparently fierce widow of the first perpetual curate, died in 1822 she left very generous bequests to her servants, who included some local people. To James Dean, 'having been a steady and good lad for some years' went £100 and the furniture of his room. James never became more than a labourer; he was a son of the oddly-named Ivory and Maria

45 The demolition in 1989 of the last of Thomas Trevethan's houses exposed the flimsiness of workmen's cottages in those days. 23 Bridge Street was built about 1806.

Dean who were living near the *Red Lion* in one of the cottages soon to be rebuilt by Charles Woodbridge. Fifty pounds went to Mary Glinister 'my washer woman', probably married to a labourer named Edward. Both Dean and Glinister families needed poor relief at times.

TALES OF TROUBLE

One or two little histories emerge which engage the imagination. In 1794 wedding rings were bought for John Groome and Mary Gristwood (costing 6d.), and Henry Elmes and Sarah Coombes (costing one penny!). These were shotgun marriages. Henry Elmes was kept in custody until the ceremony was over, and four months later baby Elmes was baptised. Groome lived in another parish.

In a vignette worthy of Dickens, Elizabeth Bedford died giving birth to her fifth child, Maria, who was baptised on the day of her mother's burial, 21 March 1821. The parish put the baby to nurse (she lived two months) and sent Elizabeth's two eldest children, William and George, aged 11 and seven, to the workhouse, leaving Elizabeth and Thomas, aged five and four, with their father James, an agricultural labourer. Another branch of the family flourished later at 9 High Street as tailors and parish clerks.

'Benham's wife' and two children – they had not been long in Pinner – were taken into the workhouse in October 1827 while their settlement was investigated. The husband was found and next July £6 was spent conveying them all to him in America.

Sarah Cox produced an illegitimate son named James in 1821, and her sister Mary did the same five years later. The sisters probably grew up in one of the group of small cottages at West End. Mary's James was born in the workhouse and partly raised there. Sarah's son produced about ten children, legitimate, of his own.

Illegitimate children were likely to be an expense to the parish, and the vestry tried hard to fix responsibility on the father. At least 41 were born between 1790 and 1833. Sarah Hitchcock and Jane Barrett produced two each, Elizabeth Shuffle, probably one of the Shuffle girls who were farmed out, produced three.

Sarah Hitchcock was the most overtly scandalous. A son Joseph was born to her in 1797, and when a daughter Elizabeth was baptised in 1799 the clerk wrote 'her husband many years beyond sea'. But Sarah, probably living at the site of 23 Bridge Street, already had two little boys by her husband John, whom the vestry found after Joseph's birth to be on HMS *Resolution* at Halifax, Nova Scotia. We never discover whether he deserted his wife or had been snatched by a press gang. Sarah remarried in 1814. The overseers hired her eldest son William to John Lawrence in 1802, and her second, James, to the Marylebone cow keeper in 1804. Her two illegitimate children died in infancy.

The parish clerk's comments were not always reliable. Against the baptism of Mary Allen in August 1810 he wrote pointedly that her mother Sarah's husband 'was buried 18 February 1809', yet the burial register clearly shows the year of burial was 1810, not 1809. One wonders if Mrs Allen knew about the comment.

Some fathers of the illegitimate were 'respectable'. Thomas Trevethan was the builder of the poorhouse and therefore of some substance, married with three legitimate children. In 1796 Trevethan was required to give security for his second bastard child – not named. Perhaps his illegitimate children were born in the very place he had built. William Davis was the postmaster and baker at 7 High Street, who sometimes supplied the workhouse, and with a son of the same name who continued the business. One of them got Jane Barrett with child in 1824 and was ordered to pay £20 for its support – George Barrett was baptised in September. William the younger did marry but during the 1830s lost his two children in infancy, and his wife at the birth of the second, and never recovered his spirits. By 1841 his stepmother and her second husband Matthew Cook had taken over his business and in 1851 William was working for another baker, Paul Bradbury at 15 High Street. Twenty years later, in his 70s, he was unemployed and living outdoors with James Davis, probably a half-brother.

There is a poorhouse mystery which has never been solved. Albert Pell, M.P., writing of his childhood days at Pinner Hill House about 1830, remembered that there was a long iron rod along one of the poorhouse walls: 'On this rod ran an iron ring, with a short chain and shackle. To this shackle the village idiot was fastened by his ankle, and so, passing from right to left and left to right in the blazing sun or the bitter wind, took his exercise and wore away his life.' Pell did not say who he was. We can only hope Mrs Bates showed him some kindness.

Accelerating costs prompted many parishes to unite into unions, as allowed by the Poor Law Amendment Act of 1834, which confined all relief to the workhouse. Boards of Guardians, elected by the ratepayers, employed paid officials. So, Pinner became part of the Hendon Union and its poor were sent to the big new workhouse in Hendon, designed to cope with several parishes. The little Pinner house was let to John Beaumont, wheelwright, who divided it into five dwellings. The building was demolished when the Metropolitan Railway extended beyond Pinner in 1885.

Coping with a larger Pinner

POPULATION

The population had been increasing for decades and the government instituted the first census of population in 1801. These are the earliest census figures for Pinner.

year	1801	1811	1821
total population	761	1078	1076
inhabited houses	140	167	181
number of families occupying	151	216	203
uninhabited houses	11	7	3
families occupied chiefly in agriculture	80	114	134
ditto trade, manufacture, handicraft	33	48	41
ditto other	38	54	28
males	408	533	523
females	353	545	553

For later years only the totals of population are available:
1831 – 1270; 1841 – 1331; 1851 – 1310; 1861 – 1849; 1871 – 2382.[27]

The unusually large increases of people in Pinner between 1801-11 and 1851-1861 resulted from a net influx from elsewhere – comparison of baptisms and burials with the census figures shows this. Babies from 224 families had been baptised between 1790-1812 and over two-thirds of their fathers had not been born in Pinner. The overseers' task of spotting likely new burdens on the rates was not a simple one.

We cannot find the reason for the first surge, nor whether it began before 1801. The social crisis reflected in the poor law records was probably what checked it. In the following twenty years a slight outflow must have countered the excess of births over deaths.

Many of the new people came from neighbouring parishes – the names are familiar and movement between them had been a constant factor over the centuries. But now Pinner was also affected by the greatly increasing national drift to London. Some of these people stayed in Pinner for short periods, or for good, and some of its own people moved on. In this locality the movement had nothing to do with railways, and probably little to do with improved roads. This travel was almost certainly by foot.

NEW HOUSES

In Pinner between 1801 and 1821 the increase in the number of families from 151 to 203 was accompanied by an increase of 33 in the number of houses, occupied or empty. The following schedule shows the probable extra dwellings provided between about 1750 and 1850, excluding the High Street because adaptations there were so frequent and fluctuating as to make it impossible to reconcile the situation at any one date.

type	new	subdivided	total
houses	3		3
cottages	4		4
pairs	7	6	13
row of three	6	4	10
row of four	5		5
row of five (originally the workhouse)	0	1	1
row of six	1		1
row of eight (called Rabbit Hutches)	1		1
approximate total	27	11	38

It is clear that the demand was for inexpensive dwellings. Only the single houses were intended for people of any substance. The cottages and rows were let predominantly to agricultural labourers, gardeners, servants, building workers like carpenters, bricklayers, house-painters, and an occasional railway worker, groom, or sweep. These houses, at the lowest level of village society, are the hardest to identify because the perennial necessity to make them cheap meant that they did not last long, and the building or rebuilding of an ordinary house was rarely recorded before 1900. The pressure for accommodation caused by the rising number of people was met in two ways, by the subdivision of existing houses and the building of new ones.

The subdivision of timber-framed houses had long been practised, and now several more of these old houses were partitioned, fitted with additional staircases and front doors and given new windows. Of these only Waxwell and Manor Cottages, Bee Cottage and Orchard Cottage now stand. The ones used as farmhouses were seldom divided.

Landlords and speculators found that the plethora of small plots created along roadsides at enclosure – especially at Pinner

46 Joseph Woodbridge made this row of three tiny cottages just to the left of the *George* about 1818.

Green or Common and in the marsh – provided ideal sites for new little cottages. Intended for the lower end of the market, they were usually in pairs or rows of three or more. The local builder played a leading role in the provision of new stock, buying the land and putting up the houses, either as a speculation for sale, or to rent out. Until the 19th century carpenters were the main constructors of the cheaper sort of house, providing a framework to be filled with plaster or brick. Carpenter Thomas Trevethan (the roué who built the workhouse) bought old cottages and redeveloped

them if he could, using timber frames. His last surviving house, 23 Bridge Street, was pulled down in 1989, revealing a frame of thin softwood, some of it reused, and an inner and outer skin of lath and plaster, the external surface scored to resemble blocks of stone. The walls were hollow – the last resident said they were a playground at night for mice. Trevethan's successor, Joseph Woodbridge, seems to have used the same method for the houses in Pinner Hill Road, but for his houses in Marsh Road and Chapel Lane he used timber frames covered in weather boarding, then much in vogue for cheap houses. From about 1840 the Woodbridges, the Ellements, and most others, built in brick. Of this group only 42-4 Pinner Hill Road and 2 Chapel Lane now stand.

The colloquially-named Rabbit Hutches in Pinner Hill Road, once called Coronation Cottages, were built about 1837, a single-storey row of eight, weather-boarded, with horizontally-sliding sash windows and outside water and drainage. The centrally-placed door opened into the living room-cum-kitchen, at about ten foot square the largest room, and there were two bedrooms and a scullery. They lasted until the late 1920s, and in their early days were probably desirable; the occupiers included a few construction workers and gardeners, but most were labourers.

The average small cottage, new or a conversion, had a living room and service room or scullery with two bedrooms above; cooking facilities were usually in the living room, and occasionally the room above could be heated. The staircase rose from the rear room, normally boxed off with its own door, as the later Unity Place, or, a little more classily, in a single flight between front and back room, shut off from both, as at 42-4 Pinner Hill Road. A staircase rising from an entrance hall, however small, signified a little more pretension, as at Rose Cottage (32 West End Lane). Until the arrival of mains water and sewage, water supplies came from an outside well, usually fitted with a pump, and the commonest place for the toilet was an earth closet in a hut at the bottom of the garden. This was true not only for

47 The eight Rabbit Hutches in Pinner Hill Road, site of 29-39, and some of the children who lived in them. They must have been the most curious-looking cottages in Pinner.

cottages but for most houses below the best. Not every house had its own facilities; as late as 1860 even the shops at 33 and 37 High Street had the legal right to use the well belonging to 35, while the three weather-boarded cottages by the *George* had a communal well and so did the two terraces of three at West End, which also shared toilet facilities. One or two brick privies survive as garden huts behind Unity Place, built about 1853.

Whatever the rate of movement in and out of Pinner, within the parish there was no great continuity of residence in particular houses, except in the case of property owners and occupiers such as farmers and tradesmen. Throughout the 18th and 19th centuries agricultural labourers and their like moved readily from landlord to landlord, back and forth across the street or lane – occupancy in the High Street was particularly complicated. With money so tight and unemployment always in prospect the varying size and earning capacity of the household must have been the major factor.

THE PROLIFERATION OF SHOPS

In the 1820s people would have noticed the way shops were appearing in the High Street. That decade brought directories of Middlesex by Pigot and by Robson which were the first to include Pinner, and the first attempt to list its local trades. Neither comprehensive nor annual, they are nevertheless very valuable in showing that outlets for traditional supplies were multiplying and that new sorts of goods were being supplied.

There were varying combinations of commodities on sale, the oddest mixture being that of John Leach, who added pork butchery to his shoemaking business in 1832; he was probably at Dears Farm. Only one full-time baker is listed and only one regular butcher. An ironmonger made a first appearance by that name in 1823, and it is no surprise to find he was also a smith. There was also a coal merchant, supplying another want which must have existed before, but about which nothing is known. In Pinner, the description 'perfumer and hairdresser' was probably an overblown version of the barber. For the first time a dressmaker and two straw-hat makers surface, all women. This sort of business, dressmaking and general sewing in particular, may have been going on for a long time without finding its way into the records, for it would have been carried out by women inside the home. When female traders did appear in the records, it was usually because they were carrying on the business of a deceased husband, as in the case of Elizabeth Bradshaw, widow of Thomas the baker. One trade which seems to have been completely new was that of bookseller and stationer, with its implication of a demand for reading and writing materials. One can but guess where it came from in general, but in particular it may have come from the pupils of Mr James Bogue's school for young gentlemen. A second new business had also appeared, with no need of a shop, James Carel's nursery in West End Lane between Elm Park Court and Hazeldene Drive. Carel had been in Pinner since the beginning of the century, propagating a new apple which he called the Pinner Seedling. This variety is still grown at The Grail in Waxwell Lane.

The following traders of the 1820s and 1830s, with addresses where discovered, were listed in the early directories:

Food: John Banks – grocer and chandler, 29 High Street; George Webb – grocer, linen and woollen draper, baker, 31-3 High St.; William Davis – grocer, linen and woollen draper, baker, post office, 7-9 High St.; William Crutch – grocer, blacksmith, ironmonger and oilman, 19 High St.; Charles Woodbridge – grocer and carpenter, Bridge St south of The Red Lion; Elizabeth Bradshaw – baker, 15 High St.; John Kerley – butcher, 58 High St.; John Bevan – butcher; Charles Jaques – miller and mealman, at windmill, Pinner Hill Road.

Clothing: John Leach – shoemaker, probably at Dears Farm; William Dodd, Thomas Eedle – shoemakers; William Murch – tailor and habit maker, site of 56-8 Bridge St.; James Bedford – tailor, 11 High St.; Mary Beaumont, Elizabeth Lee – straw-hat makers; Sarah Baker, wife of William – dressmaker, 7-9 High St.

Heavy trades: Samuel Dear – blacksmith; John Beaumont – wheelwright, 27 High St.; Daniel Dell, William Polton – carpenters; William Page, Vincent White – bricklayers; James Gude – plumber, painter, glazier.

48 This watercolour, datable to 1812-22, is the earliest picture of the High Street. West House is very prominent, the *Victory* still has its garden, there are shop fronts at 29, next to the *Queen's Head*, and at 25 further down, and 32-36 have picket fences. Pigs and fowl scavenge the roadway. The artist was probably Susan Procter, wife of William.

PINNER – T.L.A.   Aug 30 1827.

49 Almost a companion piece to the watercolour, T.L.Aspland's drawing of 1827 confirms some of its detail. There are shop fronts at 33-5, but not yet at 39. Equestrian Villa is there in its pre-temperance tavern condition. The shed in the roadway is a mystery – this is the only evidence of it.

Miscellaneous: William Spittle – coalman, at the *Queen's Head* where he was the licensee; William Moore – general dealer, High St.; Henry Beates – perfumer and hairdresser; Abraham Church – bookseller and stationer, 22 or 24 High St

SHOP FRONTS

Shop fronts began to appear in the High Street. The fashionable front in Regency and early Victorian times was the bow window, and the first watercolour of the High Street, painted about 1820, shows one at no. 29, later Joseph Banks' grocery shop, and another at no.25, which was possibly William Moore's general shop. Banks' shop appears again in the drawing made by T.L. Aspland in 1827, when Banks was there, and beyond the *Queen's Head* can be seen the two bow windows of George Webb's emporium. Pinner was keeping up with the world.

There are remnants of two bow windows in the High Street still, the oldest shop fronts in Pinner. The most obvious is at 24, installed perhaps by Abraham Church, the stationer of 1832, turned draper by 1841 (the glazing bars were renewed and enlarged early in the 20th century). The less obvious one has been repositioned in the east side of the extended shop front of 18 High Street, less complete than the other, but with older glazing bars.

The Chalk Mines

Chalk was worked on at least two sites in the later 18th century, on Pinner Common and at the Woodhall quarry.

Those on Pinner Common belonged to the lord of the manor. By 1803 they were well-established on the east side of the common, roughly from Latimer Gardens

50 The high galleries of the chalk mines beneath Grimsdyke, with their side galleries and regular bands, have been specially illuminated for this photo. Some names are just in view on the ceiling.

to Albury Drive, but need not always have been there. The tenant of this 12-acre site was Charles Blackwell, owner of the brickworks at Harrow Weald, for whose business chalk was an essential commodity. The workings included a lime kiln and appropriate buildings. Within a few more years they were worked out and the field was restored with great effort to agricultural use, though the risk of the ground sinking reduced its rental value.

After the Waxwell pit was exhausted quarrying continued north of Uxbridge Road on Woodhall land. Dingles Court is set in the Woodhall quarry, whose banks are visible behind them. The workings were extended by driving adits into the higher slopes. These methods ceased about 1830 in favour of mining, and shafts datable to 1830, 1840 and 1850 were sunk close to Grimsdyke south of Norman Crescent. The galleries below ground were some six to seven metres high, the chalk walls interlaced with bands of flint. The only access for workers and product was by the narrow shafts, about 5ft wide, with raising and lowering by ladder or rope. The pillar and stall method of working was used. Fairly regular workers toiled, probably in the agricultural off-season, and many have left their initials or names on the ceilings in candle soot, among them John Hill, J. Gumm and S. Beaumont. The Woodhall quarry was operated by the tenant until it was leased separately to Charles Blackwell in 1830. The lime was burned in the Woodhall quarry, latterly by Joseph Archer who lived in a cottage there. Mining ceased sometime before 1880, made uneconomic by railway traffic.

In the 19th century a chalk mine at Pinner Hill Farm was opened by either John Sellon or Albert Pell, in the field Sellon bought from Tubbs soon after enclosure. Mining may have been the idea behind the purchase. The mine is deep, 35m, and has a small network of sharply arched galleries, 2.5m high. Pell's young son Albert went down it with his friend Alexander Pym and they were shown how to mark their names on the ceiling in candle smoke. One day a worker forgot to take his clay pipe home with him, and it lay on its ledge there for nearly 150 years, until found when the shaft was explored in 1980.

A couple of cottages stood beside the mine by 1828, and by 1844 the home farm, with the requisite range of buildings, had been moved to the same site. At that time chalk could be produced worth £3 a week. Arthur Tooke probably closed the mine soon after he became the owner, for his new farm buildings crowded out the mine workings, and the shaft was adapted for a well. He may have opened a new mine on the other side of Pinner Hill Road, because inaccessible galleries lie there.

VI

Victorian Times

New times on the land

THE PRELUDE

It might have been expected that the Harrow Enclosure would usher in great improvements in local farming, but in fact uncontrollable conditions had a restraining effect.

The years from 1800-30 were bitter ones all over the country, marked by depression and bad weather. On the continent 1830 was a year of revolution. In England serious rioting broke out in the Kentish countryside and quickly spread through the southern and home counties. Farm machinery was broken, fires raised, and menacing letters signed by Captain Swing were sent to farmers and employers. Meetings were held to organise for higher wages, and in consequence of one such attempt several labourers from Tolpuddle in Dorset were transported to Australia. Within a 25-mile radius of London, however, commotion was much less, and in Middlesex only about a dozen incidents were reported. In Harrow a farm at Preston was set afire and Lord Northwick received a letter from Captain Swing.

The rain of 1828 was the worst in living memory in Harrow; it ruined the hay, it mildewed the wheat, it damaged the sheep. No-one wanted to buy sheep, and all agricultural prices had dropped. During that decade half a dozen of Lord Northwick's tenant farmers pleaded vainly for a reduction in rent, and two had to give up. Thomas Foster, whose property included some cottages in Love Lane, went 'all to pieces', and farmer Sam Greenhill's distress was so extreme by 1829 that he hanged himself in one of his fields at Roxeth. In 1831 an attempt was made to help labourers by letting 13 acres in the old Roxborough Field on the edge of Pinner – far from everywhere! – as allotments, but the soil was too water-logged for root vegetables to succeed.

The number of residents without land or a trade were growing. They faced rising unemployment and were more frequently dependent upon public charity and the poorhouse. Landowners had benefited, however modestly, but the smaller farmers were not well equipped to adopt new methods and thrive as the markets shrank, yet they and the tradesmen, along with the better-off owners, faced spiralling assessments for rates to sustain their poorer neighbours.

The social distance between farmers and their employees was widening. The farmer's family no longer wanted to eat in the kitchen with the hands or share the living-space, and began to retreat into domestic privacy. In Pinner, new wings with parlours and dining rooms still stand witness to this early 19th-century trend at Pinner Park, Woodhall, and Oxhey Lane farms, whilst also marking them out as among the more successful farms.

It was their size, of course, which gave these particular farms a better chance of surviving the hard times, along with those farmers who had benefited most at enclosure, particularly members of the Hill and Weall families. Information is too scarce to judge how much improvements in method, or new directions in production, contributed to success. Some machinery was introduced – by 1865 horse-powered threshing machines had been installed at Woodhall, Pinner Hill and Pinner Park farms, and at Hill's buildings in Rayners Lane (OS map 1865), but hay farming was dominant and reached its peak towards the end of the century. Itinerant hay makers abounded in the proper season. London's wheat could now be transported from the further reaches of England, and even from overseas. As the demand for hay too began to drop, livestock farming for meat rose, despite refrigeration, and dairy produce especially increased, with Titus Barham of Barham Park in Wembley proving an enviable local example with his Express Dairy.

WOODHALL FARM

At the start of the 19th century Woodhall Farm promised to become a herald of improvement when William Loudon from Scotland rented it in 1807. His son was John Claudius Loudon, later renowned for his pioneering theories of agricultural practice and building, and for writing the first encyclopaedia of gardening. At the threshold of this career John, recuperating at Woodhall with his father, enthusiastically redesigned it with the quadrangular yard then preferred – which both sheltered the livestock and allowed the farmer to keep everything under his eye from his house on the fourth side – plus a horse-powered threshing machine, and a plan for draining and reshaping the fields. The anticipated cost was £1,800. Loudon described them in his book *Observations on Laying Out Farms in the Scotch Style Adapted to England*, published in 1812. But these were only plans, not accomplishments. The father having died in 1809, John sublet Woodhall to Robert Bourne, taking for himself a lease of land in Kenton Lane, where he proposed another new farm, which was also included in his book. The landlord of Woodhall (and Kenton) was George Drummond, of the wealthy banking family, a man who might have been expected to respond to the challenge of building what was then called a 'model farm', were it not that he was a wastrel. He did provide a new wing to the farmhouse, very much like Loudon's design, and slightly remodelled the rest, but that was all. There was hardly time for this to happen while the Loudons were there, so it is doubtful whether John himself ever stepped through the pretty doorway into the lofty new rooms. A couple of fields were drained, which may have happened at any time in the century. Loudon later excoriated the farmers of Middlesex generally as wretched managers, prejudiced against accepting advice, using outdated implements which were badly made, and cursed with labourers ruined in their morals and health by the public houses. His parents he commemorated with a memorial of his own design, a very tall, tapering obelisk with an arched base and a fake coffin protruding front and back at half height. It is ironic that the most eye-catching memorial in Pinner churchyard should commemorate a very short-stay resident by another who expressed a very low opinion of the locals.

PINNER PARK FARM

At Pinner Park James Hume, tenant from 1806 to 1824, was partly of the new breed. It was for him that the new wing of the house was built. He introduced a mechanical thresher, but his work on the farm buildings was soon nullified by the use of poor materials. Waking up to the position in 1841, St Thomas' Hospital found the farm buildings precarious and the land 'in the last stages of poverty, covered in moss and couch grass'. After restoration their agent, Mr Trumper, proclaimed that 'the spacious cattle sheds ... commodious barn ... and large and spacious cart sheds had been built in the strongest and most substantial manner possible and may be calculated with ordinary care to stand for a century'. They have done that and more, although the smaller barn was burnt down about 1980. The large three-floored store, recently called a granary, which was shortened by Trumper because part of it had been built over the old moat and decayed, was re-erected at Headstone Manor in 1992.

HEADSTONE MANOR FARM

The swing to dairy and hay farming is more clear at Headstone than at any other local farm. In 1800 just over half its area was arable, but in 1819 the position was reversed, and by 1900 all was pasture and meadow. In 1840 it was reported that although the land produced heavier corn crops than lighter land, the heavier costs of tillage cancelled the benefit. In 1851 the landlord's son criticised tenant John Hill's 'wretched system of farming' but did not get rid of him. From an area of about 410 acres then, sales for house-building reduced it to slightly less than half by the end of the century.

TITHE FARM

There was plenty of space in the former open fields for old farms to expand and new ones to form once matters improved. The front-runner was Christ Church, Oxford which formed the huge New Farm on land it had received in compensation for the loss of tithes. The most southerly part of Pinner, roughly south of the Smart and Yeading Brooks, formed part of this. The farmhouse was in Eastcote Lane, a brand new road, and was subsequently called Temple Farm, Priors Farm, and lastly Tithe Farm. It was on the site of Rowe Walk, and the *Matrix* (previously *Tithe Farm*) public house stands in its rickyard. One of the first tenants was John Hodsdon, a relative of the Hills of Pinner, who supplied mutton from his cross-bred Welsh and South Devon sheep to a Windsor butcher for the royal table.

FARM BUILDINGS IN RAYNERS LANE

During the 1820s or 1830s Daniel Hill of Church Farm built accommodation for his labourers – a cottage with animal and cart sheds – in his new land in the long lane which had always linked Pinner to Roxeth. The Rayner family, by whose name it is now known, only arrived in Pinner from Ruislip at the start of the 19th century. George, the first one, was employed by Daniel Hill and lived with his wife Martha

51 Thomas and Eliza Rayner with son Dick at their home, 44 or 46 Eastcote Road.

in Hill's new cottage. Three of their sons became agricultural labourers too. George died in his 50s, buried 29 March 1846, and his eldest son Daniel – named after the employer perhaps – took over the cottage. There he brought up his family, and perished at the age of 45 in 1861, leaving his widow Anne with three youngsters, of whom 11-year-old Susan was handicapped in some way, preventing her mother from earning their keep. In 1864 a public appeal was launched to raise money to send Susan to the private Earlswood Asylum at Redhill in Surrey. Daniel Hill was among the first contributors. Daniel Rayner was often poor; he received charity blankets between 1849-56, and his widow received meat, bread, coal and more blankets from local charities between 1862-5. The family were gone from the cottage by the middle 1870s, when Anne went to live with her recently married son Daniel, who, from 1873-88, was landlord of the *Victory*, the small alehouse near the foot of the High Street.

George and Martha's second son George lived with his wife's mother Sarah Shepherd, who kept the *White Hart* beer shop in the High Street. Sarah raised his three young children there after her daughter Ann died in 1853, followed by George two years later. One of the children, Thomas, worked at the new gas works in Eastcote Road for most of his life and lived in one of the adjoining cottages, no.44 or 46. In 1918, at the age of 66, he climbed the gas holder to place a victory flag at the top. His descendants by two daughters were still in Pinner at the end of the 20th century.

It was this humble family of farm workers whose name is now familiar to every user of the London Underground system. The first documented use of 'Rayner' as a place-name in Pinner is found in a conveyance dated 4 October 1856, in which two fields on the west side of the later Rayners Lane, stretching from the present Greenway to Village Way, were called Upper Rayners Field and Lower Rayners Field. The roadway was presumably called Rayners Lane before or very soon after the Rayners moved out in the 1870s, but there is no written evidence. It is nameless on the 1896 OS map. It had often been called Bourne Lane because of the brooks it crossed – Lanketts or Lankers (Yeading), Smarts, and two branches of a brook at the Roxeth end now called Roxbourne Brook.

After the last Daniel Hill died in 1906 the bulk of the land on the east side of the lane was let to James Smith, and a new farmhouse was built about 1915 well to the north of the cottages. Originally named Lankers Brook Farm, from the name of the field on which the house stood, it was occasionally called Lankers Farm, Brook Farm, or Rayners Lane Farm. The building is still there, numbered 552, looking just like any other suburban house, its former yard differentiated from the surroundings by the post-war houses now standing on it, nos. 544-50. Daniel's

52 Lankers Brook Farm, or Brook Farm during the 1920s. The side of the farmhouse, 552 Rayners Lane, just creeps into the picture at left.

heirs sold the farm to Metropolitan Railway Country Estates Ltd. about 1928, and in August the last farmer, Arthur Smith, advertised for auction his 120 cattle, 200 sheep, six cart horses, and store of new hay. The Rayners' old cottage and yard was bisected by Farm Avenue.

TEMPLE FARM

Temple Farm was new, created from Emily Cottage (site of Lloyd Court) as first Ralph Ellis, then his son John, added over 90 acres of enclosure land to it. But John sold 93 acres to the Prince brothers about 1856, so the next farmer Charles Temple (c.1856-84), may have needed to rent land. Farming ceased when Agnes Marshall bought the house and seven acres for a country home in 1891. It was the only new farm to vanish before 1900.

DOWNS FARM

William and Henry Prince formed Downs Farm from the 93 acres bought from John Ellis. They lay between Cannon Lane and Rayners Lane and included Upper and Lower Rayners Fields. The brothers built a farmstead on the site now occupied by the Methodist Church, and lived there some 30 years – the road was occasionally called Princes Lane in the late 19th century. In 1887 they sold to Daniel Hill and seem to have moved to the U.S.A. Hill leased it to Joseph Gurney, coal merchant and rate collector, who operated a small-holding there until it was developed for housing in the 1930s. The land on the western side of Cannon Lane remained largely unconsolidated and available for rent till then.

HOPE FARM

Edward Powell, who rented Park Farm in Field End Road, Eastcote, built Hope Cottage on three acres of the old Newlands which he had bought in 1848, and equipped it with a few out-buildings. His tenants called themselves farmers, but much of their land must have been rented. In 1881 George Barter had a dairy farm of 61 acres based there, which survived until the late 1920s. Barter was Powell's brother-in-law. The house stood in Pinner Road, and the yew tree in its garden is now enclosed within that of 27 South Way.

PINNER HILL FARM

Further north the colonisation of the former common also proceeded in stages. The home farm of the Pinner Hill House estate, previously based near Pinnerwood House, was re-established in its present position, and run in conjunction with Albert Pell's small chalk mine.

Arthur Tooke rebuilt the farm in quadrangular form soon after he took over the estate in 1844. He installed a horse-powered threshing machine of recent design, whose granite-set horse circle can still be seen, though of the building which housed its mechanism only the foundations remain. Part of a cobbled pathway to a vanished lime-kiln is also visible. Outside, where the road bends, lies a roughly semi-circular, flat limestone slab of uncertain purpose. It was designed to run on its edge and may have been used in crushing fruit or the like. It was not a millstone.[28] The plainness of the initial farm buildings contrasts with the clock-towered stable at the roadside which Tooke added in 1862 in the flamboyant style he then loved. The tower had a tack room, hay loft, and top floor of unknown purpose. Much of the farm's area was parkland of the estate and therefore primarily pastoral. There was a regular turnover of tenants until James Gregory arrived about 1880, and the Gregorys stayed there until farming ceased in the 1930s.

MILL FARM

The new fields in the southern part of the common remained with their several owners – the Hill family and Pinner Park Farm among them – for most of the 19th century. The small Mill Farm emerged as a separate entity very late in the

53 Mill Farm, pictured at an unknown date, was clearly not built as a farmhouse.

19th century, some time after Arthur Tooke of Pinner Hill House had bought the burnt-out windmill in 1872 – in its last years the mill had ground animal feed. It was more of a small-holding than a regular farm, with only a few out-buildings and no traditional yard. A row of back-to-back outhouses, one storey high, had been converted at their street end for use as the farmhouse, whose floor was still earthen in the 1920s. James Emeny's family, which arrived in the late 1880s, sold eggs and milk at the door and was there, still selling, till the buildings were demolished for housing 1972-77. Mill Farm Close follows the old track to the mill and farmhouse.

Every one of these new 19th-century farms fell before the scythe of 20th-century suburbia.

The Main Line Railway

LONDON TO BIRMINGHAM

The London to Birmingham (later the London & North Western) Railway came to Harrow in 1837, and passed through Pinner on its way north. Disruption while the track was constructed was inevitable, and some farms lost land by sale to the railway company. A sliver was nipped off Woodhall Farm and strips were sheared through Oxhey Lane and Pinner Park Farms. Dove House and Hatch End Farms were sundered. John Boys, the owner of the former, received £1,800 in compensation, and his tenant John Tilbury £221. But at Hatch End Farm the owner/occupier Benjamin Weall proved difficult, so the company offered him almost 10 per cent above the true value to sell them the whole farm, which he did. Nor would he rent back the unneeded part at a sum the company would accept.

A station called Pinner (now Hatch End) was opened opposite Dove House in Uxbridge Road, the nearest convenient point to the village, in August 1842.[29] Eight stopping trains a day served it, three down and five up – how was that managed? – and three each way on Sundays. The journey to Euston took about 45 minutes. Third-class travel was available only once a day, which reflects the initial low demand at that level. For the first decade and more, the prime targets of the London & Birmingham Railway were long distance and freight traffic.

The stone sleeper blocks originally used on the track were soon replaced by timber ones. They were sold, and some of these relics of the first railway can be seen forming the street frontage of Pinner Hill Farm, and piled as a column in the grounds of Pinner Hill House.

CONSEQUENCES

The provision of something new is both a response and a stimulus to demand. The new way of transport would have excited or disconcerted Pinner people just like any others. They must have gone to watch the trains, but as yet few needed or could afford them. The stage coach continued, and the population increase did not lurch upward. But gradually trains began to make a difference and brought to Pinner two developments of equal, though differing, novelty, a large school and a commuter estate.

In 1855 the Commercial Travellers School (not called Royal till 1919) transferred from Wanstead to a great new complex opposite the station. Pinner had never been home to an institution of any size since Thomas Goodwin's academy at Pinner Place. For a long time the school was self-contained in that much of the running and maintenance formed part of the curriculum, and it had extensive kitchen gardens. How far the purchase of other provisions directly benefited Pinner tradesmen we do not know. But every Sunday the children were to be seen parading to the parish church, and were afterwards let loose to spend their ha'pence. The church scarcely had room for them, and in 1859 the south chapel was built beside the chancel especially for them to use.

While the school took land off the railway company's hands it could not have brought it much traffic, since the pupils boarded. And it was a poor recommendation for the railway that the guest of honour at the opening ceremony, H.R.H. The Prince Consort, who had come by train, found himself delayed by 25 minutes.

Nevertheless, by mid-century Londoners in good salaried jobs were keen to live outside town and the railway companies and nearby landowners grasped the opportunity to accommodate them. In Pinner, Canon John Meynell built an estate of 50 dwellings on a few fields he owned opposite Woodridings Farm west of the station. It was ready by 1855. His agent, Richard Field, made much of the healthiness of the countryside and the number of gentlemen's mansions in the vicinity, and heavily overstated the ease of getting sons into nearby Harrow School, currently enjoying enormous prestige.

This became the Woodridings estate, and out from town came Pinner's first commuters – businessmen, civil servants, senior clerks, and annuitants or pensioners in a comfortable way. The railway company added the additional bait of a free first-class season ticket to Euston for each house worth £50 a year in rent – they all fell into this category – for 13 years, one year for every mile of distance from Euston. With one exception (the gothic Oak Villas adjoining the tavern) the new estate was built in the Italianate style popular in other parts of Harrow, at Brondesbury, Kilburn, and Highbury. All houses were semi-detached, and were called, fashionably, villas, with aristocratic names like Beaufort, Chandos, Wellington and so on. There were variations of detail and size. Each had two reception rooms, either five, six or seven bedrooms, domestic offices, i.e. kitchen and larder, and *two* water closets. This was new, as was the running water. The estate had a water-pumping house powered by steam, but the arrangements for sewage disposal remain obscure; deodorising before discharge into the river was its practice in 1870. The annual rents ranged from £50 to £65. The only commercial premises provided was the *Railway Tavern* (demolished 2004), so all shopping had to be done in Watford, Harrow or Pinner – but that enhanced the rural charm, and those were the days when shop-keepers were keen to wait upon customers of quality. There were 215 residents, 61 of them servants, occupying 29 houses in 1861. There were 265 residents, including 66 servants, in 44 houses in 1891, at about which date development in the neighbourhood began again.

The Woodridings residents formed an enclave situated between existing hamlets and with no direct route to the village centre, from which they were separated by Pinner Park. Nor were they carriage folk, for only four or five stables were provided on the estate (there are commercial garages on this spot now). There should have been some economic benefit to Pinner traders, and it may be significant that it

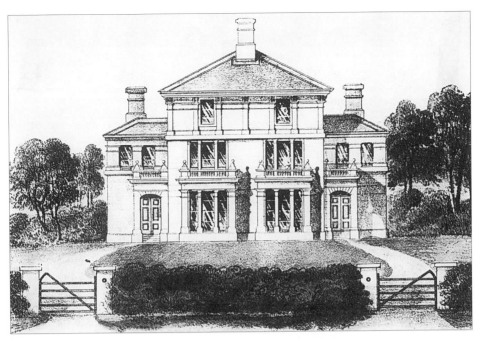

54 The Beetons lived in the right-hand half of Chandos Villas in Uxbridge Road, annual rent £50. The estate agent's advertisement exaggerates the space at the sides.

was about this time that fly-driving became a new occupation. In 1863 the vicar classified Woodridings as not 'affluent'!

Part of a Wider World

GREAT CHANGES

Pinner felt the impact of the wider world continually. The railway was speedy beyond belief. It became easier to spend a day in London, to try the horse buses there, or visit the Great Exhibition of 1851. The introduction of the Penny Post in 1841 made mail more affordable to the majority. The first local newspaper appeared in 1855, the *Harrow Gazette*, carrying national and international news, as well as local. Maybe the newsagent in the High Street sold *The Englishwoman's Magazine* – two pence monthly, started in 1852 by Samuel Beeton, who soon afterwards came to live at Woodridings estate, which contained fiction and fashion, as well as household and gardening advice. Any child whose parents could pay a few pennies could learn reading, writing and a few more things in the new National School. Nonconformist sects had returned and friendly societies with country-wide connections appeared.

Villages like Pinner and its neighbours, whose communal affairs had been managed within the manor or parish, found themselves entering new frameworks in order to cope with the growing size and cost of their social problems. Poor relief, sanitation, roads, education, hitherto directly shouldered by the local community and organised by unpaid residents, came to be managed more distantly, and professionally. When the Pinner poor were sent to the union workhouse at Hendon the problems of paupers no longer fell so obviously directly upon their neighbours. The roads of Harrow and Pinner were taken over by the Edgware Highways Board in 1863, though local overseers were still appointed to it, and failure to mend roads quickly could be blamed on an outside authority. Sanitary matters and nuisances were taken out of Pinner's hands by Hendon Rural Sanitary Authority in 1872, which swallowed the Highways Board also. Central government expanded in the 19th century; its swathes of social legislation created new ministries and multiplied jobs in newly accessible London.

NEW JOBS

As the world changed and Pinner with it, people found new occupations, though many were practised by the newcomers seeking out-of-town houses, whether the new little villas, the larger detached houses, or even the older mansions, rather than by the native-born. These were such as lawyers, stockbrokers, contractors, tea-dealers, photographers, storekeepers, jewellers, booksellers, publishers, and – symptomatic of the new developments – civil servants in the admiralty, chancery, inland revenue, customs, war office, colonies, and museums. About 35 people are reckoned to have been commuting by 1861, some 20 of them from Woodridings.

Native-born and newcomers shared in the new skilled trades. From 1841 there were railway employees – platelayers, policemen (a description which included level-crossing keepers), a driver, a signalman, labourers, and clerks (who usually worked in London) – and in 1861 there were 15 altogether. From the late 1860s there were gas workers – fitters, stokers, and an engineer. There was one electrician as early as 1871; and a fly driver. The same was true of traditional tradesmen such as bakers, tailors, smiths, builders, though it is noticeable in the alcohol trade that inns or public houses were usually managed by outsiders, whereas beer shops, authorised by the Beerhouse Act of 1830, being very small, often just a front room, and needing scarcely any capital or experience, were owned or run by local people – the *White Hart*, the *Starling*, the *Victory*. In agricultural work and general labouring only newcomers from nearby localities like Harrow, Ruislip, Stanmore and Bushey competed with native-born. Nevertheless this work was often quite specialised, and included stock care, hedging and hay-binding.

Domestic service had its own areas of expertise, and newcomers tended at first to bring most of their staff with them, particularly in the higher grades like butlers, ladies' maids and governesses, where local people lacked experience. This changed with time. The demand for gardeners rose noticeably, pushed by the desire for ornamental gardens at large houses. And so, partly from the same source, did that for laundresses. This provided virtually a new source of income for widows and wives in hard-up families because it could be done at home. Many of Pinner's laundresses lived in the small cottages strung about Pinner Green and Hill. Some newcomers brought employees with them, such as John Mayall, the court photographer who bought The Grove in 1859 and employed four assisistants in Pinner, who did not originate here.

Whereas in 1801 about 50 per cent of Pinner's workers depended on agriculture, the proportion in 1851 was just over 40 per cent and in 1881 about 15 per cent. The following table of workers compares the numbers in occupational groupings at the censuses of 1851 and 1881 (compiled by Ken Kirkman using the Booth Armstrong classification).

	1851			1881
agriculture	213		domestic	292
domestic	135		agriculture	133
manufacture	62		distribution	80
distribution	29		professional	75
building	26		general labour	72
professional	22		manufacture	68
general labour	9		building	57
transport	8		transport	54
miscellaneous	3		miscellaneous	52
	507			883

After marking time for a decade the population of Pinner rose by 40 per cent, or 539 people, in the ten years to 1861, of whom 215 can be attributed to the Woodridings estate and about 200 to the Commercial Travellers School – without the school it was 26 per cent. It had risen another 30 per cent by 1871. The 1901 total of 3,366 was four and a half times that for 1801.

Schools

THE SITUATION IN 1833

Education of the majority was one of the forces changing Pinner. A national Education Enquiry in 1833 showed the following provision in Pinner, which was typical of the variety available in the surrounding parts of Middlesex.

type	boys	girls	total	
Sunday school	36	51	87	
an infant school	25	35	60	revived 1831
a daily school with	5	8	13	
a daily school with	22	0	22	began 1822
two daily schools with	0	42	42	
two daily schools with	14	15	29	
two boarding schools	32	8	40	began after 1818
	134	139	293	

The Enquiry stated that: the Sunday School still received £10 annually from the Harrow School Governors, with further maintenance by subscription; the Infant School was supported wholly by the clergyman except that parents paid 1d. per week per child; the boarding schools were wholly at parental expense; Mrs Goditha Martin's money was still available.[30]

Sunday Schools had been founded by Robert Raikes in the 18th century and did give tuition. However, many of those who attended the one in Pinner must also have been pupils at others, for in 1841 there were only c.220 resident children between the ages of five and 12, the school years (plus 199 between 12 and 18). The daily schools were presumably paid for by parents. Pupils at the boarding schools were not necessarily local, and Pinner children may have boarded elsewhere.

PRIVATE SCHOOLS

Directories list some non-parochial schools, though perhaps not all.

1823-5	James Bogue	boys' boarding school, at Pinner House
1826	William Procter	boys' boarding school
1832-4	Sarah Polkinghorne	day school
1832-4	James Buckley	day school
1832-40	Catherine Pay	day and ladies' boarding school
1840	George Richardson	boys' day school

Procter may have taken over Bogue's school. The rates lists suggest that Mrs Polkinghorne was on the site of 33-5 Bridge Street, and Miss Pay at Church Cottage in Church Lane.

In 1841 Miss Caroline Doogood or Toogood had a boarding establishment at Mount Cottage (site of the house called Blackgate) in Church Lane, with 14 boarders aged from four to nine years, boys and girls, plus her two little sisters. She was only 21 years old herself, but father and mother, both retired teachers, lived next door at the Bay House. After 1841 there were far fewer boarders. Between 1851 and 1861 she gave it up – perhaps she married – and for the next 20 or so years it was run by Louisa Davis, wife of Alfred, a landscape artist.

Several of the wealthier residents employed governesses, usually for children of both sexes, from four to ten years old. There were as many as five in the peak year of 1871. At the parsonage in that year the Rev. Hind had six children for his 23-year-old governess Ann Read, while ten years earlier at Wellington Villa, Woodridings, wine merchant Arthur Bloxham engaged Gabrielle Gissault from Paris to teach his brood of seven.

THE VILLAGE, OR NATIONAL, SCHOOL

The National Society for Promoting the Education of the Poor in the Principles of the Established Church was established in 1811, and promoted day and Sunday schools. It made a grant to the Pinner Sunday School in 1816, when 103 pupils attended. About the same time Nonconformist churches founded the British and Foreign School Society. After the 1833 enquiry the government made annual grants toward the setting up of schools by both Societies. Under these arrangements a National School in Pinner, promoted by the vicar, and no doubt incorporating the infant school, was set up in 1841 on land given by the lord of the manor, to be maintained by school pence and voluntary contributions.

Pinner lagged behind Roxeth, Great and Little Stanmore, Ruislip, Northolt and Hendon, where the National Society had already helped set up schools. It was soon followed by the other villages of Harrow – Weald, Sudbury, Kenton, with Greenhill and Wealdstone rather later.

Set opposite the foot of Pinner High Street, the new single-storey building had one room for boys, one for girls and infants. The date 1841 was worked into the brickwork of the southern wall. There were 190 pupils in 1851, that is *c.*70 per cent of the eligible children plus a few younger and older ones. James Brooks and his wife Amelia came from Clerkenwell to be the first master and mistress, and rented the middle house of the nearby converted workhouse. Nothing more is known of the Sunday School.

The censuses list several schoolmistresses. There was Jane Gude (1841), aged 60, mother of James the plumber who lived on the site of 42 High Street; Sophia Crutch (1841, 1851) a widow with children of her own living in a cottage behind the vicarage; Anne Lee, aged 24 (1851, 1861) living in the old cottage in Chapel Lane with her father Edward, a coachmaker; Charlotte Jones, aged 40 (1851, 1861) living behind 53-7 Bridge Street with her labourer husband Sam. These ladies may have taught the infants at the National School, or kept dame schools, traditionally places where infants were taught their letters in the home of a woman who need not herself be very learned.

A bigger National School was opened in Marsh Road on 27 March 1867, with five rooms. School Lane was created to give access, and is now the only trace of Pinner's National School. The new master and mistress were 22-year-old Henry Berry and his wife Mary, appointed in October 1866 in good time to inaugurate the new building. They resided in a new house attached to the school. The initial

55   This was the National School from 1841-65 – the railway embankment came later – and then the parish hall. The Parish Council met here till 1934, the Civil Defence used it in wartime, and from 1946 until 1960 it was the public library.

average attendance was 56 boys, and 80 girls and infants; for 1900-1 the parish report said the numbers on the books were 111 boys, 103 girls and 60 infants, but the average attendance was 83, 75 and 43 respectively.

Three years were spent in the infants' school, learning reading, writing, arithmetic, singing, religious knowledge, drill, and general moral lessons – one of the primary purposes of education. In the six following years geography and history were added, and needlework for the girls. In 1877 Latin and French were tried out for a while on the boys, and freehand drawing in 1891. In 1880 Mrs Tooke of Pinner Hill House gave a couple of lessons on moths and butterflies, and then some more on elementary botany. Ladies of the parish often helped, particularly with tuition in needlework, and usually included the wife or daughter of the vicar, or the wives of school managers, who were often local gentry, such as Mrs Tooke and Mrs Graham of Nower Hill House.

In 1873 the Berrys were replaced by John and Philippa Walker, the ones who tried Latin and French. In 1878 Charles and Isabella Billows, 27 and 28 respectively, were appointed, and remained in charge until their retirement in 1916.

The master and mistress were assisted by pupil teachers, newly-left youngsters who served a five-year apprenticeship at £10 a year, progressing to £20, until going to a teacher training college at age 18, where two years' study would earn a teaching certificate. The head received £5 a year for each pupil teacher. In practice many pupil teachers remained in Pinner as assistants without going to college. At the end of the century it is not at all clear whether assistant master William King was certificated or an ex-pupil. In the infant school the teacher was helped by monitors, older pupils still learning themselves. The background of the pupil teachers in Pinner was similar to that of the children they taught; Mark Mullins, son of a gardener, James Cox, son of a plate-layer, Emily Hitchcock, daughter of a plumber, Emily Garnham, daughter of an agricultural labourer, Rosa Wakeham, daughter of a shoemaker. Emma Hayden is worth noting; daughter of Samuel, an agricultural labourer, she lived with her schoolmistress aunt Charlotte Jones after her mother's early death. She was certificated, maybe as a result of experience only, and was mistress of the infant school from 1874-81 but did not often get good reports from the inspectors. Discipline and attainment in particular were criticised. In 1881, seeing the writing on the wall, she left.

The Education Act of 1880 made school attendance compulsory, even though school pence still had to be paid. The managers decided on a flat fee of 3d. per week, raised to 9d. the following year for non-parochial children. (In 1886 a large number of boys from Northwood who were attending Pinner school went back when a master replaced a mistress in charge of Northwood school.) Collection was sometimes difficult – Edward Ball, of the cottages at Headstone Farm, was refused admission on 12 December 1881 owing to long arrears of school fees, but re-admitted in the afternoon on part payment and a promise of the rest. From October 1891 education in the infant school was wholly free, though the upper schools charged 1d. per pupil, no family to pay more than 2d.

The teachers' log books give a good daily picture of school life. Wet weather often kept children away, because of inadequate footwear or impassable lanes, and so, of course, did snow. Epidemics are recorded, and occasional child deaths. Boys were punished with the cane for throwing stones or playing truant. And there were many school treats; gifts of fruit and cake, half days of jollification and tuck at a local spot, like the grounds of Pinner Hill House or at the *Cocoa Tree*, visits to the zoo, half days off.

From 1879 there are references to boys going to work for the railways, and in 1881 Mr Billows commented that 'nearly the whole of the 6th and 7th Standard boys [are] bent on becoming Euston Clerks'. We know of some: Harry Cox, to

Euston booking office 1879, Alfred Odell to Euston in 1880, William Dalton, William and John Wakefield of West End, and William Williamson to Euston in 1881 and 1882; Charles Prince as booking clerk to Pinner station (1886) and Arthur Rixon to Northwood Station (1887). George Williamson went as clerk to the Metropolitan Coal Co-operative Stores (1890) and Arthur Humphreys as clerk to the St Pancras Local Board (1894). The part Mr Billows played can be seen from his log book for 18 June 1880: 'Gave greater part of the day to Alfred Odell who attends an exam. at Euston for a clerkship on the 22nd. Took him in Newspaper Reading, Penmanship, Dictation, Spelling and Interest.'

It was a strenuous life, even in small things. On 10 January 1887 Charles Billows wrote in the log book: 'Taught a new song to the lower standards. As the assistant master does not sing I find it very difficult to be constantly singing to the whole school.' His hoarse sigh is audible still!

Pinner at Worship

THE CHURCH OF ENGLAND

At the start of the 19th century the fabric of Pinner church was half a millennium old, and showing it. In 1811 a ceiling was made to conceal the decrepit roof, and the chancel arch was patched up. In 1849 there was still an early-English triplet window in the south wall of the chancel, a little old glass in the south window of the south transept, and remnants of a perpendicular rood screen – all of which went in the alterations of 1859.[31]

The rising number of parishioners at the end of the 18th century caused problems of accommodation, because the high Georgian pews which filled the church were difficult to rearrange. Many of them were appropriated or allocated to particular residences. There was already a little gallery in the tower, possibly an old ringing floor, which had been altered in 1805 to seat five people instead of three.

56 The interior of St John's before 1859. The ceiling is boxed in, the Royal Arms are above the chancel arch, box pews extend into the chancel, and Hutchinson's and Clitherow's monuments still hang respectively at north and south sides of the chancel. There is no south chapel, so the pipe of the heating system can go straight through the window to the outside.

A new gallery was the solution for most churches, and in 1815 one was inserted across the west end of St John's, supported on the two end pillars and some slender iron columns. It was to be used also for a Sunday School of up to 100 children, so the National Society weighed-in with a grant of £30 towards the expected cost of £100.

The arrival of the Commercial Travellers School aggravated the seating problem, so in 1859 a south aisle was added to the chancel to accommodate the children, and the high box pews were replaced by more commodious open pews.

Church attendance was high, stimulated by the evangelism of the Noncon-formists, and the spread of education, which itself was heavily influenced by the churches via the National and British schools. A special census of national church attendance on 30 March 1851 found an average of 40 per cent.

In 1863 the Rev. William Hind completed a form for the Statistical Committee of the Bishop of London's Fund. He estimated that there were about 150 dissenters in the parish and that several Anglicans attended their chapels either for convenience, or because they could not get into the parish church, though he did not say whether the overflow was the result of appropriated pews or high attendance. He said the church had 716 seats, all but 200 appropriated. (If it were full and the Dissenters are added then some 43 per cent of Pinner inhabitants attended Christian worship.)

There had been a church choir of sorts, because the churchwardens made seats for the singers at the west end of the nave in 1805, before there was a big gallery, but there was no musical instrument, according to Albert Pell of Pinner Hill, before they installed an organ in the big gallery about 1847 and appointed an organist, Mr Mull, at £20 p.a. By that time there was a proper school building.

A major restoration in 1880 has preserved the church for us. William Tooke of Pinner Hill House chose the architect, John L. Pearson, and paid the bill, nearly £5,000. No significant violence was done to the character of the church. The outside was cleaned of rendering, the tower repaired, the dormers reconstructed, door and window facings replaced in Bath stone, and the brick vestry rebuilt in stone. A niche over the porch was rediscovered. Inside, new roofs were made for the nave, chancel and south aisle, the west gallery was removed and the capitals and bases of the columns repaired. Choir stalls were made in the chancel. The new chancel aisle was enlarged to take a new organ donated by William Barber, and its east window, a replica of the medieval triplet destroyed in 1859, was moved to its south wall. A grateful public erected a drinking fountain to Tooke's memory on Nower Hill Green, whose name has since been changed to his.

PARISH PRIESTS

Harrow and Pinner parishes were transferred from the diocese of Canterbury to that of London in 1836, and in 1868 the Wilberforce Act accorded the status of vicar to every parish priest who was not a rector. William Hind, therefore, became the first vicar of Pinner. The following vignettes of incumbents are necessarily brief, and do not do justice to the role of each in the community nor his attention to duty, especially regarding the school and the fostering of local organisations. All of them had a gentleman's upbringing.

John Venn (1830-33) was an evangelical, a low-church man. To keep the sabbath holy he urged employers to pay wages on Friday or early on Saturday, so that shops need not open on Sunday mornings. The window-glass in the porch, the oldest in the church, was his gift.

Thomas Burrow (1833-61), another evangelical, was the illegitimate son of a half-caste West Indian mother. His quarter-century witnessed many changes in Pinner, including the opening of a new cemetery in Paines Lane in which he was one of the first to be buried. The east window of St John's commemorates him, a window which hugely irritated one of his successors, Charles Grenside. Burrow is said to have forbidden his daughter to marry Daniel Hill of Church Farm; Hill repined, and when he died in 1906 there were no Hills to succeed him.

William Hind (1861-75), born in Ireland, was a scholar. His paper on St John's church was printed in the *Transactions of the London & Middlesex Archaeological Society* in 1868, and he contributed to and edited works on the flora of Harrow and Middlesex. He installed the north chancel window with squirrels around the border in memory of his parents.

William St Hill Bourne (1875-80) was a small neat man whose large family soon obliged him to move to a better paid living at Haggerston. He wrote hymns which were popular in his lifetime.

William Pinnock (1880-85) was another scholar who wrote much on church history, and carried on in a small way the compilation of school books from which his father had made a good living. It is said that when the bells were being rung at his welcoming ceremony he was himself carried high off the ground by the bell-rope he tried to toll. The Lord brought him safely back to rest.

Charles Grenside (1885-1910) won plaudits for his charm of manner and voice. He initiated the parish magazine in 1887, with its official insert of bible teaching, household hints and fiction, and followed it with the more short-lived *Pinner Almanack*, a review of the past year compiled by himself. He was the first local historian of Pinner. He gave the tall font-cover in memory of his wife.

OTHER DENOMINATIONS

In his statistical report of 1863 William Hind showed five Roman Catholics and two Jews in the parish, whom it has not yet proved possible to identify.

There were two nonconformist chapels, both in Chapel Lane, which only received that name because of their presence. Several places in Middlesex built Methodist and Baptist chapels sooner than Pinner did, including nearby Eastcote. Pinner Methodists were meeting in Chapel Lane by 1830, according to a mortgage dated 26 November 1830 which stated that the

57 Pinner's first Methodist Chapel appeared on the north side of Chapel Lane in 1844. The railway was built close to its right side in 1885.

barn and stable of the old sub-divided cottage near the north-eastern corner of the lane was 'converted and used as a Wesleyan Chapel'. This may mean that the cottage itself was not a meeting place, as is often supposed. The trustees bought a plot west of the cottage from the owner Edward Lee in 1843, and the Steward of the Hammersmith Circuit, to which Pinner then belonged, laid the foundation stone of the small brick chapel on 1 April 1844. When the railway was built in 1885 the Methodists chose to stay alongside until noise and vibration drove them to newly erected premises in Love Lane in 1916. Their old site lies under the later western set of tracks.

Fifteen years after 1844, in the words of William Hind, 'a wealthy Baptist came to reside, and he erected an Iron Chapel, which drew away a large part of the congregation from the other Chapel'. He was George Attenborough, a Regent Street bookseller living at West House, who had leased another piece of Mr Lee's land between the Methodist chapel and the old cottage and opened the new chapel in 1859. Hind said that 'at the same time dissent became openly hostile to this Church, and for a time caused much trouble and uneasiness'. The most distinctive Baptist minister was the heavily bearded William Treneman from Cornwall, resident at Cornwall Cottage in West End Lane, who was vigorous enough on the verge of his 80s to be the school attendance officer as well, and to marry for the second time in 1898, whisking his much younger bride off on honeymoon. The Metropolitan Railway obliterated the chapel, and a new one of yellow brick, seating 180, was built in Marsh Road, where it remained until a larger church was opened in Paines Lane in 1910 (from 1945 the United Free Church). The Marsh Road building was used as a working men's club until it became Pinner's first synagogue in 1951, and was rebuilt in 1980.

Social Affairs

FRIENDLY SOCIETIES

In the deteriorating conditions of the previous century some people had preferred self-help, rather than full dependence on the poor law, and by 1800 a large number of friendly societies had been registered, organisations for mutual support of members in times of sickness, unemployment or death. They also offered convivial meetings, frequently centred upon a public house, with occasional celebrations, and were not unlike the brotherhoods of medieval days.

There were three friendly societies in Pinner. First off the mark was the Benefit Society of the United Brethren of Pinner, founded in September 1817. By its rules new members must be aged between 12 and 40, with admission fees graduated according to age, and no-one already suffering a chronic illness could join. Members paid 1s. 3d. a month and the benefits were 12s. a week for the first 52 weeks of incapacity, 6s. for the next 26 weeks, and 5s. weekly thereafter until the termination of the illness. The death benefit was £5 for a member, and also for one wife. The vestry took account of benefits in fixing its poor relief payments, deciding in March 1819, for example, to allow John Lea 2s. weekly during illness in addition to his 'clubb' money, and the same to James Greenfield, 'in addition to the half pay he receives from his clubb'. In the early years the society would also pay half the cost of a substitute for members drafted into the militia. In 1860 subscriptions were 6s. 1d. a quarter, but benefits remained the same, though the death payment was doubled.

The second society was the Promoters of Friendship, which sold a plot at Pinner Green to the brewer Clutterbuck in 1834. They met at the *Queen's Head*, and their stewards were John Levy, a Pinner gardener, and Christopher Bugbee, a sawyer of Roxeth. This is all that we know of it.

Third was the Manchester Unity and Independent Order of Oddfellows, set up in Pinner in 1845 as the Loyal British Queen Lodge of Pinner no.3861 by Thomas Ellement, carpenter, James Gladman, shoemaker, and Harry Mayo, publican. Early rates are not known. It probably replaced the Promoters.

The Brethren, and probably the Promoters, were merely local societies, whereas the Oddfellows were part of a nationwide one. The Brethren's rules forbade meeting in a public house, or the drinking of beer at meetings; its treasurer was always to be the incumbent. By contrast the others met at the *Queen's Head*, with the landlord as treasurer of the Oddfellows. Brethren and Oddfellows had gentlemen as honorary members to lend dignity, and in the Brethren's case to act as trustees, but all the organisation was otherwise done by members. The Oddfellows were the first to hold festivities, beginning in the 1850s, with procession, banners, bands, sports, and the flag flying from the church tower. The Brethren held their first dinner in July 1860, with an address by Lord Ebury of Moor Park, followed by a public jamboree, in which hundreds of non-members were let in to enjoy tea and cake and dancing to the music of the Harrow Rifle and Quadrille Band, and their flag flew from the church tower.

In 1860 membership of the Brethren was about 300, many living at some distance from Pinner. By the end of the century the Oddfellows were dominant, having 214 members in 1902 and 225 in 1909, compared with the Brethrens 105 in 1900 and 96 in 1903. Each drew members from the same families, though scarcely a handful belonged to both. Membership was weighted towards skilled artisans and tradesmen. Members in distant places grew greatly in both societies as some moved away but kept their membership. In 1900-3 there were about 200 locally-based members of the two, ranging from labourers to tradesmen and a few farmers, which might have represented 25 per cent of the male workforce. After the National Insurance Act of 1911 set the welfare state in motion societies like these were needed less. In 1913 the dwindling Brethren were absorbed into the Oddfellows.

At the Brethren's inception Admiral Spranger of The Hall had endowed them with property in Barrow Point Lane – a new single-storey brick cottage with three rooms and a kitchen – to bring in rents. The Oddfellows in 1866 invested their own funds in nos.1 and 2 Manchester Villas (now 33-35 Waxwell Lane) to provide rental income. They met in the subsequently added Lodge Room (no.31 – also let to a succession of small schools), having used the *Oddfellows Arms* for many years. The lodge was originally single-storey, but was heightened and converted to residential use about 1992.

The Brethren's cottage has gone but there is a still a distinct flavour of the Oddfellows at the south-west end of Waxwell Lane. The *Oddfellows Arms* was built by Thomas Ellement on part of a plot he bought in 1852 with the help of a loan from his society. On the other part Samuel Jones and Joseph Hayden built nos.4-14 in 1853, naming them Unity Place. Manchester Villas have already been mentioned.

OTHER ORGANISATIONS AND SOCIETIES

The last third of the 19th century was remarkable for the efflorescence of clubs and societies. Most were fostered or led by middle-class people who felt duty bound to improve the outlook of, and provide wholesome diversions for, those less fortunate.

Some groups supplied a provident or welfare function like the friendly societies. The Clothing Club, the Coal Club and the Nurse Fund were provident, thrift funds. Welfare prompted the Work Society, which gave out garments to be made at home and paid the worker the profit made when they were sold at the Parish Hall.

Many more aimed to provide education, social intercourse and entertainment, like the Working Men's Club, established in Pinner about 1870. The Mothers' Meeting met weekly. Younger people could join the Girls' Friendly Society, or the Young Men's Institute, which provided mental and physical activity – it was trying to accumulate a library in the 1880s. The Band of Hope tried to cater for all ages. A Church Lads Brigade was begun in 1896, formed by James Arthur, one of the founders of the movement itself who lived in Pinner at the time. Nearly all of these were affiliated to national organisations. Sunday School flourished and there were bible classes for both sexes.

There were occasional educational classes; Philip Odell, gardener at The Hall, gave classes in 'science' at the *Cocoa Tree* which led to public examinations. Pitman's Short-hand classes were held there in 1880, attended especially by hopeful boys soon to leave school. In 1896 classes in laundry work were given free, at state expense, at the Parish Hall to help girls thinking of earning money in this way. The

PENNY READINGS.

PARISH HALL, PINNER.

President.
Rev. W. M. HIND.

Secretary & Treasurer.
Mr. F. A. M. NICOL.

General Superintendent.
Mr. CLOWES.

TUESDAY EVENING, MARCH 30, 1869.

Programme.

Reading	{ Napoleon's last look upon France	B. Simmons	Rev. W. M. HIND.
Trio	Memory	Leslie	Mr. AND THE MISSES HUMPHREYS.
Reading	Faithless Sally Brown	Tom Hood	Mr. B. PENNINGTON
Duet	The Seaboy's parting	Boildieu	Mr. and Miss Z. HUMPHREYS
Reading	Happy Thoughts	Burnand	Mr. CLOWES
Song	Alice, where art thou?	Archer	Mr. N. HUMPHREYS
Reading	The Desert Born	Tom Hood	Mr. LEE
Song	Swallow		Mrs. BERRY
Reading	The May Queen	Tennyson	Mr. B. PENNINGTON
Song			
Reading	Mrs. Caudle in France	D. Jerrold	Mr. CLOWES
Glee	May Day	Müller	Mr. and the Misses HUMPHREYS and Mr. CLOWES

GOD SAVE THE QUEEN.

Admission One Penny.   Front Seats Sixpence,
By Tickets to be had of Mr. EDWARDS, Chemist, Pinner.

Doors open at a Quarter before 8;   Commence at 8 o'clock.

58 Penny Readings 1869

Men's Discussion Class at the end of the century was quite ambitious – Can we be certain about anything? Is the Devil dead?

Fêtes, bazaars, jumble sales and concerts were part of the local scene, helping to concentrate community feeling. Often they were in aid of a local cause, such as the Fire Brigade or Young Men's Institute, or a national one like Waifs and Strays. A local landowner usually provided the venue for outdoor events, which included National and Sunday School treats and the Pinner Horticultural Society Annual Show. The Tookes of Pinner Hill House, William Barber at Barrow Point House, the Birds at The Hall, were the most forthcoming. Charles Bird owned the fire engine and captained the volunteer brigade, and their displays of drill and rainbow hose-spray effects were popular at many events. Equally popular was the Pinner Brass Band, which gave its first concert in 1882 and graced many an outdoor occasion.

Concerts, dramatic evenings and Penny Readings (seats one penny and sixpence), took place in the Parish Hall, which had been the first National School. The first of the readings was called Pinner Readings, held in 1868 to raise funds for a reading room, probably the refurbishment of the old school. The performers and readers were local people and provided a good spectrum of Pinner society – John Lee the butcher, George Boreham the butler at Pinner Hill House, George Norton of Bridge Street, William Woodbridge of the carpenter family, William Clarke the coal dealer, Gladman the cobbler, William Clowes of The Lawn and Bennet Pennington of Manor House in Waxwell Lane, both gentleman – several of them newcomers with town jobs. The Pinner Ebony Minstrels, formed in December 1880, gave many a show. Almost every musical event involved Norton, Clarke or Beaumont. Beaumont lived at Glastonbury Cottage, rebuilt as 21 Waxwell Lane, and later became the leading light of the Boy Scout movement in Pinner. From 1882 there were lantern slide shows, and the war correspondent of *The Graphic* gave a lecture in 1888. The circus came to Harrow Town from time to time, and once visited Pinner. Pinner Fair was an annual high-spot, and an occasion when many people who had left Pinner came back to see family and friends.

SPORTS

Pinner was no exception to the Victorian inclination towards organised team sports, though the leadership came from gentlemen. William Barber founded Barrow Point Cricket Club in 1878, providing a pitch in his grounds. He had admired Nelson Ward's pitch at West House, but that was only used for family games. A match played on Pinner Green in 1790 between teams from Pinner and Rickmansworth is the only reference prior to Barber, and there is no evidence of continuity, though the club believes itself to date from 1835. One of the Pinner players in 1790 was Thomas Ellement, probably the first of the clan in Pinner, who came from Rickmansworth, and perhaps proposed the match. Barber encouraged members of the Young Men's Institute to play and instigated concerts in support of the club. The 1888 fixtures included matches against L.N.W.R. and Grenadier Guards teams. When Barber left Pinner in 1890 it was renamed Pinner Cricket Club and Arthur Helsham-Jones of Pinner Hill House offered the use of a field, which later became Montesole Playing Fields. The presidents were men like Barber

59 This is thought to be Pinner cricket team sometime between 1870 and 1900.

and Helsham-Jones, but the first recorded captain (1888) was William Wetherall, a clerk, born in Pinner and educated at the National School, who lived at the current 12 Chapel Lane. Rather marvellously, a ladies' team from Pinner was fielded against one from Harrow in 1888, known only from sketches by Gerald du Maurier. Like tennis, this was probably a private affair.

Professional football clubs were burgeoning at this time. The first football in Pinner was rugby football, beginning c.1882, and played on Little Common. A team played ten fixtures in 1883 against others like Twickenham and Kensington. It seems to have faded after the soccer club was founded in 1892. This played friendlies until it joined the Harrow & District League in 1896, and was soon able to field a first and second team every week, winning the Middlesex Junior Cup in 1909-10. It used the recreation ground in West End Lane, and then Montesole Playing Fields, having to make do with changing facilities at the *Bell* for both. The first club colours were black and red. Gentlemen led the way again. The founder-players were the Stone brothers, fresh from University College School, whose father John, clerk to a joint stock company, lived at 1 Lonsdale Villas, Woodridings, still standing as 40 Wellington Road, and the first president was John Graham, gentleman, of Nower Hill House. The committee, however, included cricketer William Wetherall and others like him. Players were commonly in both cricket and football teams.

Tennis in Pinner was a game for the gentry at home. A few matches played against a Harrow team at Barrow Point or The Hall in the 1880s were private affairs and had no connection with the clubs of the 20th century.

Cycling was very popular at the end of the 19th century, one reason, according to the Rev. St Hill Bourne, for falling attendance at church. When W.S. Gilbert, who lived at Grimsdyke, came upon Lisa Lehmann of Birtsmorton (58 Waxwell Lane) cycling along, he exclaimed the sight was as unexpected as a vision of the Virgin Mary. Cycle races were part of the Diamond Jubilee Sports – winner Henry Gregory of Pinner Hill Farm – and Harrow Cycling Club held race meetings. London cyclists enjoyed country trips, and members of the Oceaola Athletic and Cycling Club of Waxwell Lane would go for a spin on their penny-farthings.

The Headstone Races – farmers' races – took place in a field at Headstone, north of Southfield Park, but after a few years they were abolished following riots, thieving and assaults – of which the gentlest was throwing someone into the moat – perpetrated by marauders from London in 1899, or so it was alleged.

Gambling probably lay behind several less well-reported events, recalled in 1951 by 79-year-old Ted Evans of Pinner Green, which usually involved animals. There was hare-coursing on one of Daniel Hill's fields south of Southfield Park, cock-fighting in a yard behind 4-6 High Street, and dog-fights between bull terriers at locations kept secret. One of the dog owners was Jimmy Dean, a sawyer for Woodbridge who lived in an old cottage next to Mayfield at Nower Hill, and was himself a fighter. He took part in bare-knuckle prize fights just behind the old chalk workings (Dingles Court) north of Uxbridge Road.

60 Headstone Races card

TEMPERANCE

The ancient relaxation of 'going down the pub' was encouraged by the Beerhouse Act of 1830. By 1870 there were seven new beershops or public houses in Pinner – the *Starling, Hand in Hand, Victory, White Hart, Oddfellows Arms, Railway Tavern* and *Letchford Arms*, and in the following couple of decades both the *Red Lion* and the *George* were rebuilt. Big breweries had acquired all of them by 1907.

There was a corresponding increase of effort by the promoters of temperance, found in especially large numbers among the swelling ranks of nonconformists, and people who signed the pledge of abstinence were awarded a badge of blue ribbon. In 1884 there was a week-long temperance mission in Pinner, and Mrs Treneman organised the blue ribbons.

Temperance taverns were set up to provide drinks other than alcohol, such as tea, cocoa and cordials – this was the time when many favourites like sarsaparilla and Vimto first appeared. William Barber of Barrow Point House laid out £1,200 in 1878 to build a temperance tavern at the top of the High Street, replacing the left side of no.64. Designed in the Old English style by architects George and

Peto and named *Ye Cocoa Tree*, it had on the ground floor a coffee room, and a kitchen where customers could have their own food cooked, while above was a reading or club room for the use of local workmen, on payment of a subscription. The old part at the rear was adapted as a lodging house. The Band of Hope held many of its meetings there. The *Tree*'s actual success in the fight against alcohol is not known but it flourished as a tea-room, popular until the 1920s for day outings by individuals and organisations from London and nearby villages, and fields in Cannon Lane were hired to accommodate pavilions, swing boats, donkeys and the like for visitors' enjoyment.

61 Catherine Langthorn, whose many letters to her son in Australia have survived, was the wife of a labourer who was often unemployed. Her sunken cheeks are probably caused by lost teeth.

The alcohol problem was not just a matter of drunken brawls – some were reported in the local newspaper – but also of spending too much of the wages on drink, probably the more insidious worry. In 1887 Catherine Langthorn wrote to her son William in Australia of her relief on the latter account when his father and younger brother attended the Blue Ribbon meetings.

MISBEHAVIOUR

Misbehaviour was much the same as in earlier periods – pilfering, assault, drunkenness, disorderliness, cruelty to horses, poaching. Less usually, in 1885 two poachers were given five years' penal servitude for attempting to murder two gamekeepers at Hatch End, and Lotty Bird, aged 26, was charged with disposing of the body of her illegitimate child in the stoke-hole at Ravensworth Villa (either in Paines Lane or at Woodridings), where she was a cook. Appeals for a police station in Pinner, beginning in 1859, were not satisfied until the present building was opened in 1899, just in time, as it turned out, to deal with the Headstone Races riot.

The Metropolitan Railway

The Metropolitan Railway caused so many visual changes in Pinner that it must have seemed to burst upon the scene. Brought through the centre of the village in a cutting, it required five bridges, three over the track, at the junction of Marsh and Pinner Roads, in West End Lane and at Cuckoo Hill – and two under it, in Marsh Road and Chapel Lane.

In fact it was long foreshadowed and was intended to by-pass the centre. In 1873 Parliament accepted a plan for the London, Harrow and Pinner Railway, which would terminate between The Grove and Cannon Lane Farmhouse (site of the *Pinner Arms,* lately the *Whittington*). A new plan in 1878 proposed that the terminus should be at Pinner Green. In 1880 Harrow Metropolitan Station opened. In 1884 the third and last plan plotted the route actually taken, with the station to be set somewhere between the Marsh/ Pinner Road bridge and the High Street. At a public meeting most residents seemed to prefer the latest route, the chief objector being the National School, which thought the line too painfully close and suggested moving itself to a new site. Benjamin Weall of Rugby House in Church Lane was the lucky or unlucky owner of most of the land involved – his opinion has not been preserved. It was, however, his father who had held the London & Birmingham Railway to ransom at Hatch End.

Three establishments in Marsh Road were demolished. These were, moving north from School Lane, The Elms, Marsh Farm, and a couple of cottages. It was decided to place the station on the site of Marsh Farm. By 25 May 1885, two days before Pinner Fair, the line was ready for use and thereafter steam trains ran every half hour to Baker Street. The first station building is still there, minus its chimneys and ironwork entrance canopy. The *Harrow Observer* commented blandly that some thought

62 The Langthorn house in Chapel Lane which was demolished for the railway. A songbird hangs at the door.

the railway would destroy Pinner's rusticity and residential character, while others thought it a boon.

The extension to Rickmansworth required four of the five bridges mentioned plus an embankment between Marsh Road and Chapel Lane, which meant removal of the former poorhouse, the Baptist Chapel and 11 cottages in the lane. The Langthorn family's cottage was pulled down for the southern end of the Chapel Lane bridge. Catherine Langthorn wrote to William in Australia that Pinner was 'quite spoilt' and lamented 'you will never find the dear old spot where you used to play killing pigs and keeping shops again, the railway goes right through it'. Her husband James found temporary work on the construction, though her daughter Kate, alas, was more interested in the navvies than her mother liked.

To counter the competition from the new line the L.N.W.R. (previously L.B.R.) began a bus service from the village centre to connect with the main-line trains. The little two-horse bus, entered from the rear, able to carry eight inside and two beside the driver, ran from 1885 until 30 April 1914. The maximum fare was 4d. For 27 of those years the driver was George Bridge, called Bussy, smart, erect and efficient. He lived at 2 Leamington Cottages, and then at 1 Park Cottages, both in The Chase, and stabled the horses and bus across the way in the stables (nowadays Alderwasley, 16 Nower Hill), once belonging to Mayfield Farm. In May 1914 George became a ticket collector at Pinner and Hatch End Station, and met a grisly end when he fell between train and platform one dark, rain-wet evening in January 1917.

Because the Metropolitan station was in the heart of Pinner, not on the periphery like the main-line station, more people were able to benefit from the

63 George Bridge waits with the Pinner omnibus between a flowery *Red Lion* and the Fire Station *c.*1910. The bus has a rear entrance, and there is luggage up top. The cottages between were Oakland Cottages.

link to the capital. The speedy connection offered by the Metropolitan Railway would tempt development along its length. The large private properties nearer the line would be less secluded, less suitable for country sports, have less cachet. On the other hand they could be sold for development, and as the century turned the centre of Pinner began to change.

Places and People in the Nineteenth Century

THE GENTRY

The gentry still demanded and received respect in 19th- and early 20th-century Pinner, and retained a significant role in the community. Fewer of them now had titles. They usually owned or occupied extensive property or properties, like the Birds of The Hall, or the Pells and Tookes of Pinner Hill. Most of the men also had an occupation, which enabled them to maintain the land which gave them status. Law was the predominant field, but increasing numbers were in commerce, as dealers in bullion, tea, tobacco, or wine.

People with less land but similar occupations formed almost a second rank. They were often in administration of some sort, such as the chief clerk or similar grades in government, or actuaries or accountants – people like Nelson Ward, a registrar in the Court of Chancery, who rented West House; Augustus Eck of New Dove House, member of the stock exchange; and John Parkhouse of Mayfield in Nower Hill, ultimately chief accountant of the L.N.E.R., and an early specialist in superannuation.

First of all they were a source of employment, directly employing domestic servants, estate workers like gardeners, grooms, gamekeepers, and outworkers such as laundresses and day servants. Indirectly they were a channel to other work by means of recommendation or advice, according to comments in school logs and elsewhere. Many Pinner residents were said to have owed their positions in the Euston offices to the help of John Parkhouse. And, for shopkeepers and tradesmen, they were important customers.

Secondly, they dominated local organisations and events in positions such as president or chairman of almost every local activity, from the Guardians of the Poor Law to the Band of Hope. They expected to do so, they had the leisure, and quite often the expertise, it must be acknowledged. Their ladies did gracious things which required gratitude, such as taking sewing classes at the National School and donating material to the Work Society.

Thirdly, at a time when there was little nation-wide entertainment and professional entertainers were low in the social scale, the resident gentry were the celebrities at local events, opening the shows, doing the honours, allowing occasional access to their own surroundings. Mrs Trotter of Waxwell Farm sometimes threw open her grounds for a haymakers' tea. Many residents recalled the winter scenes at The Hall at the start

64 Mrs George Bird often made the grounds of The Hall available for village functions.

of the 20th century when the grounds were decorated with lights and everyone was invited to skate on the lake.

Nineteenth-century maps show Pinner's mansions as having ornamental gardens with ponds or lakes and flower beds, kitchen gardens enclosed by walls, glass-houses and conservatories, where exotic plants and vegetables like melons and pineapples were grown, and ice-houses, which preserved the stuff year-round. A few had 'moats', which usually originated as 18th-century clay-pits to provide brick-making material for the house – Pinner Hill House, The Lodge and perhaps Dove House, were examples. Some had tiny man-made islands in the Pinn – one can still be seen off Eastcote Road opposite Lyncroft Way. Some had a small farmery for a pig, a cow, or poultry, though there is little evidence in the form of staff that they were so used. A stable and coach-house were essential.

PINNER HILL HOUSE

John Baker Sellon, owner 1803-22, serjeant at law (or barrister), was the magistrate of the court in Hatton Garden which was featured by Charles Dickens in *Oliver Twist*. He improved the house, enlarged the estate, and, maybe, opened the chalk mine. Albert Pell, owner 1822-45, a lawyer who was knighted in 1830, moved

65 The 18th-century west front of Pinner Hill House, with slightly later bays, as it looked c.1850 before Arthur Tooke blocked it with his Victorian wing.

the home farm to its present site. His son revelled in the flora and fauna of the remaining woodland.

Knowledge of Arthur Tooke, owner 1845-71, and a solicitor practising in Bedford Row, is dominated by his passion for building. He added the huge many-gabled west wing to the house, and a new service wing, whose octagonal kitchen with high pointed ceiling harked back to the monastic kitchen at Glastonbury. In the garden he built a fancy clock tower, hung with a peal of Russian bells bought at the Great Exhibition in Hyde Park. He built two lodges, the northern at the further end of South View Road, the southern, called South Hill Lodge, at the junction of Pinner Hill and Pinner Hill Road. He built Pinner Hill Farm plainly but gave the roadside stable another ornamental clock tower of coloured brick, bearing a tablet with his crest – a griffon's head holding a sword in its beak – his initials and the date 1862. The roof and clock were replaced by replicas in 1985-6.

He bought Pinnerwood House and set up a new farmhouse of red brick, with pretty barge boards and window-headings. Pinnerwood Cottage nearby was rebuilt relatively demurely and given a date stone labelled AWT 1867.

Having acquired Woodhall Farm he only gave it a new stable, but across the road he continued to indulge his yearning. There arose Woodhall Towers, a house with a tower 75 feet tall, which had pitched gothic roofs, corbelled windows, projecting stair turret, dizzyingly patterned brick, and two tablets, one bearing his crest with the motto 'Militia Mea Multiplex' (My Duties are Manifold), the other with his initials and the date 1864. The tower had a clock, and a room on each floor. Adjoining parts sported turrets and conical roofs. This *pièce de résistance* was called Tooke's Folly by the locals and, of all of it, only the first plaque now remains. In Uxbridge Road he put a sweet pair of tied cottages (now 546-48) with patterned iron window frames.

Thomas Ellement was Tooke's builder, but the architect is not known.[32] South Hill Lodge and Pinner Hill House tower have been demolished, like the Folly. Tooke's activity was characteristic of some landowners, of whom Lawrence Baker of Haydon Hall in Eastcote was the nearest in place and date. In the 1880s Baker was studding his lands with estate cottages, mostly designed by George and Peto, the architects of Pinner's *Cocoa Tree* tavern, cottages like 29 and 124-6 Fore Street, Keepers Cottages in Coteford Close and Mad Bess Woods, New Cottages in Eastcote High Road, and the intricate Haydon Lodge at the bottom of Southill Lane.

Pinner Hill House had a full complement of servants – butler, cook, ladies maid, nurse, house, kitchen and laundry maids, footman, coachman, groom – varying from time to time. What on earth did the cook think of her enormous octagonal gothic kitchen? George Boreham, who came with Tooke as a footman, rose to be coachman and then butler. He married one of the housemaids, Eliza White, daughter of Vincent, the fly master. One of the offspring of this below-stairs romance, Emma, herself became a housemaid whilst her father was still there. George rented one of the old cottages at Mill Farm for his family at first, but later moved them to Waxwell, possibly one of the tied cottages in Uxbridge Road, even though, when a butler, he had to live-in much of the time. He used to take part in village entertainments, compèring or performing solo 'in his usual happy style'.

William, the son of Arthur Tooke, confined his building activities to the restoration of the parish church, but played a full part, almost that of a squire, in chairing and supporting many local committees – Board of Guardians, National Schools – and organisations. When he died at the age of 40 in 1884, all the shops in the village closed and curtains were drawn as his hearse passed by. Alice, his sister and heir, with her husband Arthur Helsham-Jones, entertained W. S. Gilbert at the house. In 1902 they sold Pinner Hill but kept the Pinnerwood and Woodhall estates.

The Pinner Hill estate was bought by Samuel Lammas Dore, managing director of Baldwins' Ironworks at Wilden, near Stourport, and it was not unusual for him to be visited by Stanley Baldwin, one of his co-directors, who subsequently entered politics and became Prime Minister. Baldwin was noted for his fireside chats on radio but was more famous for being Prime Minister at the time of the Abdication. Like the Tookes, Samuel shouldered many local burdens. He died in 1919.

66 Alice Helsham-Jones as the lady of Pinner Hill with her youngest daughter, Angelet, *c.*1886.

THE HALL

George Bird, a contractor who had laid out many of the new roads of Kensington bought The Hall in 1875, and soon it was refashioned to resemble Kensington houses. The family had its own fire engine – why? – and one Sunday evening in 1880 it clattered out to the rescue of Gregory's blazing bakery at 15 High Street, pipping the Harrow Fire Brigade, whose driver then drowned his frustration in drink. This event prompted the establishment of the Pinner Volunteer Fire Brigade, and the saviour Charles Bird, son of George, was chosen as captain. Of The Hall only the lodge at the Uxbridge Road entrance remains (no.609 very cleverly enlarged), and a few trees from the long avenue which led to the Paines Lane gate.

THE GROVE

The Milman family was the most illustrious of The Grove's owners and usually had more domestic staff than any other in Pinner. Sir Francis was physician to Charlotte, the Queen of George III, and his wife had inherited The Grove from her brother Sir William Miles in 1803. One younger son became Dean of St Paul's, and a grandson became Bishop of Calcutta. The 2nd Lady Milman was reputed to read a book openly in church if she did not like the sermon. In 1859 the 3rd baronet sold The Grove to John Mayall, a Lancashire-born American who was a Court photographer. His album of 14 cartes-de-visite, including the first photographs of the Queen and Prince Albert to be marketed, brought him £35,000. Other albums followed. Mayall sold the property to Francis Rummens, a railway contractor, in 1859. The west window of Pinner church is dedicated to his wife and grandchildren. Only the Lodge, 79 Marsh Road, is left, and many of the trees.

PINNER PLACE

In 1832 James Garrard bought Pinner Place from Edward Aubrey. Garrard's firm was appointed Crown Jeweller in 1843, with responsibility for the jewels at state occasions, and for cleaning them. They were involved in cutting the Koh-i-Noor diamond in 1862, a fabulous Indian stone which had been given to Queen Victoria. It was reputed to bring bad luck to men and so its largest portion, 108 carats, was set in St Edward's Crown, the one used for queen consorts.

WEST HOUSE

John Taniere, owner 1814-47, bought West House from the heirs of Thomas Bowler, who had been hanged for attempted manslaughter in 1812. Taniere changed it from a farmhouse to a gentleman's residence, and subsequent owners continued the process. The lake, smaller than now, had been created by 1865, together with the usual pleasure grounds, kitchen gardens, and stables. For the rest of the century it was usually let. From 1873-83 the tenant was Nelson Ward, grandson of Admiral Lord Nelson, who married Jessie, daughter of George Bird of The Hall. Their brood of eight included two sets of twins. About the end of the century the house was almost wholly rebuilt, to be almost wholly demolished in the 1950s. Nevertheless virtually the full estate remains today – grounds, lake, trees, landscaping. The kitchen garden has become the Peace Garden but of the buildings only a fragment of the 19th-century house, a tack room, and the staff house remain. In the garden you will find the miniature gravestones of five pet dogs who won prizes at shows during the Edwardian period. This is the only estate in Pinner which still survives

67 This watercolour of West House was painted about 1886 by Florence or Rose, one of Nelson Ward's four twins. It looks like an 18th- or early 19th-century house. Jessie and Nelson Ward are pictured left.

in its medieval size and shape, and was called Aldridges in legal documents until 1872 at least. William and Isabella Aldridge had it in 1425, and the owner in 1315 may have been John or William Alverych.

BARROW POINT HOUSE

William Barber was a barrister, professor of law, and tobacco dealer, who left Pinner in 1890 when he was appointed a circuit judge in Derbyshire. In Pinner he was an energetic promoter of temperance and wholesome youth activities, as we have seen. He was also a keen improver of his property. In 1871 Barber was renting the elaborate Woodhall Towers from Arthur Tooke and, like him, he burned to build. So he bought Barrow Point House, which the family of Ralph Carr, gentleman, had

68 The Nelson Ward children outside the window Rose/Florence had painted. From left to right they are: on seats, Agnes, Mary/Katherine, Jessie, Mary/Katherine (holding a cricket bat), Rose/Florence; behind, Maurice, Rose/Florence, Nelson.

owned for some sixty years, and commissioned first J.P. Seddon and then George and Peto to design a splendid new one. Though the second design was featured in the influential paper *The Builder* the house was never rebuilt, just slightly enlarged and given an old-world look with fake timbering. About half the land between Waxwell and Paines Lanes belonged to the house, including five old cottages along Barrow Point Lane let to labourers and the like. But Barber must have a fine garden with lake and island so the cottages went, though two of them were retained or more likely rebuilt, for his coachman and gardener. Thus he, and John Gibson a century before, had between them destroyed most of the old hamlet of Barrow Point, incorporating it into Barrow Point House and The Hall. Though Barber bought and enlarged Moss Cottage, the present west wing is the work of William Seth-Smith for Percival Birkett. Barber replaced the nearby timber-framed Weatherleys Farm with Oakfield House, possibly by his favourite architects, George & Peto. It was used as a preparatory school by Florence Thompson, daughter of one of the officers' widows who benefited from Howard Place (see below). He built a pair of fake timber cottages where Marks and Spencer's car park is, rebuilt the old cottage at the junction with Love Lane (58 Waxwell Lane), though more plainly, and yet left 18a/22a Waxwell Lane, with its five cramped cottages attached, unaccountably untouched – perhaps because he moved away. In 1898 his estate, so close to the centre of Pinner, was offered for redevelopment.

EAST END HOUSE

Made into a gentleman's residence at the end of the 18th century, the most notable resident of East End House was Henry James Pye, who bought it in 1811, near

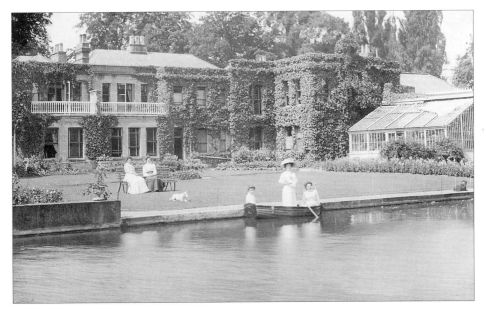

69 In 1910 a tree no longer hides the right-hand part of West House and all the windows look new. The ladies are servants and friends enjoying some time off while Mr and Mrs Hogg are away.

the end of his life. Pye was Poet Laureate, mocked in his time as a poet of birds and flowers, and never since esteemed, as the fact that his works have not been reprinted since 1828 attests. There is no evidence that his muse took wing in Pinner. Nevertheless he was a man of substance in other respects, and carried responsibilities as the M.P. for Lincolnshire and a justice of the peace. His last wife was from Pinner and, as she long outlived him, it is said a special dispensation was granted by Queen Victoria in 1862 to allow the poet laureate's wife to be buried beside him in the now-closed churchyard of St John's. Pye had also bought East End Farm and Tudor Cottage, and all remained with his heirs until the death of his grand-daughter Elizabeth Pye in 1917.

NOWER HILL HOUSE

Nathaniel Graham of Nower Hill, gentleman, married a daughter of Charles Lawrence of East House opposite. Their son John (1823-98) has left a lively account of the coach journey from Pinner to London when he was a boy on his way to boarding school in the 1830s. John's occupation was characteristic of those taken up during Victorian times by the sons of gentlemen – a chief clerk (a substantial position) at Customs and Excise. When Ambrose Heal, proprietor of the great furniture store in Tottenham Court Road, bought the house he promptly had it given a new look in the Arts and Crafts manner by his preferred architects, Smith and Brewer, with whom he was connected by marriage. Furthermore, he had them design The Fives Court opposite for his son, Ambrose junior, a beautiful house strongly affected by the influential style of Charles Voysey. Its name referred to a court for the game of fives at the rear. There is an equally beautiful memorial in the

Paines Lane cemetery to Alice, the first wife of Ambrose junior, who died in 1910, almost as soon as she had moved into her new home.

EAST HOUSE

This had been a gentleman's residence since the 17th century and to judge from pictures it was considerably altered around the turn of the 19th and 20th centuries, and some old panelling was brought in.

PINNER HOUSE

In 1866 Jason Woodbridge bought Pinner House from the heirs of Mary, widow of Walter Llewarch Williams. It was a very public sign of the success of Woodbridge, carpenter and builder, who had made his pile in Harrow and Pinner, and whose family business had been founded on church and chapel repair at the beginning of the century, and building low-rent cottages on enclosure plots. Jason was now Surveyor of Highways for Pinner.

DOVE HOUSE

Dove House had been rebuilt by the Boys family by the early 19th century. John Tilbury, a coach-maker, who had designed many carriages, among them the robust and widely used two-wheeled Tilbury, lived there 1820-45. He was a horse dealer, and boys from Harrow School enjoyed practising their steeple-chasing on his land. John Weall bought the place and added another house, called New Dove House, for letting. Both were demolished during the 1960s.

PINNERWOOD HOUSE

This was a gentrified farmhouse, a little rural retreat which Edward Bulwer-Lytton, later Lord Knebworth, rented from 1831-3. He was a great reformer in Parliament, and also an author. Lytton wrote part of his novel *Eugene Aram* in the house.

WAXWELL FARM

A farmhouse until about 1872, Waxwell Farm was leased to Edward Trotter, financial agent for the Cheshire cotton manufacturer Dewhurst, whose daughter he married, and was enlarged by him to the Old English designs of William Seth-Smith about 1895. Mrs Trotter was widely praised for the beauty of her flower garden which was painted by Helen Allingham, a connoisseur of such joys.

CHARLOTTE HOWARD

Charlotte was born before her parents married, and believed herself to be descended from the ducal Howards. Her parents were Londoners living in the fashionable new environs of Regents Park. They had acquired a house in Love Lane from a relative, and later, in will, the childless Charlotte proposed to replace it with a crescent of 19 almshouses for the widows of naval or military officers, or of clergymen. However, her intentions were frustrated when her heirs and beneficiaries wasted most of the money in lawsuits to block the will, and eventually only three dwellings were built, forming the crenellated Howard Place. The trustees had sold them long before they were demolished in the 1950s to make way for the second St Luke's Church.

HORATIA NELSON WARD

Horatia (1800-81) is noteworthy for who she was, rather than for anything she did. The natural daughter of Horatio, Admiral Lord Nelson and Emma, Lady Hamilton, she was but five years old when her father died. She spent her adult life in respectable obscurity as the wife, then widow, of Philip Ward, vicar of Tenterden in Kent. Proud of her father, but ashamed of her mother, Horatia was nevertheless careful not to advertise her illegitimacy. She came to Pinner as a widow about 1860 on the recommendation of her son Nelson, then resident at Woodridings. She lived first at West Lodge (then called Hazeldene) and not West House as is often alleged through confusion with her son, then at Elmdene, and finally at 2 Beaufort Villas, Woodridings (about 455 Uxbridge Road). Two of her children predeceased her: Philip, who died 1865, and Eleanor, who was knocked down outside the *Queen's Head* by a bolting horse in 1872, and expired in

70 Nelson's beloved Horatia, looking very much like him, during her old age in Pinner.

the shop at no.35. If you look carefully at their joint tombstone in Paines Lane Cemetery, you can discern that in the description 'beloved daughter of Admiral Lord Nelson', the word 'beloved' overwrites the original, discreetly mendacious word, 'adopted'.

THE BEETONS

The newly-wed Samuel and Isabella Beeton were the first residents of 2 Chandos Villas, Woodridings in 1856. Sam was publisher of the *Englishwoman's Domestic Magazine* and the *Boys' Own Journal*, both breaking new ground, and soon his highly capable young wife was writing the cooking and household items for the former, and commuting to town with him. Her compilation of recipes to help new middle-class brides was printed by Sam in monthly parts from September 1859, and published complete in October 1861 as the *Book of Household Management*. It sold 60,000 copies. Her practice of clearly listing ingredients, cooking time and servings was an innovation. Isabella is said to have provided soup to some of Pinner's needy in the winter of 1858. They moved to Greenhithe in 1862 and Isabella died of puerperal fever in February 1863, aged only 28. Two of her four children survived her. The Beetons' Pinner home was destroyed by a bomb in 1940, and the site, about 513 Uxbridge Road, is now occupied by a restaurant.

AGNES MARSHALL

Agnes Marshall (1855-1905) was a cook, possibly more famous in her own day than Isabella Beeton had been in hers. Both were young. Both were publicisers, reaching their public via the best means at their disposal. For Isabella it had been her husband's magazine. For Agnes, at a date when women were a little more free

71 Agnes Marshall, *c*.1891, by Edoardo Tofano.

and there were more newspapers, it was through her own cookery school, her own magazine *The Table*, four books, and public demonstrations reported in the press. She had established the school in Mortimer Street, W.1. by her mid-20s (it was wound up in 1951) and with it a shop where she sold her own branded equipment, and she pioneered ice-cream-making at home. She became a celebrity. According to the custom of those days she was known by her married name – Mrs Marshall, just like her now more famous predecessor, Mrs Beeton. In Pinner Agnes was the wife of the chairman of the Pinner Gas Works, Alfred Marshall, but it was her money which in 1892 had bought Temple Farm at the junction of West End Lane and Eastcote Road, and turned it into a turretted mansion, renamed The Towers. They were among the first in Pinner to own a motor car. The window in the north aisle of St John's, which was designed by Sir Ninian Comper and pictures Saints Agnes and Bertha, is Arthurs memorial to his wife.

INDIVIDUALS AND FAMILIES

More individuals of interest lived in Pinner from time to time than there is room to mention. Many families in the bedrock of Pinner society were noted for their length of time in the village, often lasting into the 20th and 21st centuries. Beaumont, Bedford, Dell, Ellement, Greenfield, Hedges, Hitchcock, Lavender, Lines, Manning, Wilshin are just a selection, and all of them produced characters, or worthies, deserving of more attention than can be given here.

THE BEAUMONTS

John Beaumont (1762-1844), wheelwright, came about 1785 to 27 High Street where his descendants remained, metamorphosing into car mechanics, for two centuries, until Richard Beaumont closed the business in 1994. Their oldest business records still exist, single-entry accounts of debts owing, and show that as early as 1809 John Beaumont was accepting payment by cheque drawn on the Uxbridge Bank at Uxbridge. Members of the family were active in village entertainments and sports. George William (1856-1929) was a founder of the fire brigade, and one of its few non-gentleman captains. His brother Walter (1860-1917) began the brass band, playing cornet whilst a third, Ernest Edgar (1870-1942), played euphonium. Walter started the Boy Scouts. In the 20th century Eric (1906-83), son of Edgar, had his own jazz band which used to perform for shilling dances at the *Cocoa Tree*. Once he played piano for the American red-hot-momma Sophie Tucker at a Donkey Derby.

THE ELLEMENTS

The Ellements were primarily carpenters, builders and undertakers. Thomas (1756-98), engineer of the early cricket match with Rickmansworth, came from there to Pinner about 1790. His grandson Thomas (1820-99) was apprenticed to Woodbridge and for 39 years was building manager to Arthur Tooke. He also built for himself and for the Manchester Unity of Oddfellows, and his mark can be seen yet: in Waxwell Lane, the *Oddfellows Arms*, 25-29, 31-5, 45-7, and maybe 4-14 also; in Elm Park Road, Suffolk Villa and North End Cottage; and in Cuckoo Hill Road, 1-4 and 19-21 Camden Row . He took up civic duties, serving terms as constable, overseer, and Poor Law Guardian, a habit which remainedstronglycharacteristic of his son and grandson. For George Cornelius (1855-1926) it was the new Parish Council and Hendon Rural District, to whose meetings in Stanmore he often went on foot. He had a white beard and cut an impressive figure as he proceeded in stately fashion at the head of walking funeral processions. For Thomas (1877-1954) it was the new Harrow Urban District Council. He served with distinction during the Boer War, and in the First World War closed down the business to be an engineering instructor. He was remembered as the man to go to for help and advice in dealing with authority.

72 Thomas Ellement, *c.*1890, his son George Cornelius, *c.*1920, and grandson Tom, *c.*1902.

A VILLAGE DAME

In 1896, in a house in Chapel Lane, 98-year-old Sarah Shepherd breathed her last. Her life had taken twists and turns as she coped with the changes of 19th-century Pinner, and except for its longevity hers was probably a typical life. Her parents, James and Hannah Greenfield, were poor. Sarah married a labourer, Richard Shepherd, and they had a daughter named Ann in 1821. In 1827 she produced an illegitimate son, baptised as Thomas Greenfield Shepherd, and by 1841 she was a widow. Her husband did not die in Pinner. He may have left Pinner in the dire 1820s to find

work, or abandoned his family, so that Sarah found consolation elsewhere, or perhaps he had left because of that shaming birth. Between 1825 and 1831 Sarah regularly received a shilling a week for the child from the overseers. She worked as a servant and then as a laundress. In 1861 and 1871 she was running the *White Hart* beer shop at 26 High Street, with two or three grandchildren in residence, two of whom found employment in the new gas industry. In 1881 she and her bachelor son Thomas were living in the western end of the decrepit little timber-framed cottage in Chapel Lane. Ten years later she was living in a brick house across the road with the

73 Sarah Shepherd, an anonymous pencil sketch made near the end of her life.

family of William Clarke, who managed the new coal depot at the railway sidings. There she died. Through her daughter Ann she was an ancestress of the Rayner and Ellement families.

The End of the Nineteenth Century

POPULATION

Pinner had about 2,350 residents in 1891. One third of them (729) said they were born here, 110 in Harrow, 75 in Ruislip, 357 in London, 32 in the colonies and 11 in foreign countries (most claiming British citizenship). Movement out is unquantified, though the friendly society membership reflects it. A few emigrated. The names of William and Eliza Livy in 1856, both aged about 20, William Langthorn in 1883, George Horrod and his wife in 1884, all of whom went to Australia, are known because descendants have requested genealogical information, but there were perhaps more than this. At the other end of the social scale, Francis Bird, son of George of The Hall, had emigrated with much fuss and baggage, including 28 boxes of shirts, in 1864, and eventually became state architect of Western Australia.

AMENITIES AND UTILITIES

Harrow, however, had been outstripping Pinner in growth since the middle of the 18th century, due to the burgeoning Harrow School and the virtual merging of the settlements on the Hill, Greenhill and part of Roxeth. There was, as there always had been, considerable mutual contact, investment and movement between one and the other, but Pinner liked to emphasise its separateness from Harrow and, when elected councils replaced vestries under the Local Government Act of 1894, Pinner joined Harrow Weald and the Stanmores to become part of Hendon Rural District. Harrow on the Hill became Harrow Urban District Council, and Wealdstone became Wealdstone Urban District Council. Long before this Harrow on the Hill, fortified by the powerful School interest, had asked for its own Board of Health after the cholera scare of 1848-9, and had become one of the most forward

Rural Boards in the land. It secured many of the new public services before the Hendon Union provided them for Pinner – waterworks and sewage works in the mid-1850s, and 24 street gas lamps in 1856 to replace the existing oil lighting.

The cholera which smote Harrow had left Pinner alone. Nevertheless over 100 orders were made for cleaning or building cesspools and privies in Pinner in 1854. The offenders were often the most affluent, using water closets for which there was no outfall. The lowly relied more on the slightly less problematic earth-closet. In 1857 the Vestry's Committee of Nuisances reported that some privies overhung the brook, and many private cesspools overflowed onto the land of others or into the brook. The two worst cases were the Commercial Travellers School and the Woodridings Estate both new. The first, instead of remedying matters 'prevaricated, hoping to tire out the Committee'. Woodridings 'has one large cesspool, never emptied, causing a swamp of sewage, fetid to smell, filthy to sight, dangerous to health', and when presented with a magistrate's order the managers ran a pipe from the pool straight into the brook. Much effluent still drained directly into the Pinn until Pinner got its sewage farm and outfall works at the far end of Cannon Lane about 1879-82.

The Colne Valley Water Company, established in 1873, provided water to Pinner. Prior to this it was usual for the outlying houses to have a well or outside pump, and the 1865 O.S. map shows that many in the High Street and neighbouring roads had them too. It has already been noted that some places

74 William Langthorn, Pinner boy made good in Adelaide, and his shop – the taller man is his son.

had private arrangements for sharing, and that even small cottages like the group at West End had a common well, so it is hard to understand George Barter's claim that he had to fetch water from his relatives at Eastcote for Hope Farm in Pinner Road (he moved in about 1880). Perhaps he preferred neither to provide his own supply, nor to share. Waxwell was not the chief public supply, and in view of its distance from the centre probably never had been, but people may indeed have collected the water for its reputed medicinal properties. By 1896 most wells had been converted to pumps, probably by the water company.

Dissension over need and cost delayed the lighting of Pinner High Street until about 1880, when six gas lamps were provided. The Pinner Gas Company, whose works were in Eastcote Road opposite Cannon Lane, had been set up in 1863 as a branch of the Midland Gas Company, with John Emery, grocer and postmaster at 35 High Street, and William Rosington, draper at 37, as two of the directors, and by 1872 there were about 70 consumers. When housewives began to forsake solid fuel kitchen ranges around the turn of the century Sunday dinner put too great a strain on the supply, and the gasworks manager and his family sometimes took chairs and sat on top of the 20-foot holder until the pressure could be restored.

THE HIGH STREET

By the end of the 19th century Pinner had been affected by the greater specialisation among shops – the greengrocer, chemist, newsagent, confectioner, fishmonger, watchmaker, ironmonger, seed merchant, builder's merchant and tea shop had arrived, in ones or twos. They filled the High Street and new shops were appearing at the corners of Bridge Street and Chapel Lane. Two of the grocers – Kingham's at 13-15, and Gurney's at 38-40 High Street – had double frontages, both laying claim to a large and discerning clientèle. Many traders benefited from Pinner being one of the shopping centres for Eastcote.

In the High Street bay windows were installed, some still to be seen at nos. 25, 26, 33, 36, 39, and at 35 the draper's large plate glass panes with curved tops

75 Part of the High Street *c.*1875. Jimmy Bedord, tailor and parish clerk, lived in the weather-baorded house at the left. The bay windows next door are Kingham's. The *White Hart* is at the gabled house opposite, with the hanging sign.

proudly copied West End styles. In 1880 Daniel Gurney had filled the last gap in the frontage with a row of four three-storey houses in the garden of nos.4-6. They took a long time to let, being reputedly too expensive, and gradually the ground floors became shops. In 1904 the vicar called them unsightly, and claimed that Gurney would neither let, sell nor demolish them. In 1895 a fire damaged several old buildings nearly opposite which were replaced by nos.17-23, high and handsome with an oriel and fancy timbering. No. 9, refronted in brick by Petley the grocer in 1896, still has its perforated grille in the shop front. The next year no.13 was entirely rebuilt in red brick. Both of these were in contemporary style but when the *Crown* was demolished in 1898 the replacement, nos. 1-5, like 17-23, took inspiration from the more historic buildings in the street. With the arrival of the early Edwardian no.2, neo-baroque in flamboyant red-brick, the High Street had achieved the general appearance for which it is now famed, even though shop fronts are often replaced.

NEW COTTAGES

Some old timber buildings might still be crammed full, but the housing stock had changed. About 1840 the brick cottage with two rooms on each floor had become common and spread through Pinner. Waxwell Lane, Camden Row, Rickmansworth Road, Chapel Lane and Headstone Lane became honeypots for local builders, providing additions to the housing stock, not replacements. Except for those at Headstone Lane, which were the investment of Ben Mold, licensee of *The Letchford Arms*, the most notable feature about them is that many were financed, usually in ones and twos, by local working men of modest means. They represented the investment of savings, intended for letting to produce a small income, rather than owner-occupation, and were at the same time a surety for old age. For example, Tom Read the chimney sweep built 7-8 Camden Row, which he named Caroline Cottages after his wife, but lived more cheaply himself in part of the old timber house in Chapel Lane. Sam Jones and Joseph Hayden, both gardener-labourers, jointly financed 4-14 Waxwell Lane but went on living in John Street's old timber-framed, former head tenement behind 53-7 Bridge Street. Many investors were involved in the building trades, such as Joseph Pearce, John Jones, Edward Long and Joseph Anderson, all carpenters, John Tilbury and John Evans, bricklayers, and George Phippard, stonemason, in Waxwell Lane.

The piecemeal growth of Pinner before 1900 resulted in a close proximity of the classes, physically if not socially. Each hamlet, each newly-filling road, had

76 The bottom of the High Street about the same date, with John Lee's meat on display and the *Crown* doing business next door. Washing is drying in the garden of the later *Victory*.

houses from the grand to the decrepit, the most striking examples being West End and Waxwell Lane. The five cottages once shoe-horned into 18a-22a Waxwell Lane must have been the most crowded spot in Pinner. Officially called Gibbs Yard, after the landlord Mr Gibbs of no.127, the familiar name of these one-up, one-down residences was Cadgers Court or Beggars Yard.

A DIFFERENT PINNER

Pinner had changed radically during the century, and not only because there were four times as many inhabitants at its end. The outlook was very different too. When its people were no longer tied to the land, when the moneyed class no longer had the monopoly of education, or of knowledge of the wider world, when the villagers managed friendly societies and meeting halls, when girls in service had seen how the wealthy conducted their households and emulated it in modest ways in their own homes, when residents could be photographed, when men understood gas production and office practice, when the High Street had a bank, a chemist and a telephone exchange, when a 20- or 30-minute railway service to the heart of the city rattled by, taking some of them to work – then Pinner society itself had changed and Pinner, though still semi-rural, was no longer a backwater.

VII

The Edwardians and After

Pinner Developing

THE FIRST PHASE

As the 19th century turned into the 20th and London swelled like a tree adding rings, the pace of change accelerated in Pinner and in the majority of villages around the capital. The stations were in place to provide access, buyers were waiting in town for a home in what they regarded as the country. Who would provide the land?

The answer came from those with an advantageously placed field or two, or who decided to sell their large estate and move away. Their world had begun to crumble, and the different conditions after the First World War – lower incomes, higher taxes, the near impossibility of getting enough staff – hastened the process, so that by 1939 the mansions of Pinner were defunct. And there were predators prowling, speculators hunting land that might be bought and resold for development. Pinner experienced them all.

PRETTY PINNER

Pinner's appeal as a village was well recognised. As early as 1844 a plot in Paines Lane had been advertised for 'pretty suburban retreats' and Pinner was called 'a locality which is already famed for its healthy air and scenes of landscape beauty'. Similar qualities on the Woodridings estate were stressed in 1855, and thereafter this has been the perpetual refrain of estate agents.

New residents and visitors loved it. Lisa Lehmann extolled the peace and quiet in letters, while artists such as Helen Allingham, Kate Greenaway, and John Cotman had come to paint its rural scenes. An unnamed writer in *The Artist* grew lyrical in 1898; '… here are the weather stained houses with irregular red-brown roofs mounting slowly the broad way towards the hill-top … of all places for sunsets Pinner is the most enticing. The main street, with its roofs and its smoking chimneys, its dogs and its wayfarers, is half lost in the fading glow. The light of the blacksmith's forge begins to redden the overhanging upper storey of the old cottage, the lights show, now silver, now gold, in the windows. The birds are silent. This is the hour of hours.'

NEW HOUSES

The development of Pinner as a desirable suburb began in earnest while Victoria reigned, beginning in the middle and north, where the embryonic water and drainage services were making headway, the terrain was picturesque, and there were good connections to London. The southern part, where the stiff clay presented problems of drainage, and there was no transport, was ignored.

In 1886 Daniel Soames' trustees auctioned both sides of Elm Park Road (he had lived at The Lodge), and stressed the charm while setting the tone – the materials and labour component alone of each house was to be not less than £400. The first houses, from Red Cottage to Roseneath, went up on the north side in 1889. They were soon joined by Chigwell Hurst (1890), where Mr Ashbridge planted several acres of varied ornamental trees – some of them survive, and by Ashburton (1894) in half an acre. (The adjoining neo-Georgian Chelsea House and its lodge were built in the grounds of Antoneys in 1927.)

Further north Westfield Park – a few very large houses in the style of Norman Shaw's Grimsdyke House – and St Anselm's Church, were being built on part of Woodridings Farm west of the main line station. East of it William Tebb laid out the Royston Park Estate on nearly 70 acres bought from William Weall in 1891, and by 1898 there were six houses in The Avenue, Royston Park Road and Royston Grove. Almost every plot had a minimum frontage of 50 feet and a required minimum materials and labour cost of £800. The timber, brick and render type of vernacular revival was adopted, except for the red-brick Georgian 'Landaras' in Royston Grove, now locally listed. The pace of development was acknowledged when the station name was expanded to Pinner & Hatch End in 1897, which effectively made this area the new heart of the old hamlet of Hatch End.

Nearer the centre of Pinner, Barrow Point Estate was marketed in 1898. The bulk was bought in 1905 by the Pinner Land Company, formed by London men. It straightened the Pinn and proposed three new roads – Avenue Road, Leighton Avenue, and Barrow Point Avenue – with 175 building plots along them and Love and Waxwell Lanes. Designs had to be agreed with the company, and minimum property values were stipulated.

The Metropolitan Railway had Benjamin Weall's Rugby House estate, choicely situated at the heart of Pinner, and they set out Cecil Park south of the line. Though the first houses, 18-24, went up about 1902 progress was disturbed by the war. In 1906 the great garden of the centrally placed Howard Place was divided into plots for sale, which were advocated for shops and bank, all still there. About 1907 the northern arm of West End Lane was begun on part of Pinner Place and 87-105 Marsh Road were erected on part of The Grove.

The development of Headstone Farm – Harrow View, Hide Road, Cunningham Park – was really part of the westward spread of Harrow, rather than Pinner, as was the layout along Pinner Road of the county roads, as they are called. After 1914 they hung fire, like much else, until the end of the war.

Construction moved in fits and starts over these two or three decades, for there were plenty of other developments in Middlesex. Just over 30 streets were affected by new building prior to 1914. Many builders were involved, including local firms such as J.W. Ellement, J.C. Rackham, Thomas Pither and H. Cutler. The predominating style was the vernacular revival, favouring red brick, sometimes with speciality brickwork, black and white ornamental timbering, gables and bays, all appropriately scaled to the quality of the house. At the lower end of the market

77 Young Pulford is outside his greengrocery shop at 25 High Street. The post office and telephone exchange was at no.23 from 1903-10. Now it is Bishops Walk.

were Kingsley and Melrose Roads, still of good quality, and a row of 17 cottages built at Pinner Green by William Page (18-50). However, the majority of the houses were for the comfortably off, the only ones at this stage who could move so far out of town, and typically were generously proportioned, with a large entrance hall, two reception rooms, and three to five bedrooms. Occasionally there was a small room for a maid, the mark of middle-class respectability at the start of the new century, even if she only came daily.

THE PEOPLE WHO CAME

In a trend which was to continue people came to live in Pinner from the widening sphere of the arts and the learned professions, people notable in their own time if not now. The presence of the successful artist Frederick Goodall, and then the librettist W.S.Gilbert, at neighbouring Grimsdyke House, exemplar of the current architectural style, must have lent cachet. The earliest arrivals included Barry Pain, who lived at the Red Cottage and later at The Circuits in Cuckoo Hill (now a close of that name). Pain was a writer and journalist at the turn of the 19th and 20th centuries who created a hugely popular cockney character called Eliza. Lisa Lehmann, a singer before her marriage to miniaturist and composer Herbert Bedford, came to newly rebuilt Nascot (58 Waxwell Lane) where she composed music at home; her song cycle 'In a Persian Garden' based on the *Rubaiyat of Omar Khayyam*, written in 1896, was popular for years; her musical play called 'Sergeant Brue', the first to be commissioned from a woman, played in 1904 at The Strand and Prince of Wales theatres.

John Gairdner, at West View, 696 Pinner Road, was Assistant Keeper of the Public Record Office, and an acclaimed authority on Richard III, Henry VII and Henry VIII. He contributed heavily to the *Dictionary of National Biography*. He was made a member of the Order of the Bath, and when he died in 1912 the *Harrow Observer* called him the greatest scholar of his age. A few doors away at 688 was a barrister named Ernest Jelf (1868-1949), who later moved to Church Farm and then to St Mary's Cottage, 71 Waxwell Lane. Jelf became the Senior Master of the Supreme Court and King's Remembrancer – this is the official who swears in the Lord Mayor of London and presides over the goldsmiths' jury at the annual Trial of the Pyx. Jelf was knighted in 1939. What made him different, however, was his success as a writer of ballet-plays for children, which were performed in many countries, and usually previewed in the garden at Waxwell Lane with a cast of local children. Sir Frank Rea, a director of the L.N.W.R., lived at the rebuilt Antoneys, while the company's solicitor, Percival Birkett, lived at Moss Cottage.

NEW WITH THE CENTURY

New conveniences came with the new century and were taken up by the newcomers in particular. The Marshalls bought a motor car. Telephone exchanges were established in 1903 at Hatch End and in Pinner – at 23 High Street and then, in 1910 at 16 High Street. The Fives Court still has the basic number it was allocated

78   The Pinner fire engine and its volunteer brigade is the centre of attention in Bridge Street. This is probably about 1912-15 for the Love Lane shops are in full swing. The projecting Bridge House at the right hides the *Red Lion*.

79 This was the view from School Lane, *c.*1910, after The Elms had been demolished to make way for 100-114 Marsh Road, and these are the trees which had given the house its name. Muggs stood here in medieval times. The *George* is behind the elms, and the cottages have been replaced by Monument House.

in 1904. The Police Station was connected the next year. Electricity was available in 1906 – Pinner Hill House had it, and the Colne Valley Electricity Company served Pinner from 1913. In 1901 the fête at Barrow Point included a viewing of 'Messrs Maskelyne and Cooke's celebrated cinematograph' – perhaps the first moving pictures in Pinner. Tickets covering both fête and viewing cost from 6d. to 2s. 6d.

Suffragettes were new too. The Pinner branch of the Women's Political and Social Union was formed in 1911 with Mrs Manuel Terrero of Rockstone House (77 Paines Lane, rebuilt) as Secretary, Mrs Mark Verden of 60 Paines Lane as Treasurer, and Mrs Ambrose Heal of the Fives Court as Speakers' Secretary. The extent of support in Pinner is not known. Meetings at the *Cocoa Tree* and garden parties in their homes were apparently well attended, but speakers in the High Street encountered disruption and the Terrero home was stoned in 1916. Jane Terrero had been imprisoned for four months in March 1912 for breaking windows in the great march down Regent Street.

Charles Grenside the vicar feared that the new developments menaced the very characteristics which people sought, and said so in the *Almanack*. He pleaded for the conservation of Pinner in 1896, regretting that old facades in the High Street were destroyed for new shop fronts. He urged in vain that part of the Barrow Point estate alongside the river be used for a public park and lamented in 1899 that when those fields 'are cut up into plots and covered with houses the rural charm of Pinner will be a thing of the past'. He noted the secluded beauty of Moss Lane succumbing to Dunbar Thomas's 'perky little red villas' in 1900, that 'big shops stand on what was once the shady garden of Howard Place', and small houses had replaced a row of fine old elms in Marsh Road in 1908 (nos.100-114, converted to shops 1932). And he observed that few of the young people of the village could afford these new dwellings.

But the old, the original Pinner, which had covered some six square miles, was changed further under the pressure of increasing numbers. Separateness found its first outlet in the formation of new parishes. The daughter church of St Anselm, Hatch End, superseded the old iron church of All Saints at Woodridings in 1895, and became a separate parish in 1905. It was beautifully fitted, with a rood screen in art nouveau style by Spooner and several windows by Louis Davis, whose glass can also be seen at St John's church in Pinner, and in Gloucester and Dunblane cathedrals. He lived at 'Ewelme' now 62 Paines Lane. At first the screen, paid for by Mr Skilbeck of New Dove House, was forbidden as tending to encourage a superstitious reverence of its figures, but after a furore which went as far as the ecclesiastical courts, it was allowed. The parish of St George, Headstone was formed in 1907 from those of Hatch End, Pinner and Greenhill, and the great permanent church replaced a temporary one in 1911.

Everyday Life

The activities which had flowered in Victorian times were still the staples of leisure, augmented by Scouts and Cubs, run by the Beaumonts, Girl Guides at Cannon Croft in Eastcote Road, and Rosebuds (Brownies) started by young Miss Thelma Dore of Pinner Hill. Not till the First World War were there cinemas at Northwood and Harrow, and only afterwards did motor buses make the Hippodrome Music Hall in Edgware Road accessible. All the shops were shut on Sundays and attendance at church and Sunday School remained fair, perhaps for somewhere to go. Pinner was said to be dead on a week-night after the shops shut at 8 p.m. The gas lamps were turned off at 10 p.m. Many were pleased after the Great War when a travelling library used the school on two evenings a week. Roman Catholics had met at Dudley House, Devonshire Road before St Luke's church opened in Love Lane during 1915. It contained a shrine to the now-demoted saint Philomena.

80 The village sports in 1909 during what looks like an egg-and-spoon race.

81 A little gypsy looks after the popcorn at Pinner Fair.

Youngsters played in the surrounding fields, messed up hay-cocks, fished in streams. They relished it when John Lee or George Hedges drove a couple of animals back from Watford market and they could watch the slaughter or even help in the preliminaries. They enjoyed the weekly visit of the taciturn Italian organ-grinder, occasional school celebrations, the spectacle of a real bear at the *Queen's Head* for a year or so, the annual fair with its small circus in Leighton Avenue – only the older boys were let out during the evening of fair day. Gypsies were supposed to be out of bounds, though children were keen to watch the police clear them out of their camps in Roxbourne Park, sometimes setting fire to their tents to encourage them off. Tramps were regarded more benignly and fascinated children with their oddities, particularly Tommy Gregory who used to fight trees. It is no wonder that lots of fun was found in teasing adults – policemen, the disfigured chimney sweep, those deceived by the lost purse on the ground swiftly twitched away by a hidden string. Scrumping was a favourite prank, and orchards on the ways to and from school suffered regular depredation, especially those in Elm Park Road and Bridge Street. On building sites there were half-built houses to explore and machinery and materials to be meddled with and tipped over.

In those days poverty was still a real risk for the weekly employed. Charles Paradine of Unity Place called himself fortunate because he had been blessed with good health. Illness or injury meant no wages, and perhaps doctor's bills, though membership of a friendly society might take care of the worst. A letter from a subscriber was usually needed to get admittance to hospital, and not everyone knew a subscriber. Mr Nugent of The Hall was gratefully remembered for sometimes letting his chauffeur take someone to a hospital in London. Dr Levick the parish doctor treated people on the dole (parish relief) which was the only form of social security. Neighbours were a marvellous help. If there was any chronic unemployment in Pinner it has not been recorded, though it was the habit of those out of a job to loiter round the parish hall at the foot of the High Street.

The degree of poverty is difficult to judge at this distance of time. Did poaching and the occasional theft from vegetable gardens indicate hunger, or opportunism or mischief? Lads loved to go out with Dad to rabbit with a ferret or take birds with catapults. Food would be basic, and mothers did wonders with it, especially those who had worked as cooks; clothes were frequently home-made, sometimes cut down, boots often leaked or were patched with cardboard. Some mothers took in washing and the home steamed up; many fathers grew vegetables in the garden or allotment.

Those at the bottom of the ladder undoubtedly sometimes lived hand-to-mouth but no one reported unusual poverty, or hunger. Charles Paradine talked about the means-test being applied, whereby most non-essential possessions had to be sold before dole was granted, but Harold Plummer, the assistant relieving officer in the '20s and '30s, said in his memoirs that this had not happened in Pinner. When Daniel Gurney's bequest of money to the poor of Pinner in 1906 was eventually distributed at the *Queen's Head* in 1925, the Beaumonts, watching from next door, considered the recipients were generally nowhere near poor.

The feeling of community remembered by some as existing in Pinner just before the invasion of suburbia should not be overestimated. There was still a geographical community, but with a population of around 9,000 in 1920 was it still possible to recognise everyone? In practice there were two or three communities based on differing lifestyles, interacting with each other, but linked within themselves by family and occupation. The social divisions were apparent to the children. 'There were people like my father at the gas works', remembered 76-year-old Mrs Howell of The Chase in 1978, 'then the shopkeepers and those sort of people, and the remainder were the people who lived in the big houses.' The big houses by then included the Edwardian and substantial post-war villas.

By 1918 Pinner had four stations – Hatch End (main line), Pinner, Rayners Lane and North Harrow, opened 1915 (Headstone Lane was just over the border), and three churches – St John's, St Anselm's and St George's, but was still separated from London by miles of fields. In the 21 years separating the end of the First World War from the eve of the Second those fields vanished.

82   A Bert Thomas cartoon of the First World War.

VIII

War

The Boer War

The Boer War provided a foretaste of what was to come. We do not know how many young men went off to fight, but we know of six who did not return. Charles Seaton died of fever in Matabeleland, and Ernest Ogle in action at Bloemfontein – both were from Royston Park; Trooper Gregory fell in battle; Walter Coleman, son of the former police constable died of enteric fever; Edward Apps, son of the Pinner station master, died of enteric at Bamboo Creek; the eldest son of Dr Eck of West View aso died.

Trooper Tom Ellement, son of George Cornelius, wrote home:

17.1.1900 Bloemfontein – I am living like a lord ... one pound and a quarter of bread and the same of meat per day, as well as jam, and sometimes cheese, also a quartern of rum per week to keep out the cold. I have only got one under-shirt at present; somebody comandeered my other on Sunday while I was out, but I must get up early tomorrow – there are generally one or two hanging outside the tents to dry!

Things were not so good for Trooper Dawson Billows (son of the headmaster), who subsequently took over the *Queen's Head*:

7.6.1900 Pretoria – We have been on the march ... and have covered 532 miles in 51 days including 11 days' rest ... We have been on half rations, consisting of two biscuits, a piece of beef, and a little flour per day. Some of the fellows look thin and bad on it, and dirty and scrubby too.

The parishioners prayed for victory, raised £70 for the War Fund, and went mad with joy at the relief of Mafeking in May 1900. The church bells were rung into the small hours and the band played, at dawn the Union Jack flag was raised and hymns were sung atop the tower, while the next evening a torchlight procession paraded the streets.

Several survivors received public receptions and dinners as they returned, including Captain Angus Collins, Dawson Billows, Corporal Petley (the grocer's son), Captain Parr, whose carriage was drawn by the crowd, and Sergeants-Major Ellement (a promoted Tom) and Carley (son of the licensee at the *Bell*). The *London Gazette* reported Ellement's mention in dispatches by Lord Kitchener: 'Corporal T. Ellement, near Ladybrand, on April 5th 1901, with five men, drove off a party of Boers and attacked a convoy with great determination, thereby saving six wagons.'

The First World War

IN THE FIELD

Reserves were mobilised immediately war was declared, then Kitchener called for volunteers, and in 1916 conscription was instituted. The words 'To Berlin' were painted on the horse trough outside the *Queen's Head* with an arrow pointing to the recruiting office in the parish hall. Families high and low lost sons, including the Heals of the Fives Court, the Hoggs of West House and the Kerr-Clarkes of Waxwell Farm. Second Lieut. Kenneth Forbes was the first from Pinner to fall, killed on 10 February 1915 at Armentières, aged 21, the son of Thomas Forbes of East House, Moss Lane. Private Harry Hodgins of Dove House Lodge, Hatch End, ticket-collector and holder of the D.C.M., the only son of his parents, was killed in April 1915, aged 20, probably the second from Pinner to fall. Two brothers died within five weeks of each other in 1916, Alfred and Amyas, both captains, sons of Alfred MacGregor of Glencairn, Paines Lane (site of 10). Amyas had won the M.C.

More than a score of men of all ranks were decorated or mentioned in dispatches. There is no full list of Pinner men who were decorated or fell or served, so it is impossible to give a balanced account.

The highest award of all, the Victoria Cross, was given in July 1918 to Theodore B. Hardy, who had attended the Commercial Travellers School in Pinner. Hardy, an army chaplain attached to the 8th Battalion of the Lincolnshire Regiment, already had the D.S.O. and M.C., and was in his fifties. He rescued a wounded officer from 400 yards beyond the front line, he dug men out of ruins while under heavy fire, and he helped rescue a wounded man lying within ten yards of an enemy pill-box. A month before the armistice he died at Rouen.

A couple of Pinner combatants have left first-hand accounts of their experiences. Dr James of 10th Brigade, B.E.F. wrote to the vicar on 18 September 1914:

> Through the day we march … we often fall asleep on the road, I find myself reeling like a drunken man, in fact we all feel it. … Our first day here was awful, it seemed as if Hell was let loose, we were under fire and shell the whole day, with practically no protection. We lost our Colonel and two officers, total amount killed and wounded about seventy.

Major Alan Dore of 7th Battalion of the Worcester Regiment, B.E.F. wrote to his father Samuel at Pinner Hill House on 8 June 1915;

> After a time you get to know from the sound of a shell where it is going and act accordingly. … We sent about fifty (Huns) as near to heaven as they will ever get and then shelled those who came up to repair

83 Major Alan Dore of Pinner Hill House painted in Flying Officer Corps gear in 1917.

the trenches. It's a dirty business but it's war . ... On this front both sides are like wild bulls butting against a wall and getting bruised each time.

Alan became a flyer and wrote on 15 March 1916 about reconnaissance flights over

a new part of the line which is rightly named the Labyrinth. From aloft it is an untangled skein of trenches crossing and recrossing each other in the maddest way. Only a line of mine craters looking from 9,000 feet up like those of the moon tell you where our line ends and the German begins. A town or village which figured a good deal in the French communiques last summer is simply blotted out.

He won the D.S.O. in 1917, and a bar. He survived, and later became Deputy Lord Lieutenant of Middlesex and High Sheriff of Middlesex.

Among the stretcher parties moving around down there was Edwin Ware, R.A.M.C., Pinner's parish clerk and, later, local historian. He was wounded at Ypres, 1917, and the Somme, 1918, and a painting in the Imperial War Museum is said to show him with a squad of stretcher bearers at the latter place.

One conscientious objector is known, H.C. Marten of 19 West End Avenue, serving in a non-combatant corps. In March 1916 the *Harrow Observer* briefly reported that he, along with three others, was sentenced to death at a court-martial for refusing to obey an order, but that the sentence had been commuted to ten years' imprisonment.

84 Edwin Ware, standing, and chum Henry Godfrey, both of 133rd Field Ambulance Unit, R.A.M.C. The photo was taken in 1917 at Waton, Belgium.

THE HOME FRONT

The Great War was the first in British history since 1066 to have had an impact on every section of the population. Civilians were under attack for the first time and Pinner was no exception. Zeppelins penetrated the skies over London and the first warnings locally were given by the hooter at Kodak's Wealdstone works and a siren at Pinner gasworks. On hearing it residents in Pinner and Harrow took to seeking a vantage point in the hope of seeing one come down in flames, particularly after the celebrated kill by local boy Leefe Robinson (also V.C.) near Cuffley. In a magnificent spectacle a flaming Zeppelin would buckle in the centre as each end rose and formed a circle, and burning pieces fell off as the mass of illumination sank to the ground.

The government-made film about the Battle of the Somme was on view in Harrow in October 1916 and anti-German feeling manifested itself occasionally. When the bakery at 15 Pinner High Street was taken over by a Mr Wyatt the windows were smashed because he was supposed to be German, though the business recovered and continued. In August 1918 a cyclist rode straight at Police Constable Faber because she thought by his name that he was German, and she went to prison for a month rather than pay a fine. Some German prisoners-of-war from Eastcote were sent to plough what is now Montesole playing fields.

Servicemen from all over appeared in Pinner when Pinner Place, standing vacant, was used as a convalescent hospital, staffed by Voluntary Aid Detachments (V.A.D.) In their blue uniforms the wounded would sit on the Parish Hall wall and chat to the locals. Mrs Tanner at Pinner Green had some to tea and offered accommodation to visiting wives. Granny Jewell in one of the wooden cottages beside the Pinn used to give tea to an injured soldier who leaned on the nearby bridge – the one John Edlin had repaired centuries before – and when the war was over he married her grand-daughter Laura. Some Belgian refugees in 1914 were billeted at Glenroy in Royston Park and The Croft in Cornwall Road, and were supplied with some of their clothes and furniture by the residents.

Never before had the country experienced such shortages of manpower and goods. It is said that North Harrow Station had a female station master, a Miss Berritt of Bridge Street, though this memory cannot be verified, and Thelma Dore of Pinner Hill became a 'corduroy girl' working on the land. Gentlemen's wives assumed leadership of the war effort. They organised work circles and sewing bees to make comforts for the fighting men; scarves, mittens, socks and towels were in constant demand. They held fund-raising fêtes – Mrs Heal had one at Nower Hill in July 1916, while Mrs Foster of The Towers somehow enticed H.R.H. Princess Beatrice to hers in June 1918. Mrs Regnart of Pinner Court and Mrs Causton of Gippeswick in Uxbridge Road managed the V.A.D. hospital. Lady Kerr-Clarke of Waxwell Farm held weekly afternoons for service wives at the *Cocoa Tree*.

Food became short. Rationing was finally introduced early in 1918 but was badly organised. Ernest Peters, the baker at 33 High Street, ignored the regulation to dilute bread with potato flour. Supplies sometimes ran out – Charlie Paradine remembered queuing for two ounces of margarine but getting none, while Mrs Tanner always tried to get to Stembridges, 2 Chapel Lane, when they had cheese in. In May Pinner butchers complained that mutton was only available at the rate of two carcasses between three butchers.

When the war was over, national shock and relief and found expression in the public memorials which appeared everywhere. Pinner commemorated its fallen with an obelisk at the top of the High Street, unveiled in 1921. There are no exact figures of Pinner's casualties. Edwin Ware later calculated that around 676, roughly one in six, of Pinner men served in the conflict, and about 107 of them were killed and 39 wounded.

IX

Between the Wars

London rampant

INVASION

For villages close to London the unprecedented speed at which the metropolis rolled over them presented the most significant change in their history. The widespread demand for better accommodation had been encouraged by the trend toward greater public welfare and by post-war euphoria – 'Homes fit for heroes!' chanted the politicians in 1918.

The fields between London and Pinner were gobbled up within twenty years and Pinner was no longer a geographical village. Some 300 roads were created. The population quadrupled.

The existing facilities were insufficient to provide for the new numbers, and distance made it necessary to form new centres, each requiring an identifying name. The natural focus was the railway station, and station names transferred to the surrounding neighbourhoods. Two of them were rather misleading. Rayners Lane is so long that it projects far outside the locality which took its name, whilst North Harrow defies geography. There were three perfectly good alternatives for this one – East Pinner, suggested by the Metropolitan's chairman; Roxborough, the common field which had covered much of the area; and best of all Hooking Green, the old stream crossing – but the chairman of the Great Central Railway, which had joint running rights over the line with the Metropolitan, decided on North Harrow. The station was opened on 22 March 1915, just where a farm access road passed under the line. Because no station had ever been envisaged there the embankment was low, and the depth to which the road had to be lowered left it chronically at risk of flood after downpours. The only perpetuation of the medieval place-name 'Hooking Green' is the triangle of houses north-west of the shopping area, which stands on a field called Lower Hungerlands, once part of the medieval virgate of Hugh Ellis.

Metropolitan Railway policy from 1914 to 1919 powerfully affected the character of north-west Middlesex, and Pinner with it. It coined the name 'Metroland' for the area its lines passed through, and publicised it admirably by means of its Metroland booklets, which are now famous, beginning in 1914. The countryside, the villages, the delights of rambles on foot or bicycle, and the houses one could buy to be embowered in this, but yet be within easy reach of town, were seductively presented. In 1919 a new company called Metropolitan Railway

Country Estates Ltd. was set up to develop housing alongside its western lines so as to bring customers to the railway, aiming at the middle and high value market. Other developers were keen to advertise in the booklets and they all benefited, whatever the quality. Many new residents declared they had fallen for Pinner after a day trip to Metroland.

BUILDING THE HOUSES

The usual inter-war procedure was that a developer would purchase several acres of land, either directly from the landowner or from a speculator who had bought it in anticipation of the demand. The developer then arranged the building of the roads and their connection to the main sewers, water, gas and electricity – Middlesex had benefited especially from the County Council's great main-drainage scheme with an outfall at Mogden near Isleworth, completed in 1936. At this point he would normally sell groups of plots, or even the whole, to speculative builders, who in turn would construct a few show houses from which the buyer commissioned the one of his choice. The builder often provided easy access to a building society. It was a highly competitive industry and advertising was aggressive.

The character of the market altered between the wars. In the first decade the pool of purchasers or lessees was enlarging but it did not yet extend below those with an income of £3 or £4 a week, which effectively excluded non white-collar

85 Some builders took on huge developments, for which the mini-locomotives and trucks of a contractor's railway were valuable. Here the hedges of Tithe Farm go down before Nash's new roads.

workers. As the great depression took hold of the country London found itself escaping the worst because of its economic diversity, so more people migrated in as a consequence, which in turn maintained pressure upon housing. Building costs fell a little, investors put more money into building societies, and it became easier to raise a mortgage, while cheaper houses grew in number as more estates were built to lower specifications. The peak year for the number of houses built in Greater London was 1934. About £3 a week was still needed to buy, but the range now included most sorts of white-collar worker and the highest-paid manual workers. The average weekly wage in the country as a whole was £2 15s.0d.

THE BUILDERS

It is not always possible to distinguish developer from builder, and an estate may have been known by the name of either, or by a given name. The builder had the higher profile. In Pinner the most notable firm was founded by Albert Benjamin Cutler, senior, from Tottenham. He began modestly in Harrow in 1909, but almost all of his work was done in Pinner and the firm lasted until the late 20th century. His son Horace worked in the firm but entered local politics in 1952. Mayor of Harrow for 1959-60, leader of the Greater London Council from 1977-81, he was knighted in 1979. Albert lived locally, first at 21 Beresford Road, then at 43 Marsh Road and lastly at 22 Eastcote Road, which has a coloured glass window bigger and better than any other he produced, showing a hunting scene. Cutler was closely associated with the developer Imperial Property Investment Co. Ltd (replaced in 1931 by Amalgamated London Properties Ltd), commemorated by Imperial Drive, purchasing their land as and when he could cope with it. In the 1930s he tackled much larger amounts, and bought independently, but by then he had additional family companies, A.R. Thomas Ltd. and Garnett Ltd.

So much was going on that many other developers and builders, large and small, found opportunities. Most builders were outsiders – Comben & Wakeling, Costin, Laing, Taylor Woodrow, Telling, Wimpey, to name a few of the larger ones, while William Old, Rackham, Pither, J. Fowler, and Edward & Sons were local firms. Smaller firms either filled in on large estates, as A. Robinson did at Harrow Garden Village and Tithe Farm, and H. Pickrill did for Cutler, or bought a few plots, built, and bought more as sales allowed. Ellements continued to build throughout the century, but usually just individual houses. The larger enterprises are generally noticeable by their relative uniformity, while the street built by several betrays many differences. Variety surely reached its peak in Southfield Park at North Harrow, on Hugh Ellis's virgate. Eighteen or so builders were responsible for its 60 houses, one of which, no.20, was an early example of prefabricated housing by the Universal Housing Co. of Rickmansworth. This company later built post-war prefabs.

STYLE

The basic style of Pinner's new houses was vernacular revival, with gabled roofs, bay windows, porches, and walls of pebble-dash relieved with brick, tile or half-timbering. In general the less expensive the house the more watered-down the style. On a large undertaking there were very often small differences of detail in facade and layout so that a street was not wholly uniform. A few art-deco examples appeared, sporting sun-trap windows or green pan-tiled roofs. The majority of houses were two-storeyed and semi-detached but there were plenty of detached ones also, plus a good number of bungalows and a few blocks of flats, usually three storeys high.

New Pinner

VARIATIONS

While there were all sorts of gradation in quality and price, new building in Pinner fell into two broad price zones. The dearer north and west had a fairly even mix of detached and semi-detached houses. The east and south were dominated by the semi-detached and here, it has been said, the semi can be studied in all its wide variation. A few of the larger developments are mentioned below, but alongside, or even within, them were countless other endeavours, large, small, or individual, which completed the roads.

THE NORTH AND WEST – HATCH END/WOODRIDINGS, FROM 1923

 Woodridings Farm folded, selling 32 acres in 1923 for Hillview Road, Grimsdyke Road, and The Broadway. More Dove House land went in 1929 for Anselm Road and Park View. The rest of medieval Woodridings, in the south-east angle left by the Royston Park Estate, was filled by a multitude of builders via developers who have not yet been researched. The house called Clonard was let to Our Lady of Lourdes Convent and Girls' School while its land was turned into Clonard Way and Cedar Grove, the former a private road lined by individually designed houses. Nearer Uxbridge Road the houses become semi-detached and are noticeable for their ramped parapets, arched window bars, and the frequency of houses with white walls and green roofs in the hacienda style. These were Comben & Wakeling houses for the most part. Other builders included Laing, Nash, and especially the local firms Pither and Rackham. Rowlands Avenue echoed the pattern of its western neighbours.

WOODHALL AND PINNERWOOD, FROM 1932

Further west the great combined Woodhall-Pinnerwood lands of the Helsham-Jones family, and the Pinner Hill estate of the Dore family, both formerly Tooke property, had been released just before the outbreak of the Great War, which scuppered plans for both. In December 1913 Alice Helsham-Jones sold her 513 or so acres to the Pinner Land Syndicate (1913) Ltd for £60,000. The following year the Pinner and General Land Co. Ltd was floated to buy the land for £75,000 and develop it on high-class lines, having regard to its 'charming surroundings' and proximity to several golf and tennis clubs, as well as to public transport, for the company anticipated that the Metropolitan Railway would shortly place a new station within five minutes' walk of Uxbridge Road. In this they were wrong.

However, building did not begin until 1932 when the Pinnerwood Park Estate was designed by Martin Jackson for the Artizans, Labourers and General Dwellings Co. Ltd (later Artagen), a company which originally provided working-class housing in the 19th century. This estate however was aimed at middle-class people, albeit the lower end. It was the only large scale, homogeneous undertaking at the north, though the intention to erect 2,500 dwellings around a central shopping area and church failed, even before the Second World War intervened; only some 400 were built, without the public facilities. Garden-suburb principles were followed, tree-lined roads with grass verges, cottagey houses, some grouped into closes, with picket fences, brick walls and wooden windows, casement or sash. The favourite house plan was the semi-detached pair in the form of the medieval house with projecting wings. The estate is neat and harmonious and was made a conservation area in 1989.

PINNER HILL, FROM 1922

Samuel Dore had been contemplating the development of his 123-acre estate for housing but the London Joint Stock Bank Ltd refused to finance him 'in the present circumstances'. His letter was dated 11 August 1914, exactly one week after Great Britain entered the war. The war depleted Dore's resources further, for he had investments in Germany, and he died in 1919. His sons sold the place for £18,000 in 1922 to F.W. Griggs, who turned it over for £20,000 to his company, Country Garden Estates Ltd and built a very select private and gated residential area, with just four internal roads. Full advantage was taken of the woodland and the trees with which Sir Albert Pell had screened his avenues. It was heavily advertised over the next few years. The houses, having two or three reception rooms, four or more bedrooms, every labour-saving device, 'designed by distinguished architects ... each a gem in a perfect setting', all individual, would stand in plots of at least half an acre, with a minimum frontage of 70 ft, set in winding avenues without pavements on the wooded heights of Pinner Hill where bluebells grew, and enjoying magnificent views from between the trees. The publicity conveyed an aura of country living, and sports facilities were emphasised. Each garden had plenty of room for a tennis court, and there were five golf courses nearby. In 1927 Pinner Hill Golf Course was laid out on 137 acres of this and the Woodhall wonderlands and Griggs and his two brothers were members. The lowest house price fluctuated from £1,575 in 1923, to £1,750 in 1925, and down to £1,250 in 1926, probably representing differences in quality and size as much as financial upsets.

The estate was declared a conservation area in 1990 and four of the houses have been locally listed as of architectural importance. Two of them, Naseby and Oakwood, were built for the Griggs. The other two, Monks Rest and Pond Cottage, further indulged rural fantasy, examples of the eccentric vernacular revival house whose old, mellow and realistic look was achieved by incorporating genuine old timbers or parts of old buildings. Their architect was Blunden Shadbolt, a specialist in woodland settings, to whom Country Gardens Estates gave considerable publicity in conjunction with the Ideal Home Exhibition of 1924, at which Monks Rest itself was on show. Afterwards it was dismantled and transferred to Hillside Road. Pond Cottage was built for a songwriter, D'Auvergne Barnard, in 1926.

MOSS LANE, FROM 1924

The part north of the river was built up before the First World War, mostly by Dunbar Thomas of Elmdene, a speculating auctioneer. The southern part, including East End Way, was released to various purchasers from 1924 by Edward Montesole, the new owner of East House.

WEST END FARM, FROM 1923

The Hilliards, whose ancestors had bought from William Street in the 18th century, sold the farm during the early 1920s, in several parts. The individuality of the houses suggests small projects, even in High View, which was probably the largest single land sale. The houses fronting West End Lane between Cuckoo Hill Road and the school make a pleasing group.

THE TOWERS, FROM 1930

The grounds of The Towers were bought by developer John Buckley in 1930, and five streets soon appeared, Rochester, Malpas, Cranbourne, Winchester and Colchester Drives. Most of the houses were detached, with four bedrooms, probably built by Laing. Lloyd Court was laid out over the site of The Towers itself, which was sold and demolished between 1937 and 1940. It was named after the vendor William Lloyd, son-in-law of Alfred and Agnes Marshall. A few ornamental evergreen trees still stand about.

ELM PARK COURT

This is the most distinguished group of flats in Pinner, and is listed. Designed by H. F. Webb in 1935-6, the three blocks are ranged behind an arched entrance and have green pan-tiled roofs, white stuccoed walls and angular art-deco detailing. They were luxury flats, from two to five rooms, fitted out in wood, having each a balcony, whose annual rents, £85-£185, bought central heating, constant hot water, refrigerator, garage, and private tennis courts. The advertising was classic 'live in the Country yet be on top of Town' – quaint village, drag hunt, golf, private schools. How could it then bring down the tone by noting there was a bus stop just outside the entrance? Pinner Court and Capel Gardens in Pinner Road are very similar flats.

THE CENTRE

The Metropolitan Railway filled its Cecil Park estate north of the railway with Grange Gardens, which curls between Church Lane and the High Street. It was the only known interruption of the High Street frontage. Old cottages were replaced about 1934 by Grange Court, which remains the most recent building along the frontage. Beaumont Mews is off-street.

EAST AND SOUTH – ROXBOROUGH AND HOOKING GREEN, FROM 1919

At North Harrow the spread of Harrow had moved swiftly westward from Surrey Road, the last one to be finished before August 1914. One old resident said that most of the houses in Canterbury Road seemed to have been built while he was on his summer holiday. Cutler was the major builder. A few blocks of garages were included for letting but it was not yet thought necessary to provide every house with one, or even space for one. Nevertheless, some of the houses were fitted with a bell to the kitchen, and a fourth bedroom might be called the maid's room. Here Cutler's logo first appeared: four tiles grouped diamond-wise on the upper bay.

86 Grange Gardens is laid out over Odell's woodyard, *c.*1934 ...

87 ... And then the adjoining cottages are pulled down – High Street view.

HEADSTONE, FROM 1925

In 1925 Hendon Rural District Council bought Headstone Manor House (known as Moat Farm) and 25 acres of land in order to provide a recreation ground. Much of Headstone, especially on the Harrow side, had already been sold to developers, and now the rest followed, along with nearby land owned by trustees of the Weall estate. The council widened Headstone Lane and made a new road, Parkside Way, from Southfield Road to Harrow View; because of the Yeading Brook there was only a footpath link to Station Road until 1936-7. The buyers were Headstone Manor Estates and their major builder, A.J. King.

PINNER VILLAGE AND RIDGEWAY, FROM ABOUT 1923

These were Cutler's largest projects, covering most of the area between the Watford line and Harrow Garden Village, once part of Lankers Brook Farm. It had hills and trees, a walk was to be retained beside the Yeading Brook, and Cutler referred to it romantically in 1926 as 'the enchanted ground'. Prices ranged from £685 to £845. Bungalows were introduced in 1933 and pebble-dashing became less frequent. His houses were plain but graced with beautiful coloured-glass pictures in front doors and stair windows – cottages, countryside, rivers, ships, light-houses, rising suns – lovely to see when the house lights are on.

CANNON FARM, FROM 1934

Filling the space between Whittington Way, Cannon Lane and Yeading Brook, these houses have more brick ornament than Cutler's, and similar coloured glass, though it features more fruit and flowers. The builder was A.R.Thomas Ltd.

CANNON CROFT, FROM 1932

Sweeping chalet roofs and art-deco houses feature more heavily on this estate than on others. Built by the General Housing Co., it takes its name from a late 19th-century house whose land it used. The post-war Ellement Close follows the line of its drive and several ornamental trees can still be seen nearby. The Croft open space is said to have been the owner's unsuccessful private airfield.

HARROW GARDEN VILLAGE, FROM 1927

This, the first development in Rayners Lane, lay north of the station of that name. The land was bought from Daniel Hill's heirs by the developing company, Metropolitan Railway Country Estates Ltd, which hoped to get the station name changed to Harrow Garden Village. It provides a classic illustration of how things were done. The builder, E.S.Reid, organised sidings at the station for the delivery of heavy materials. The nine types of house on offer cost from £895 to £1,350, having four bedrooms and space for a garage. Most were semi-detached, a few detached, many in half-timbered style. The Village was laid out on garden suburb principles, with small closes, greens, set-back corners, and old trees left in place, particularly along Rayners Lane. With amazing chutzpah Reid claimed that its character and charm were 'assured for all time'. More believably he pointed out that the houses were easily bought – deposit £50-£100, weekly repayments 28s. 5d. to 42s. 2d., no surveyor's charges or legal fees; they were easily reached – two lines, 228 trains daily, the fastest taking 20 minutes to town, third-class three-month season ticket to Baker Street for £3 2s. 3d., first class for £4 15s. 6d.; and they were easily kept with a tiled, labour-saving kitchen. It was heavily advertised in Metroland, naturally. An estate bonfire 60 feet high was lit on Guy Fawkes night 1932, publicised by the *Daily Sketch*, with proceeds sent to local hospitals.

TITHE FARM, FROM 1930

Between 1925 and 1939 T.F.Nash Ltd. created three huge estates in this part of Middlesex – at Eastcote, where Nash lived during the 1930s, latterly in Bridle Road, at Kenton, and here at Rayners Lane. Christ Church Oxford sold Tithe Farm south of

88 Nash's huge advertisement in Alexandra Avenue crossed from about number 411 to 418. Through the arch can be seen, from the left, the station ticket kiosk, Nash's sales office, and the coal merchant's tiny hut, which lasted until it was destroyed by arson in 1986.

the Piccadilly Line to Nash about 1930 and there arose an estate of close to 40 roads, about 18 of them lying within southern Pinner. It was the largest scale development in Pinner. Nash's system was stream-lined. He used the railway sidings, and was one of those who had an estate railroad; the Wealdstone Joinery Works mass-produced many of his components; he had a vast fleet of heavy transport vehicles; he had cohorts of cars to take prospective buyers around his growing neighbourhoods. He produced a 72-page brochure, and his advertising was tremendous. He erected a 35-ft-high illuminated wooden arch across Alexandra Avenue, from number 411 over to 418, with 'Nash Estates' emblazoned on it. Set close together in terraces of three, four or six, with a few semi-detached and none detached, the houses gave roads a more uniform appearance than elsewhere. Nevertheless, there were plenty of small differences in detail and layout, the streets were tree-lined, some with grass verges, and every house had either a garage or garage space at the rear to which a network of service roads gave access. Nash houses were the most economical in Pinner, ranging from £595 for a middle terrace house, three up, two down, to £750 for semi-detached, four up, two down, with integral garage. Shops with maisonettes above were built in quantity near Rayners Lane station, and the slope of Alexandra Avenue was lined with blocks of flats.

COUNCIL HOUSES, FROM THE MID-TWENTIES

Local authority housing played a modest part in the growth of Pinner. The Housing and Town Planning Acts of 1919-25 made councils responsible for providing low rent housing, bathrooms included, with the help of government subsidies. One reception room, three or more bedrooms, and pebble-dashed exterior was the usual rule. Harrow was among the most energetic councils in those years. The 285 houses built in Pinner Hill Road formed the second largest venture in the borough, the group of 53 in or near Pinner Road at North Harrow one of the smallest. The later ones of those at Pinner Hill, on the west, were experimental, using asbestos and timber in a mock-Tudor style. Within a few years they were leaking badly, were condemned after the Second World War, and were replaced by flats from 1968.

People's recollections are that most of the tenants came from Pinner, or from other parts of Harrow, notably Wealdstone. A policeman's daughter remembers moving to Pinner Hill from Camden Row via Cadgers Court and Hedges Cottages in Bridge Street. There was not the importation of large numbers from outside such as happened east of London at places like Dagenham, and no particular animus was aroused. Nevertheless, Comben & Wakeling complained in 1935 that the acquisition of 142 acres for an L.C.C. estate east of Headstone Lane was affecting the value of its houses north of Uxbridge Road.

Suburban Life

So huge an influx of people could not be assimilated into the existing community, into local jobs and social circles. The newcomers had different expectations, and were constrained by circumstances to form new networks. Four things distinguished them. The breadwinner worked in town, his day lengthened by travel. His wife spent most of the day amidst an expanse of similar houses, half of them a good distance from shops. All fell mostly into the lower part of the age range. All of them needed shops, schools, churches, weekend activity and entertainment

ADMINISTRATION

In the midst of this Pinner was reunited with Harrow in 1934 when Harrow Urban District was formed from Harrow on the Hill, Pinner, Wealdstone, Harrow Weald and the Stanmores. Pinner was divided into two wards, North and South. Harrow became a municipal borough in 1954 and a borough of Greater London in 1963.

A new burial ground was established in Pinner Road in 1931, and eight years later the fire brigade moved in alongside, leaving their old shed beside the *Red Lion*. The gas company replaced its Eastcote Road gasholder with a bigger one by the sewage farm at the end of Cannon Lane in 1924. When the sewage farm closed the Harrow U.D.C. nursery used its space.

TRANSPORT

The transport lifelines for the commuters were the Metropolitan and Piccadilly lines. Though the Uxbridge branch of the Metropolitan had been electrified in 1905, the branch through Pinner had to wait until 1925. Steam haulage to Pinner was thereafter largely confined to the coal sidings.

On 30 April 1914 the LNWR replaced the old horse bus by extending the route of its motor bus, already running from Harrow and Wealdstone to Harrow. From the early '20s more routes ran to or through Pinner, operated by different organisations. Route 183 was one of the earliest, going from Hendon to Pinner Green in 1927, and on to Northwood Station in 1930. Winter's Taxi Service in Station Approach began the 208 from the *Red Lion* to the top of Pinner Hill in

1930. Bus 221 linked the *Red Lion* and North Harrow Station in 1930, and the 181B went from the *Red Lion* to Uxbridge in 1932. The *Red Lion* persisted as the name of the Pinner terminus long after its demolition in 1961. Bus routes were easy to vary, and vary they did, producing a transport historian's dream. In 1933 nearly all of them were absorbed into the newly formed London Passenger Transport Board, together with the underground trains.

Some road plans did not materialise. For example, there was to have been a ring road using The Ridgeway, Suffolk Road, Whittington Way, Lyncroft Way, and West End Lane; even when nos. 1-21 West End Lane were built in 1956 space for a roadway was left between them and the river to link the last two. Another example is St Thomas Drive, which had once been intended to continue northward across Uxbridge Road and connect with South Oxhey.

SHOPS

Three major new shopping centres appeared, around or close to Hatch End, North Harrow and Rayners Lane stations. Many of the national or local multiples opened branches – Express Dairies, United Dairies, Dewhursts (butcher), Home & Colonial, Cullens, Salmons (all grocers), Mac Fisheries, Boots the Chemist, Woolworths – and the same was true for the banks, especially the big five: Barclays, Lloyds, Midland, National Provincial, and Westminster. More individual were the bakers, greengrocers, newsagents, tobacconists and confectioners. Hardware stores were usual, as well as outfitters, shoe shops, drapers, haberdashers, jewellers, hairdressers, estate agents and a tea-shop or café; places to eat out were in little demand in the suburbs of those days. There was often a toyshop and a florist, and there might even be a small furnisher. Specialists like dentists, solicitors and

89 Bridge House and four cottages alongside come down to make way for nos.10-12 Bridge Street, *c.*1934. There is a bus stop where the front steps were. The *Red Lion* lasted until 1962.

accountants installed offices above shops. North Harrow and Rayners Lane had branches of the Watford Co-operative Society, and the former could boast a motor-car showroom. Small parades containing at least the staple shops of grocer, greengrocer, butcher, hardware and newsagent were inserted where Whittington Way met Cannon Lane, and at Pinner Green.

The original shopping centre almost trebled in size. Bridge Street was widened and only the *Red Lion*, the shops curving round into Love Lane and, for some strange reason no.23, which had been Thomas Trevethan's house, were retained. The *Red Lion* went in 1961, and no. 23 in 1989. Two of the old businesses transferred to new premises – Ellement the undertaker and Smith the baker. Many of the new ones were chains and banks. Of all these, and the Love Lane curve, only Ellement's, Boots, Woolworth, and four of the banks are there now. In Marsh Road 100-114 were converted to shops, and Jubilee Parade (137-183) went up in 1936. The *George*, and Carolyn (106, children's wear) are the only unchanged businesses.

SCHOOLS

Schools were swiftly provided by Middlesex County Council. Pinner Park in 1931, Cannon Lane 1934, Longfield 1935, and Grimsdyke at Hatch End 1939. In the same year Pinnerwood School was built to replace the National School, whose staff and pupils transferred to it. Headstone Lane Secondary School was built in 1929 (now Nower Hill High). Pinner County Grammar School (closed 1982, now Heathfield School for Girls) appeared in 1937, while the other grammars at Harrow County (1911) and Harrow Weald, 1933, were also accessible.

Although most children went to local authority schools a high proportion of the new residents of Pinner desired the genteel image which was put before them, and a host of small private schools rose to meet their demands, especially before the Education Act of 1944 made grammar schools free to the academically able. A private school marked status as newcomers Cecil and Ann Chapman found in 1930 when they decided to send their two children to the National School, on the basis that all the teachers would be qualified. Many neighbouring children were forbidden to play with them, and some party invitations were cancelled. It took months for the situation to change. Yet Cecil was a chemical engineer with Monsanto, and his house at 39 Cuckoo Hill Road had cost £1,700. Some tradesmen used the private schools – Woodman (hardware), Piercey (butcher), Kingham's manager (grocer), but the Ellements continued to go the the National School. Reginald Bridgeman of Waxwell Farm Cottage employed a governess when his daughters were young.

Many private schools did not outlast the founder. A few took a small number of boarders. Infant schools were in greatest demand, but several catered for older children, the boys hoping to go to preparatory schools or to private or state grammars between the ages of nine and 11, the girls also going on in a similar way, or perhaps staying there instead of going to a state secondary school. The curriculum was geared accordingly. Sport, music and drama were strong selling points, maybe at extra charge. The following are just a sample of the better known schools.

Woodridings School (1898-*c*.1960) had a purpose-built house near the corner of Uxbridge Road and Altham Avenue, taking primary and junior mixed and senior girls. Although in 1956 it had 170 pupils aged from four to 16, it was suffering from the not uncommon small-school drawbacks of having no science facilities and no sixth form – for this girls had usually gone on to St Helen's in Northwood.

St Mildred's School (1903-1939) for boys and girls, also called Pinner High School, was at Wilby House, now gone, in Love Lane, but did not offer secondary education. The founder, Miss Conder, had come from Primrose Hill High School, which probably accounted for the school colour being yellow.

Reddiford School, founded 1913 by the White family at 36 Cecil Park, continues, as an independent trust. It was always kept small, and in 1974 adjusted its age range to match that of state first and middle schools.

St John's School was founded at the vicarage in 1920 by C.E. Norman and the vicar, the Rev. C. Rowland. It settled at Barrow Point House in 1924, after a brief stay at 77 Paines Lane, but outgrew the place and moved to a new site on the western side of Potter Street Hill in 1970. It catered for boys up to 14 years, who wore purple uniform.

The Knoll School (1921-63) began at 34 West End Lane in 1921 as Mrs Vernon's Froebel day school, moving to The Dingles in Uxbridge Road in 1932. After the Second World War it had 120 pupils aged three to 11, but became unviable.

St Andrew's School (1923-95) at 42 Gloucester Road, North Harrow, from 1932 to 1995, was for mixed infants and juniors and girls up to 18. After linking with Innellan in 1971 this became the senior school. The combined rolls reached 400, though were down to half by 1995.

Innellan School, founded about 1930 at Morningside, 44 Love Lane, was mixed infants and juniors. Miss Schooling's establishment for girls up to 12 years at North Harrow joined it in 1939, and in 1971 Innellan became the junior department after linking with St Andrews. It survived St Andrews.

Tall Trees in High View (1940-79) was a latecomer, founded by Mrs Hilda Verden. Only primary education was offered, but on Rudolph Steiner principles. Attendance reached about sixty.

The Convent of Our Lady of Lourdes ran a small school for mixed infants, juniors and older girls at Oxhey Rise, and then at Clonard, both in Oxhey Lane, from about 1925. Some were boarders. It closed in 1950 because it was not recognised by the Department of Education, and functioned as an old ladies' home until 1968.

Atholl House (1930-95), boys preparatory, day and boarding school, was, at 458 Rayners Lane, the most southerly. It had 100 pupils at closure.

The Royal Commercial Travellers School flourished for the first half of the 20th century. The father of a deceased pupil built the grand Elliott Hall in 1904 to the red-brick Perpendicular design of H.O. Cresswell; it was endowed later with a Willis organ. Accommodation and facilities were added or renewed for another 50 years but its natural clientèle was gradually won away to the state sector, and by 1967 the school was no longer viable. After closure the premises were used by the Harrow College of Further Education and St Theresa's School.

CHURCHES

In religious matters, North Harrow and Rayners Lane tended to be grouped together. The Church of England created the parish of St Alban in 1930, replacing the mission hall by the present light-brick church in 1937, the only one ever designed by A.W. Kenyon. He adopted an Early Christian style, with barrel vaults and aisles, but gave art-deco touches to the windows and interior detail. In 1960 it was given a mission church dedicated to St Martin, set at the corner of Cannon Lane and Eastern Avenue, though since 1985 it has been the New Testament Church of God. Pinner south of the Piccadilly line is in the parish of St Andrew Roxbourne.

The Roman Catholic church of St John Fisher was built in Imperial Drive in 1939, a gaunt brick exterior enclosing a minimally Romanesque interior. For 18 months previously Mass had been said in the *Headstone Hotel*. The Methodists, having met in a house in Southfield Park, built a hall in Pinner Road in the 1930s, adding a church in 1957. They had no establishment in south Pinner until 1956 when they bought the defunct Downs Farmhouse and built a church there. The Baptists began a church in Imperial Drive by Vicarage Way in 1934, dedicated to the memory of a young missioner who met an early death in India, Janet Hoare – her father became the first minister. They had been using the Sarsfield Hall at Rayners Lane. Two years later a smaller church was erected at the north in Rowlands Avenue.

90 Rayners Lane, just north of Lankers Brook Farm, under assault from developers. H. Pickering advertises at the right, though this was mostly Cutler land. On the hillside 2-4 Highfield Avenue, partly hidden, and 6-8, were built 1931-2.

The Quaker Meeting House, the first in Harrow, was erected in 1935 in Rayners Lane at the corner of The Close. The Brethren established a hall on Pinner Hill, 1929, on land provided by James Emeny of Mill Farm, one of the congregation, and another in Parkside Way in 1932. A similar group opened the Elmfield Chapel in Imperial Drive in 1933. Christian Scientists built a church in Elm Park Road in 1937, having met in Oddfellows Hall in Waxwell Lane since 1920.

At St John's Church the Rev. Claude Rowland (1910-32) introduced high church practices and the Rev. Eric Barnes (1936-65) continued along the path. The chancel aisle was dedicated as a Lady Chapel in 1938, and a rood was placed within the chancel arch in 1955. Father Barnes, as he liked to be called, was called up in 1941 for temporary service as a chaplain to the Royal Navy. Most of the fine furnishings of the church were given in the 20th century, including the coloured windows of the north and south aisles and the Lady Chapel.

OUTDOORS

It was part of the suburban dream that the newly colonised areas were verdant and spacious – publicity liked to portray curtains blowing at windows which opened onto perpetually sunny weather. This was indeed true for much of Pinner, for parts of it became Green Belt land, that corridor thrown around London in an attempt to stop its sprawl meeting that of nearby towns. The belt was established in 1938, having been under active consideration for a decade, and the golf courses, vestigial woodland, and farms of northern Pinner, and of its neighbours Harrow

91 Woodman's of Pinner, known for garden supplies over a far wider area after the war, began in the 1890s as a cornchandler at 21 High Street. Boosted by suburban gardeners, it spread into four shops and had several acres of nursery east of Cuckoo Hill, pictured here at an unknown date. The bridge over the railway is at the back. (Desmond Hubble once lived in the bungalow at the far right.)

and Ruislip, were safe. Pinner had been particularly lucky in 1930. St Thomas's Hospital was preparing a scheme to develop the bulk of Pinner Park Farm as a housing estate, having sold some portions for sports grounds, when the Hendon R.D.C. scheduled it as open space and bought it, sharing the cost with the County Council. Discussion in Hendon Council had been almost violent, and only the casting vote of the Chairman, Frederick Cope, carried the day. Praise be to him! His house, The Orchard in Headstone Lane, has been replaced by Winston Court.

The market in hay fell apart as the motor car superseded horse power. Of the three farms which persisted, Pinner Park turned to dairying, delivering its own milk from 1924, Oxhey Lane combined arable with dairy, while Pinnerwood Farm abandoned dairying in 1961 to become a stud farm. Residents could delight in walking the footpaths through them and, later, in watching the milking at Pinner Park.

Plenty of space for sports grounds was available and they were well used. New ones appeared at Pinner Green – the Montesole Playing Fields, named after Edward Montesole of East House, Chairman of Hendon R.D.C., who had campaigned energetically for the Green Belt; at Headstone Manor and at Roxbourne Park. There were tennis facilities in several smaller parks. You could take your choice of several tennis clubs, the Headstone in Pinner View, the Hatch End, secluded behind Clonard Way, the West End in Cuckoo Hill Road, the Pinner in Little Moss Lane, or the Towers, in Cranbourne Drive. There was a golf course at Grimsdyke, as well as on Pinner Hill.

The Pinner Cricket and Rugby Football teams played at Montesole. The Pinner Football Club used the pitch in Cuckoo Hill Road, and in the late '30s progressed from the second to the first division of the Spartan League. Two notable footballing brothers of the early 20th century came from Pinner, sons of Frederick Gregory, licensee of the *Oddfellows* 1896-1907. Son Frederick 'Fay' (1887-1937), was a professional at Watford Football Club from 1911-26 and captained them

92   The Pinner/Middlesex Drag Hunt in the farmyard at Pinner Park sometime in the 1930s. Fred Hall, Master from 1932-9, is offered a stirrup-cup by his daughter Dorothy. The Master of Hounds is at the extreme left.

for three seasons. He was licensee of the *Victory* between retirement and death. Valentine 'Val' (born 1888) became a professional at Watford in 1911. He was sold to Wolverhampton Wanderers after the war, and was their captain when they lost the 1921 Cup Final to Tottenham Hotspur.

The Pinner (afterwards the Middlesex) Drag Hunt, whose first Master was Fred Hall of Pinner Park Farm, kept field sports alive – Cyril Ellement remembered that all the farmers and gentry took part. On one occasion it was joined by the Prince of Wales and the Old Berkeley Hunt. Members occasionally rode back to the farm via the High Street and Wakehams Hill. The hunt was formed in 1931, but found its terrain increasingly reduced by development.

CLUBS AND SOCIETIES

Other pastimes abounded, so diverse and numerous that only a few can be mentioned. The new residents were enthusiastic gardeners and the Pinner Horticultural Society was soon complemented by new associations. The Pinner Working Men's Club continued until 1939 though part broke away in 1920 to form the Vagabonds Club, which installed itself beside the Pinn at the corner of Marsh and Eastcote Roads. The Vagabonds' hall was a great boon to other associations, especially for dances, but was demolished for the Pinn Medical Centre.

The dance was a favourite social activity and meeting place. No surprise, then, to find that dancing classes sprang up in church halls and the like. Miss Sarsfield's School of Dance and Drama gave its name to the Sarsfield Hall in the sub-basement of 311 Rayners Lane (then 71), entered from the rear. Miss Ogle taught dancing at the *Cocoa Tree*. Both remained long in the memories of those who were young at that time. The new public houses catered for dinners and dances and chose to call themselves 'Hotel' on this account. The *Headstone* at North Harrow (1929), the *Rayners* at the corner of Village Way East (1937), and the *Whittington* in Cannon Lane (1939, now the *Pinner Arms*) were all such.

Amateur dramatic societies absorbed great energy. The Pinner and Harrow Musical and Dramatic Society, 1921-39, produced popular musicals such as 'H.M.S. Pinafore', 'The Vagabond King' and 'Floradora'. The Pinner and Hatch End Operatic Society, founded in 1922 as Pinner Operatic Society, and still in being, concentrated more heavily on Gilbert and Sullivan's work, but since 1985 has had to go outside Pinner to find a suitable venue. The Pinner Players has flourished since its beginnings as the Popular Players Dramatic Society in 1936 – Sir Ernest Jelf was its first president. It changed 'Popular' to 'Pinner' when it resumed after four years' voluntary suspension in 1944.

CINEMA

Television made little impact before the Second World War but the popularity of films was huge. Pinner had three cinemas, all served by different distributors, which meant that each week people could see three different films, if they wished. Courting couples liked to sit in the back row and get friendly in the dark. A fourth cinema was briefly envisaged opposite Cecil Park in 1946.

The first to open was the Embassy at North Harrow in a ceremony performed in October 1929 by Betty Balfour, star of British silent films. Seating 1,700 and having a cafe, it was a classical '20s structure faced with cream glazed tiles. The end came in May 1963, when it was replaced by a supermarket and the North Harrow Bowl.

The Langham in Bridge Street was part of a small chain called the Modern Cinema Company, and perhaps for that reason was rather restrained in style, deriving its decoration from a green tiled roof and bands of green and black tiles across its smooth cream-tiled front. It opened in January 1936 and lasted until September 1981, by which time its tiles had been masked. It had taken the place of Dear's Farm and was demolished for a supermarket.

The Grosvenor at Rayners Lane, seating just over 1,000, became part of the Odeon chain. Baroque in dimensions, it is of the plain-render and metal-window type of art-deco. F.E. Bromige designed this now-listed building, whose principal decorative feature is a giant central volute like an elephant's trunk suspending a triangular column, which bore the name and used to revolve; the foyer has a sunken cafe area and the auditorium is sleekly streamlined. The main film in the opening programme, October 1936, was The Country Doctor, based on the story of the Dionne quins, whose remarkable birth had filled the news a few years earlier. This cinema closed in 1986 under the name of The Ace, since when it has had several different uses. It had functioned the longest of the three.

A FEW SUBURBANITES

Pinner's good transport connections with London and the contacts it offered ensured its continuing popularity with those in entertainment and communications. It is worth highlighting a couple of them out of the many.

William Heath Robinson (1872-1944) and his older brothers Thomas and Charles were very successful illustrators and artists, though William's clever cartoons of mad and inventive machines brought him the longer lasting fame and made his name part of the language, as in 'a Heath-Robinson contraption'. William and Thomas lived in Pinner for a number of years, William at Alfriston, Wellington Avenue, Hatch End from 1908-13, and then at 75 Moss Lane until 1918, and Thomas, who once repainted the sign of the Queen's Head, at three places, lastly and longest at 45 Elm Park Road. Calling themselves The Frothfinders the three brothers and their friends formed a walking club which visited local pubs, and for a few years at the end of the 20th century the George was renamed the Frothfinders and Firkin.

One of William's great friends was Herbert (Bert) Thomas, the cartoonist who came to Pinner early in the First World War and lived in Devonshire Road, Hatch End before buying Church Farm in 1923. Bert was published in The Strand Magazine, London Opinion, and Punch, among many others. His drawing 'Arf a Mo, Kaiser' – Kaiser must wait while Tommy has his smoke – perhaps his most famous design, was used to help raise £250,000 for tobacco for the First World War troops. He drew several cartoons for The Villager, but moved away in 1944.

Another prolific cartoonist moved to Pinner Hill in 1928 – was it something in the air? – Gilbert Wilkinson, contributor to Punch, The Passing Show, Illustrated, and particularly the Daily Herald.

Reginald Bridgeman (c.1885-1968) was a less widely known eccentric. Old Harrovian, ex-diplomat and dandy, pink-tinged scion of the aristocracy, Bridgeman lived at Waxwell Farm Cottage from 1923. He was chairman of the Hendon Labour Party and campaigned for paid holidays, colonial independence, a higher school-leaving age and pension reform. In 1927 he backed his beliefs by building a crescent of 14 cottages opposite his own home for letting at uneconomic rents to working men. They, now named Waxwell Close, survive as a conservation area, but the cottage has given way to Olwen Mews, named after Mrs Bridgeman.

SHADOWS

The public events of these years were momentous but their reverberations in Pinner are obscure.

Unemployment caused a distinct increase in the number of strangers knocking on doors and offering to dig the garden, clean the doorstep or mend shoes. During the General Strike of 1926 the father of 10-year-old Edward Warburg of Paines Lane drove an old Wolseley car as a bus between Pinner and Harrow, where volunteers were running a reduced train service to town. One of the Parkhouse family of Nower Hill told Edward he had driven a train to Scotland.

The rise of fascism left few overt traces here. Oswald Mosley was elected M.P. for Harrow – as a Conservative in 1918, as an Independent in 1922 – and then in 1923 he joined the Labour Party. All that was well before he adopted the black shirt and led the British Union of Fascists, and by then he was not in Harrow. 'Hitler and the Nazis' was the title of a talk given to the Friends of Pinner Church in April 1933 by Major Draper, a distinguished airman and peace campaigner. The major admired Hitler's firm and stable government, applauding in particular the anti-communism of the Nazis. He considered the press allegations of brutal methods were distortions. But, just over a year later, Hitler exterminated about a hundred opponents during the Night of the Long Knives.

Joachim von Ribbentrop, the German ambassador to England 1936-8, used 99 South View Road. One of the Griggs brothers met him at an event, and hearing that he needed a refuge from the embassy suggested a plot on his Pinner Hill estate. Ribbentrop wanted a German architect and materials, but used Griggs's workmen. It is said the staircase had a motif of swastikas. The house, financed by the embassy, was named Sans Souci after the Prussian palace at Potsdam. Ribbentrop was seldom in England and cannot often have stayed there, though he did visit the Golf Club House once or twice, and his secretary Trudi visited Alan Dore in Cuckoo Hill. Goering's sister was using it at the outbreak of war. The British government took it over and used it, along with the Golf Club House, for Air Force personnel. The name remains but there are no swastikas now.

Meanwhile the young all over Pinner presumably charlestoned and flapped, tried cocktails, perms, the sporty look and Oxford bags, and marvelled with their elders at the aerial exploits of Charles Lindbergh and the abdication of Edward VIII.

X

The Second World War and After

Another World War

Pinner's war history is the national history writ small, a tale of loss, anxiety, precautions, making-do, endurance and recovery. Every person was involved in the effort. Most of the able-bodied men were called up into the armed forces while home defence systems were formed, reformed and extended. Most activities fell within the scope of Civil Defence, originally called Air Raid Precautions (A.R.P.); the Home Guard, originally the Local Defence Volunteers; or the Women's Voluntary Services for Civil Defence (W.V.S).

THE FALLEN

Particulars of the war-related dead of Pinner are still being collected, but the latest available figures total 575. Of these 141 have no known grave and 208

93 Flight Lieut. A.F.P. Fane, lover of speed.

were buried abroad, in 36 countries over four continents, having been involved in most of the major campaigns. Eighty-two were civilians, the youngest just over a year old (bomb in Capthorne Avenue). Many local men and women, both fallen and survivors, were decorated for bravery but the records are not complete.

No life lost was of less value, or caused less anguish, than any other. For each there is a tale worth telling, but, as with the First World War, space permits only a few random examples, not a balanced account.

The Rev. T. Bailey, assistant priest at St Anselm's, was killed with the Church Forces in Italy. Peter Yarrow, from the big house called Blythwood in Uxbridge Road, went down with H.M.S. *Hood* in May 1941, one of two sons lost in the war. Flight Lieut. A.F.P. Fane (at The Hall 1923-8), formerly a racing driver, flew Spitfires for the Photographic Reconnaissance Unit and took a picture of the German battleship *Tirpitz* from 200 ft up in a particularly daring venture in March 1942, which proved invaluable in the consequent attack upon it. He died on duty in July. Squadron

Leader Brian Lane, D.F.C., of 17 Barrow Point Avenue, was shot down and lost over the North Sea in December 1942 shortly after he published *Spitfire – the experiences of a fighter pilot* under the pseudonym B. J. Ellan. Bert Thomas's son Peter was killed in action in North Africa in 1943 and Reginald Bridgeman's son Humphrey in Italy in May 1944. Desmond Hubble was an agent of Special Operations Executive (RF Section), parachuted into France in June 1944 and captured almost immediately. On the prison train to Buchenwald Concentration Camp he teamed up with the better-known 'Tommy' Yeo-Thomas ('The White Rabbit'), but was executed by slow strangulation in September. He grew up at 64 Moss Lane, and then, as a married family man, at 21 Wellington Road (1934), Green Woods, Cuckoo Hill (1937) and 611 Uxbridge Road (1939). Back home, John Murray of Longley Road, sent down the mines as a Bevin Boy, died in an accident at Maltby Main Colliery in July 1944. Thirteen men died in the hands of the Japanese. One who did return after more than three years as a prisoner in Japanese camps was Edwin, son of E.M.Ware, the local historian of Pinner.[33]

94 Squadron Leader Brian Lane D.F.C., in battle dress with his Spitfire.

CIVIL DEFENCE

Pinner lay between several targets of enemy aircraft – H.Q. Coastal Command at Northwood, H.Q. Fighter Command at Bentley Priory, and the R.A.F. Airfield at Northolt. The first bombs to fall on Pinner came at the beginning of the bombing campaign in August 1940, with high explosives near St Alban's Church and on Pinner Hill. There were many incidents. The most deadly night was 1 October 1940 when

95 Captain Desmond Hubble of the R.A. who became a secret agent.

Mrs Jessie Waldron and her two little children, of Edward Road, were among nine killed. The most widespread assault was on 16 November 1940 when 19 bombs fell in a line from Evelyn Drive to Love Lane. Three VI flying-bombs (pilot-less planes, doodlebugs) dropped in summer 1944. One hit Parkside Way near Pinner View, another fell behind 49-53 Cumberland Road, damaging also the British Restaurant. Eleven people died in these two impacts, both in June, including three each from the Sage and Jenner families. A third VI near Rowlands Avenue, and a V2 rocket at the entrance to Pinner Road Cemetery were casualty-free. In all 28 people were killed by bombs falling in Pinner.

96 'Clay bagging' at A.R.P. Warden Post 32, 21 West Way.

About forty-two ARP Wardens' posts were set up in Pinner, usually in private houses until the permanent brick posts were built. Post 21 still stands in Station Road, North Harrow near Canterbury Road. Until the sand arrived for the sandbags they were filled with clods of best Pinner clay hacked from the grudging Pinner ground. Wardens patrolled during alerts, and hollered at householders breaking the blackout: the teashop at 11 High Street was fined three times for blackout offences. The post in the parish hall at the foot of the High Street later became the District H.Q. West House was the centre of the Heavy Rescue, Demolition, and Poison Gas Decontamination Services – the shrub and creeper-covered structures still there on the street frontage were part of the decontamination section. The chief First Aid Post was at the Methodist Church Hall in Love Lane, whilst the Free Church and Edwardson's Building yard, both in Paines Lane, were Ambulance Depots. During alerts it was the practice to disperse the vehicles around the neighbouring streets to minimise the risk of damage. The Christian Science Church in Elm Park Road was fitted for use as a Rest Centre in time of emergency. Pinner church tower was used as a look-out point, there was a defence post of trench and sandbags at the top of Wakehams Hill, and a Home Guard observation platform perched in the ancient oak on the golf course on Pinner Hill. Wires were strung across George V Avenue to discourage planes from landing, and obstructions were put in fields at Pinner Park and Headstone Manor with the same intent. A searchlight was

97 'Ready for Gerry' at Post 32.

stationed in Pinner Park, and flares, searchlights and anti-aircraft fire from R.A.F. Northolt were visible and audible. Planes coming home used to do the victory roll over Nursery Cottages in Roxbourne Park. The church clock was silenced and no bells were rung, except once officially to celebrate victory in Egypt in November 1942.

Air-raid shelters remained long in the memory. The most favoured sort in Pinner seems to have been the cupboard under the stairs, for the children, or the garage, reinforced, because the Anderson shelter in the garden, half underground and roofed with corrugated steel, with bunk beds, was difficult to dig out and nasty to use in the Pinner clay. The later Morrison shelter for indoor use, made like a steel reinforced table, was better. Public shelters were provided early on, dug-out, like long Andersons, at the foot of what is now the Memorial Park, at Little Common, Montesole Playing Fields and Hooking Green, and on most school premises – many lessons were effectively lost when children filed into them. Smaller brick and concrete public shelters were built in some streets, such as outside the *Queen's Head*, at the foot of West End Avenue, in Lyncroft Avenue, and several in The Close, on Pinner Hill council estate.

The Home Guard was instituted on 14 May 1940, and in Pinner men volunteered next day, despite the presence of Pinner Fair. Within a month they numbered 700. The immediate object was to resist a possible airborne invasion and guard supply dumps, and soon they were lucky enough to have one rifle between three men. They became B Company of the 13th Middlesex Regiment of the Home Guard, under the command of (headmaster) Major Norman, with H.Q. at St John's School. In 1942 service became compulsory for certain groups. Supplies of equipment improved, of course, and the platoons took their responsibilities most seriously.

THE WAR EFFORT

Food rationing in Pinner was organised after 1942 from the Food Office at 40 Bridge Street. Emergency foodstuffs and cooking equipment were stored at Headstone and Pinnerwood Schools, and at the Free Church. From 1943 British Restaurants were opened in Bennetts Park, now part of the Memorial Park (a large one seating 200, closed 1951), at Station Road in North Harrow, and at Rayners Lane behind the cinema (1944-51, demolished 1986). Here a shilling could buy a three-course meal and a coffee (ersatz, no doubt), one penny less for tea. For those who could afford it, regularly or now and then, it was great for eking out the rations. Only the North Harrow building still survives, alongside an old A.R.P. post. Parks and spare land were appropriated for allotments in the Dig for Victory campaign, and gardens were dug up too, giving yet one more necessary activity for any spare time. Waste food was collected for pig-swill and delivered, free, to residents' piggeries in Bennetts and Roxbourne Parks, in return for selling half of each slaughtered animal to the authorities. Chickens were kept at home but owners were supposed to have neighbours registered with them for eggs.

The W.V.S. was at 64 High Street, then in the club premises of Elm Park Court until the Inellan School premises at 44 Love Lane were requisitioned as their H.Q. Part was used as a Forces canteen and the Y.M.C.A. ran another in the old Baptist chapel in Marsh Road. The W.V.S. helped with hospital supply, National Savings

98 In Station Road, North Harrow stand Pinner's only surviving British Restaurant and A.R.P. warden's post.

schemes, salvage collections, clothing exchanges and organisation and liaison of every kind.

Four War Savings Weeks were organised nationally, full of local fund-raising events – War Weapons Week (1941), Warships (1942), Wings for Victory (1943), and Salute the Soldier (1944). The Colne Valley & Northwood Electric Supply Company built a warship float which was named HMS *Pinner*. The demand for supplies and money was constant. There were local points for the collection of waste and scrap of all sorts, with particular drives for metal in 1942 and books in 1943. On top of this Pinner contributed £6,250 to the Red Cross, £514 for prisoners-of-war, £527 for two ambulances, £250 for a mobile canteen, and many other smaller sums. Typical of individual initiatives was the Kelly Knitting Group. A.R.P. warden and mother of two, Edna Barton of The Drive off Imperial Drive, organised the knitting of knee-socks, mittens and balaclavas for the men of H.M.S. *Kelly*, because the son of another warden mother was serving on it. The other wardens at the post made street collections to buy the wool, and once a month they held a tea-and-chat afternoon for the knitters. When the *Kelly* was put out of action they knitted for the Royal Navy in general. Local organisations often arranged Christmas dinners and entertainment for service men and women. Circumstances strengthened camaraderie; the long empty hours at A.R.P. Post 7 at 53 Pinner Hill Road gave birth to Pinner Green Social Club, and Pinner Sketch Club was born at another Post.

The war effort involved almost everyone, either voluntarily or by registration. Nights were particularly demanding. People who had worked all day had to take their turn as A.R.P. wardens; others who worked in London had to share in the task of fire-watching at business premises, not necessarily their own; each street had a firewatcher to give immediate attention to incendiary bombs; meals had to be snatched between turns of duty here and there. This sometimes went on night after night. Sixth-formers helped firewatch at school, Scouts and Guides were organised for messenger and first-aid work; at 17 youngsters had to join the Home Guard or nursing auxiliaries; at 18 the uniformed services took the fittest.

Dislocation was constant. The most powerful was the conscription of so many, particularly menfolk, into the services, constantly continued as school

99 The Colne Valley Electricity Co. staff in the alley behind Bridge Street with their float for Warship Week 1942.

100 'Aluminium for Airplanes' – one day's collection of aluminium utensils at the W.V.S. depot in Bridge Street, 1940.

leavers matured into adults. Many Service units were billeted in Pinner for varying periods, using large houses which were falling out of use, such as The Hall, Nower Hill House, Blythwood House (the old Yarrow home), West Lodge and Pinner Hill House, which last two were used on a long-term basis for the W.A.A.F. Many individual houses were also requisitioned for forces personnel.

The 1940 blitz drove numbers of Londoners out to Pinner, which was not an official evacuation area until the flying bomb offensive of 1944. Many Pinner people left then, but tended to be replaced by evacuees from the 'bomb alley' of south London, despite the continuing danger. Chigwell Hurst provided temporary accommodation for people bombed out locally. Over thirty small businesses were evacuated to Pinner, usually office or warehouse sections, because either their premises were blitzed or they could be operated from their owner's home. The biggest, Messrs. Williams Williams, wholesalers of Bread Street, used the new block of shops beyond the Langham cinema. Part of Smithfield's meat market used the garage behind the Embassy cinema at North Harrow.

In time enemy prisoners-of-war were sent to Pinner, to a tented camp in the (now) Bannister Playing Fields near Hatch End. These were of the sort thought suitable to be used on essential work in London. After Italy surrendered, Italians were often allowed out unescorted, and so, towards the end, were some Germans. Some were invited to tea by local families. But there was uproar in November 1944 when a thousand Italians were moved into some houses at Pinnerwood recently vacated by servicemen, ahead of bombed-out local people or Londoners, because the Geneva Convention required that P.O.Ws. were not kept under canvas. After

questions were asked in Parliament the prisoners were shifted to huts at Rayners Lane beside the line to South Harrow. The canteen hut was adapted as a social club for council tenants in 1953. After the war P.O.Ws. worked on the L.C.C. estate at Headstone.

Because holiday places were very restricted, public entertainments were offered, especially during the long summer school breaks in 1942 and 1943. The old recreation ground in West End Lane was used for many open-air events, and the great barn at Headstone Manor was adapted as a makeshift theatre. 'We never closed' might have been the motto of Pinner Fair, which still functioned every year, though it had to end before blackout time, and prizes and some stalls were more homely than usual. Darts, or similar stalls with pictures of Nazis or Hitler as targets always did well.

Rota the Lion seems to have been thought of as part of Pinner's war effort, but in truth he had lived in a stout cage at 49 Cuckoo Hill Road since before the war. His owner, Mr Thompson,

101 Rota the Lion on his way from 49 Cuckoo Hill Road to the London Zoo in May 1940.

managing director of Rotaprint, had won him in a bet and Rota received lots of publicity in the media. Rota fascinated and disquieted the neighbours. They feared he might escape if an air raid damaged his cage, and moreover his owner found him difficult to feed – no ration book – so in 1940 he was boarded at the zoo. Later Thompson gave him to Winston Churchill. Rota (1938-55) fathered 30 cubs, three of them named Alamein, Tunis and Bizerta by Churchill after victories in Africa.

VICTORY

Spirits began to lift early in 1945 as victory came into sight, despite the continuing rocket raids. Advertisers regretted the continuing dearth of goods, but forecast that the wait would not be much longer. Collections began for a memorial to Pinner's dead. At the junction of Nower Hill, Marsh Road, and Pinner Road the signpost was reinstated.

Once victory in Europe was declared on 8 May many joined the national rejoicing, celebrations and lights in central London. In Pinner people tore down their blackout curtains, the church was floodlit, flags were hung across roads, and the electrical shop at 22 High Street made a Union Jack in lights. Street parties were the thing in Pinner and everywhere, and were very ingeniously provisioned in spite of rationing. Children scoffed jelly and cake as they had not done for years, or perhaps never had. Music and dancing sometimes followed in the evening. There were more after the Japanese surrender in August. Later in the year Harrow Council's celebrations at Headstone Manor included the biggest bonfire since the one in 1932 at Rayners Lane. The Pinner Green Social Club treated 800 children from North Pinner to a party on 17 November.

PINNER MEMORIAL PARK

Just as in 1918, there was an urge to create a memorial to the fallen of Pinner, and it finally settled upon the creation of a park for all to enjoy. It would cost £15,000 to buy West House and its remaining eight-and-a-half acres of grounds to combine with Bennetts Park. In the old wartime spirit most organisations and numerous individuals strove to raise the funds, whose rise was shown on a large indicator fixed to the parish hall. The first edition of *A Panorama of Pinner Village* was a fund-raising publication. In 1947 Cutlers, owners of the site, reduced the price to £14,000, the purchase was made, and it was given to Harrow U.D.C. as Pinner Memorial Park. An illuminated Book of Remembrance was housed in a shrine room, rather than in a separate structure, as planned. Just over an acre at the south-west was put with Council land to provide a group of bungalows for old persons, the tall conifers along Dickson Fold marking the original edge of the grounds.

Post-war Pinner – a summary

GENERAL DEVELOPMENTS

Shortages continued for many years. Aggravated by war damage the demand for housing was pressing. One hundred prefabricated houses from America were put up at Rayners Lane in 1945, south of the line and east of the station. The following year Antoneys was leased to the Jewish Refugee Committee to use as a children's residential home and a nurses' training school in 1946, and soon The Hall was converted into eight self-contained council flats.

Nevertheless, pre-war plans were taken up again as conditions eased. In 1946 a public library was installed in the parish hall and, as agreed in 1939, Harrow Council bought Pinner Hill Golf Course for Green Belt land. The use of many grand houses which were now unoccupied had to be considered. The war had stopped Cutlers' plans to replace West House with a new estate, so it was available for the memorial park. Pinner House was fortunate, bought by Harrow Housing Society Ltd in 1948 as a home for old people, and run at first as a hostel because building materials were scarce. Pinner Place, one of Cutlers' pre-war purchases, was demolished in 1953 for Ashridge Gardens. Chigwell Hurst and Ashburton, only a few decades old but certainly spacious, were replaced in 1957 and 1958 by maisonettes and flats perpetuating their names, though retaining some of Mr Ashbridge's trees. Milmans Court (flats) was added by the council in 1966.

The Grove and its nine or so acres were acquired for council housing in July 1949. Flats were preferred to houses so as to preserve the trees – 180 flats of one, two or three bedrooms in blocks of two and three storeys. Antoneys, bought by the council in 1948 for £9,050, was demolished in 1952 to make way for another development of flats, again respecting many of the trees. A proposal to do the same with The Hall in 1955 was successfuly resisted by residents on the basis that the council houses would reduce the value of properties in a good class area. The estate was redeveloped privately. A council plan to replace 51 Moss Lane with old people's flats was defeated on the same grounds in 1959. Yet in 1957 the council was invited to complete development of Albury and Evelyn Drives in the Pinnerwood Estate.

Nearly twenty Buildings of Special Architectural or Historical Interest in Pinner were listed for the first time in 1951. The High Street became Pinner's first Conservation Area in 1968, and nine others have been added: Tookes Green, East End, Moss Lane, Waxwell Lane (south part), Waxwell Close, Pinnerwood Park Estate, Pinnerwood Farm, Pinner Hill, and West Towers. Headstone Manor and the bank and ditch boundary of Pinner Park are Scheduled Ancient Monuments. Nevertheless a large number of old buildings, chiefly workmen's cottages, have gone since the war, the latest being Thomas Trevethan's 23 Bridge Street in 1985. Like most of the others it was of poor quality and very small by today's standards. On the other hand Woodhall Towers would surely have been listed if it had lasted but a score of years beyond 1962, when it was pulled down.

New infant and junior schools were needed; West Lodge School in 1954, St Theresa's Roman Catholic School, using part of the former Royal Commercial Travellers School, in 1968-9, and St John Fisher's Roman Catholic School at North Harrow in 1976-7. Just over the border at Hatch End were Chantry School in 1949 and the one secondary school, Blackwell County, now Hatch End High, in 1950.

St Luke's Roman Catholic church was rebuilt in 1957, and in 1972 Hatch End Free Church completed its prewar building in Rowlands Avenue. The one-time Baptist Chapel at the corner of Cecil Park was bought for use as a United Synagogue in 1951, and rebuilt in 1980. About 1995 a second synagogue was begun in Woodridings Close.

102 Woodhall Towers, demolished 1962, is seen here *c*.1930 during its brief life as a hotel, displaying medieval turret, Gothic chimney, Romanesque apse and Tudor patterning, all in Victorian brick.

The fair still takes place in the High Street and bus shelters, traffic islands and other street furniture are taken down to increase the space. There is a love-hate relationship with the fair, which disrupts life for a day and a bit, but yet is rare for its age and for being a street event.

THE PINNER ASSOCIATION

'Each man kills the thing he loves', wrote Oscar Wilde. The rush to live in Pinner endangered its very attractions, the chunks of open countryside, the leafy lanes, the ancient farmsteads, the village centre. 'In a quiet unspoilt corner near to the Old Village … a valuable property ripe for development', trilled the Nower Hill House sale brochure self-defeatingly in 1939.

But there was hope. The movement for preservation was already in motion, led by the Society for the Protection of Ancient Buildings and the Ancient Monuments Society. On 21 March 1932 the Pinner Association was set up by residents old and new to watch over the government and amenities of Pinner. From the beginning its membership was great, and it is still one of the largest amenity societies in the country. It did not always achieve success. The fight for Dear's Farm was lost in 1934, and that for Cuckoo Hill Football Ground 30 years later. And Pinner, ever self-conscious, opposed in vain the incorporation of Harrow with the Stanmores.

Its many successes, hard won, include the preservation from demolition or savaging of the *Victory*, Sweetmans Hall, and Bee Cottage. In 1950 it forced London Transport to remove a giant advertising hoarding 45 ft long and 12 ft high from the hugely prominent space between the parish hall and Chapel Lane. It campaigned for the top of the High Street to be re-zoned so that shops were excluded from the green and Paines Lane. Of enormous significance was the solid opposition in 1966 to the plan to demolish 15-27 High Street (yes, even the timber-framed 25-27!) and replace them with shops, flats and a multi-storey block just behind. In this the Association was a pioneer in presenting its own alternative plan. It followed with the High Street Civic Improvement Scheme. Constant vigilance is necessary to keep this, one of the best of the few remaining village high streets in Middlesex, from being ruined. The two supermarkets which later flanked it had to be built low enough not to spoil the skyline, with pedestrian access from each to the High Street to maintain circulation.

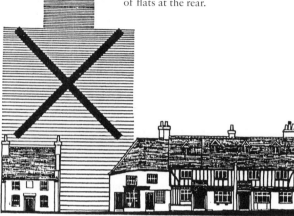

103 The Pinner Association's impression of the 1966 proposal to replace 15-27 High Street with three storeys of shops, offices and accommodation, plus a shopping precinct and a multi-storey block of flats at the rear.

Equally significant has been the matter of West House. An attempt to have this medieval estate bought for open space in 1933 resulted in the purchase of just six acres at the east, named Bennetts Park. The Association marshalled the fund-raising campaign to acquire the rest for the Pinner Memorial Park. Since the 1990s the Association has been striving to have the now closed, dilapidated, partly demolished and vandalised house restored as a shrine, a community centre, and a William Heath Robinson museum.

AND YESTERDAY?

The chief visible differences in Pinner over the last forty years are the lining of streets with parked cars, despite the spread of car parks; the proliferation of eating places, moving into the place of small shops rendered unprofitable by the preference for supermarkets; the replacement of large houses and gardens, or the filling of any spare space, by new, generally small, houses with minuscule gardens, or by small blocks of flats; and the rising of office blocks in the vicinity of the Metropolitan station. One of the most remarkable social changes is the proportion of inhabitants of largely commonwealth origin, by now long established in the community and in all its aspects.

Since the expansion of the 1930s it has been difficult to view Pinner as the entity it once was. It now means the old centre and its environs, exclusive of North Harrow, Rayners Lane, and Hatch End, which think of themselves as distinctly separate places. What happens in them is no longer focused upon, nor emanates from, the old heartland. This smaller Pinner tries to guard its image. The High Street is referred to as the village, and proximity to it is considered a selling advantage by estate agents. So is the leafiness of its lanes, but redevelopments and the conversion of gardens into parking space put those hedges and trees under heavy pressure.

There have been many complex changes. I do not propose to examine them, believing them at this short distance of time to be the province of the social, rather than the local, historian.

Appendices

1 – Buildings in Pinner

Many buildings referred to in the text have gone, or have had more than one name. The list includes those originating before about 1850. The names and dates are the earliest firm ones; there is earlier circumstantial evidence for many. For the date of *standing* buildings, consult the text.

number	on figure 2 (page 8) or figure 5 (page 15)
place-name	the first known, though not necessarily at the time of the first date
type	means the original sort of holding: C = copyhold; F = freehold; HT = head tenement; ST = sub-tenancy; W = wastehold.
first date	the first at which a named owner or tenant is known, which is not always the earliest date known – see above
first person	the owner, tenant or occupier at that date
other names	these are cross-referenced in the list
demolished	not all dates are known

no.	place-name	type	first date	first person	other names	present location
1	Alveryches	HT	1425	William Aldridge	Aldridges	West House, West End Lane
2	Alveryches – part	ST	1395	Isabel Rawlings		Chapel Lane, south, under bridge *demolished 1885*
3	Antoneys	F	1518	Thomas Cooper		Antoneys Close *demolished 1952*
4	Ashill Cottage	W	1685	William Whelpley		64-66 Pinner Green *demolished c.1920*
5	Barrow Point House	ST	1550	John Bird		Barrowdene Close *demolished 1970 approx*
6	Barryes	F	1475	Henry Edlin	The Corner	field Headstone Lane/Uxbridge Road *demolished by 1880*
7	Bay House	ST	1660	John Stanbrough		Church Lane
8	Bee Cottage	ST	1446	Richard Canon		23 Waxwell Lane
9	Blakes	HT	1396	Thomas Blake	Newes	Church Farm, High Street
10	Bowryngs	HT	1432	John Bowring		31-35 Love Lane *demolished 1950s*
11	Camden Cottage	W	1587	Gregory Colsey	Northwold	Abbey Close, Cuckoo Hill *demolished 1950s*
12	Canons	HT	1394	Richard Canon		Hereford Gardens *demolished 1930s*
13	Chantry House	F	1538	Richard Edlin		151-3 Uxbridge Road approx *demolished 1765 approx*
14	Chestnut Cottage	F	1712	James Watts		Church Lane
15	Clobbes	HT	1470	Robert Neel	not located	Chapel Lane north side *demolished by 1600*
16	Cockparkers	HT	1420	John Alverych	not located	Wakehams Hill, north side *demolished by 1600*
17	Crouchers	HT	1386	John Croucher		Weall Court, School Lane *demolished 1860 approx*
18	Dears Farm	ST	1457	William Aleyn		77 Bridge Street *demolished 1935*
19	Downers	HT	1422	Roger Downer	East House	East Glade *demolished 1954 approx*
20	Downs Farm		1860	T & H Prince		Cannon Lane *demolished 1970s*
21	East End House	ST	1486	Richard Reading		Moss Lane

22	Elm Lodge	F	1761	Edward Bailey	The Orchard	Winston Court, Headstone Lane *demolished 1960s*
23	Emily Cottage	F	1823	Ralph Ellis	The Towers	Lloyd Court, West End Lane *demolished 1935 approx*
24	Estends	HT	1424	William Estend	Marshes	East End Farm Cottage
25	Females	F	1532	William Morton		Holly Lodge, 16 West End Lane *demolished by 1750*
26	Gardiners	HT	1412	John Rowhed	New House	Elmdene, Church Lane
27	*George, The*	W	1533	William Hill		Marsh Road *demolished 1885*
28	Grove, The	F	1463	Richard Marsh		Grove Avenue *demolished 1950s*
29	Gulls	HT	1393	Thomas Reading	Coldharbour	82 Paines Lane *demolished by 1800*
30	Hall, The	F	1664	Robert Beake		Old Hall Drive *demolished 1953*
31	Hall, The	C	1667	Thos Norrington	The Old Hall	Old Hall Drive *demolished 1730 approx*
32	Harrow, The	C	1648	Richard Downer	The Chequer	Myrtown, Church Lane *demolished 1930 approx*
33	house	C	1810	Winter + Bateman		Old Hall Drive *demolished 1820 approx*
34	house	W	1412	Elis		Chantry Place, north side *demolished 1950s*
35	house	C	1632	Edward Leigh		127 Waxwell Lane *demolished by 1840*
36	house	W	1667	Henry Goldstone		7 Moss Lane approx *demolished 1800*
37	house	W	1617	Elizabeth Heyward		Pinner Green *demolished 1870s*
38	house	W	1549	Thomas Clark		Pinner Green *demolished 1870s*
39	house	W	1567	Richard Whelpley		Pinner Green *demolished 1870s*
40	house	W	1588	Robert Lawrence		Pinner Green *demolished 1930s*
41	houses (four)	STW		Bird		Barrowpoint Lane – south *demolished 1880 approx*
42	Ivy Cottage	F	1673	Ralph Page	Hazeldene	125-155 West End Lane *demolished 1970s*
43	Lankers Brook Farm		1914	H B Cox	Rayners Lane Farm	554 Rayners Lane
44	Lawn, The	ST	1567	Thomas Reading		Elm Park Road *demolished 1814*
45	Leonards	HT	1547	Francis Bird	The Lodge	Elm Park Court, Elm Park Road *demolished 1930 approx*
46	Letchford House	F	1547	William Edlin		Headstone Lane
47	Lewins	C	1384	John Lewin		1-3 West House Cottages *demolished 1950s*
48	Lewins – part	ST	1397	Elias Newman		West House grounds, south west *demolished by 1900*
49	Marlpits	C	1513	Robert New	Waxwell Farm, Grail	125 Waxwell Lane
50	Moss Cottage	ST	1496	William Lewin		2 Moss Lane
51	Muggs	ST	1373	William Croucher	The Elms	100-114 Marsh Road *demolished 1885*
52	Neels	HT	1395	John Rede	Pinner Place	Ashridge Gardens *demolished 1954 approx*
53	Nowermans	HT	1476	Henry Estend		199-201 Nower Hill approx *demolished by 1865*
54	Nowermans – part	ST	1409	John Cooper	Mayfield	22 Nower Hill *demolished 1880 approx*
55	Orchard Cottage	ST	1428	John Dell		3 Waxwell Lane
56	Oxhey Lane Farm	F	1693	Samuel Edlin		Oxhey Lane
57	Paynes	F	1422	John Payne	Paines Place	Paines Lane east, south of Pinn *demolished by 1800*
58	Pinner Hill Farm	F	1820c	Albert Pell		Pinner Hill Road

59	Pinnerwood Cottage	F	1623	John Clerk		Pinnerwod Cottage, Pinner Wood *demolished 1860 approx*
60	Pinnerwood House	F	1465	John Clerk		Pinnerwood House, Pinner Wood
61	Ponders	HT	1418	Richard Ponder	Nower Hill House	185-7 Moss Lane *demolished 1960 approx*
62	Poplar Cottage	W	1555	John Hatch		83 West End Lane at rear *demolished 1920s*
63	Pynnors	F	1422	John Pynnor		Ashill Drive, south end
64	Rayners Lane Cotts		1830	Daniel Hill		corner Rayners Lane/Farm Avenue *demolished 1920s*
65	Readings	HT	1486	Richard Reading	Tudor Cottage	Moss Lane
66	Rose Cottage		1675	Simon Edlin		32 West End Lane *demolished 1850 approx*
67	Rowheds	HT	1474	William Rowhed	The Croft	41 High Street *demolished by 1850*
68	Roxethes		1391	Richard Roxeth	Church Cottage	Church Lane
69	Sharpes	HT	1432	John Sharp	Waxwell and Manor Cottages	18a/20a Waxwell Lane
70	Sharpes – part	ST	1507	William Street		58 Waxwell Lane *demolished 1890 approx*
71	Sharpes – part	ST	1433	William Hegge	Howard Place	St Luke's Church *demolished 1950s*
72	Smiths	F	1436	Richard Smith	Parkgate	West Chantry *demolished 1822 approx*
73	Spinnells	F	1630	Chris. Clitherow	Pinner Hill House	Pinner Hill Golf Club House *demolished 1780 approx*
74	Streets	HT	1429	John Street	Hayden House	57 Bridge Street at rear *demolished 1930 approx*
75	Streets part	ST	1448	Thomas Derewyn	Fir Cottage	37 Bridge Street approx *demolished 1930 approx*
76	Streets part	ST	1445	Thomas Street		Chapel Lane, rear of Woolworth *1930 approx*
77	Strudlers	F	1499	Thomas Stroder	Brickwall House	Pinner House, Church Lane
78	Sweetmans	HT	1393	John Reading		Sweetmans Hall, West End Lane
79	Sweetmans – part	ST	1526	Henry Bird	The Cottage	75 Bridge Street *demolished 1935*
80	Terrilands	F	1632	Richard Basse	Chiswick House	Chiswick Court *demolished 1960 approx*
81	Wapses	F	1429	Richard Waps	Tindalls, Dove House	Dove Park, Hatch End *demolished 1960s*
82	Waxwell House	C	1655	John Edlin	Dingles	Derby House, Chesswood Way *demolished 1960s*
83	Weatherleys	F	1669	John Street	Oakfield	49-51 Paines Lane *demolished 1890 approx*
84	West End Farm	F	1750	Henry Street		West Lodge School
85	West Lodge	F	1747	Wiliam Street		West Lodge School *demolished 1950s*
86	windmill	W	1617	William Crane	Mill Farm	Mill Farm Close *demolished 1872*
87	Woleyes – part	C	1393	Robert Elis		Chantry Place, south side *demolished 1830 approx*
88	Woodridings Farm	F	1726	Lord Hunsdon		434 Uxbridge Road, at rear *demolished 1950s*

2 – Buildings in the High Street

house number   is the one used in 2003 and see figure 8 (page 20)
first date   the first at which a named owner or tenant is known, which is not always the
                earliest date known
first person   the owner, tenant or occupier at that date
original type   the first description

house no.	first date	first person	original type
2	1629	Henry Edlin	waste land
4	1389	Richard Reding	cottage
6	1389	Richard Reding	garden
8	1389	Richard Reding	garden
10	1389	Richard Reding	garden
12	1389	Richard Reding	garden
14	1389	Richard Reding	garden
16	1389	Richard Reding	garden
18	1386	Richard Kember	cottage divided in 3
20	1386	Richard Kember	cottage divided in 3
22	1386	Richard Kember	cottage divided in 3
24	1386	Richard Kember	cottage divided in 3
26	1465	William Cotterell	cottage
28	1465	William Cotterell	cottage
30	1465	William Cotterell	cottage
32	1592	John Edlin	cottage divided in 3
34	1422	John Downer	cottage
36	1422	John Downer	cottage
38	1422	John Downer	cottage
40	1422	John Downer	barn
42	1383	John Wilks	cottage
44	1383	John Wilks	garden
46	1657	John & Ann Bird	cottage
48	1390	John Tournor	garden
50	1390	John Tournor	cottage
52	1390	John Tournor	cottage
54	1390	John Tournor	cottage
56	1390	John Tournor	cottage
58	1391	Richard Downer	waste plot
64	1722	Thomas Huckell	house and garden
1	1476	William Denby	cottage and garden
3	1476	William Denby	cottage and garden
5	1476	William Denby	cottage and garden
7	1476	William Denby	cottage and garden
9	1504	Joan Whitberd	cottage
11	1504	Joan Whitberd	cottage
13	1547	Thomas Dodds	cottage
15	1421	John Cole	cottage
17	1512	John Fernes	cottage
19	1512	John Fernes	cottage
21	1658	Robert Wayland	cottage divided in 2
23	1658	Robert Wayland	cottage divided in 2

25	1419	Alice Kember	cottage – Copped Hall
27	1419	Alice Kember	cottage – Copped Hall
29	1418	John Pope	cottage
31	1389	William Sutton	cottage
33	1416	John Palfreyman	cottage
35	1416	John Palfreyman	cottage
37	1416	John Palfreyman	cottage
39	1416	John Palfreyman	cottage
41	1397	Shepper	head tenement

3 – The Population of Harrow

All names found in Harrow Court Rolls 1315-16, comprising nine views of frankpledge and courts baron, and a pannage list, were recorded. Where it is obvious that one person is the subject of more than one entry the surplus entries have been removed. So have persons who apparently died some time before. Females have been treated as dependent (as well as the three servants shown) except for those who appear in the pannage list, or who act in conveyances without husbands; alewives are not necessarily independent, nor are female litigants or offenders.

Some householders are not mentioned in the court rolls in the normal way – there are at least 53 who appear only in the pannage list for example – so there may well be others. Thirty-one of the names in the pannage list are illegible and, if known, may have been found to be among the other names in the court rolls; this number, therefore, has been removed from the total names for 1315-16 to reduce duplication. No adjustment has been made for the occasional son who may be in a dependent position.

All males and independent females in the adjusted list have been regarded as potential heads of households. However, the figures are approximate, and may be overstated or understated. Where residence can reasonably be determined the Pinner element is a fairly consistent percentage of the total figure for Harrow and confirms the pre-eminence of Pinner among the hamlets.

In 1315-16 the adjusted total of persons named was 478. The deduction of 50 dependent females and 31 pig owners whose names were illegible leaves 397 potential householders, of whom 32 were female. The number reasonably identifiable as living in Pinner was 104. Pannage was paid by 206 people in all, including the 31 anonymous ones.

A similar exercise for 1320-1 and 1334-47 produced broadly similar findings.

Notes

1. A. Cole, in *English Place Name Society*, vols 19, 21.
2. Castle, S., 'Excavations in Pear Wood, Brockley Hill, 1948-73', *TLAMAS*, vol.26 (1975) n.26.
3. Curia Regis Rolls Vol.XIV, no.1115, and Vol.XVI, no. 2031; E. Ware, Pinner in the Vale, no.251.
4. Lambeth Palace Estate MS. 2068.
5. Calendar of Charter Rolls, 1327-41, 360.
6. Calendar of Patent Rolls, 1381-5, 77.
7. B.M. Add. MS 29794, m.1d.
8. Calendar of Patent Rolls 1441-6, 168.
9. J. Sayers, *Papal Judges Delegate in Canterbury in the 13th Century*.
10. Lambeth Palace, Reynolds Register, fo.126v.
11. Lambeth Palace, 121 Stafford; PCC LL Stokton.
12. E.M. Ware, *Pinner in the Vale*, no.72.
13. LMA Acc.76/421.
14. Bodleian MS Rawl. B 389 B.
15. Information from Billie Reading-Lewis and Crolian Edelen, both of U.S.A.
16. Lambeth Palace, VH 96/629.
17. PCC 13 Langley.
18. LMA Acc.76, 1655-6.
19. *Trans. Historic Society of Lancashire & Cheshire*, vol. 32 (1880) pp. 158-63. The book is in the Joseph Mayer MS Collection at Liverpool University Library.
20. PCC Dossett, will of Richard Clerk; LMA Acc.249/211 inventory of Richard Clerk.
21. Extract from The Orrey Papers (p.72), at Harrow Reference Library.
22. See papers in the Oriental & India Office Collection of the British Library.
23. Guildhall MS 11936, 256, pol. 382281. William Bodimeade's insurances of 25-7 and 32 High Street 1767 and 1773 give information about several traders – see *The Villager*, no.31, p.25, and Guildhall MS 11946, 218, pol. 319454.
24. Science Museum, Simmons Collection.
25. LMA, Old Bailey Sessions Papers 1783, nos. 4 and 11.
26. Guildhall MS. 11936, 341 pol. 526827
27. *Victoria County History of Milddlesex*, vol.4, p.181.
28. T. Smith, 'Pinner Hill Farm', *Greater London Industrial Archaeology Society, Newsletter* 73 (1981).
29. P.G. Scott, *The London & Birmingham Railway through Harrow 1837-1987* (1987).
30. E.M. Sturdy, 'Charity and State Education in Harrow 1384-1959', diploma thesis at Harrow Reference Library.
31. J. Sperling, *Church Walks in Middlesex* (1849).
32. B. Cherry and N. Pevsner, in *Buildings of England – London 3: North West* (1991) say that J.P. Seddon designed some of Tooke's cottages. In fact the designs were for W. Barber in 1885 and 1896 – see J.P. Seddon; *Catalogue of Architectural Drawings in V & A* by M. Darby – and do not seem to have been implemented.
33. Most of this section is based, by his kind permission, on the research of Hilary Thornley.

Sources

NOTE ON BOOKS, SOURCES AND DATING

The books and sources consulted have been so many that full footnotes or even a comprehensive list have been impossible for a work of this length, which I regret enormously. In Parts II and III the dates of most local events, including those in brackets, derive from the roll of a manor court held in that year. There has not been room to give footnote references for them all. The modern calendar has been used.

BOOKS AND SOURCES COVERING MORE THAN ONE PERIOD

First recourse should be made to the *Victoria History for the County of Middlesex*, volumes 1, 2 and 4 (hereafter *VCH*) rich in reference to other sources; the Local History Collection of the London Borough of Harrow (hereafter LBH); and E.M. Ware's *Pinner in the Vale*, 1955-7, including his papers at LBH. London Metropolitan Archives (hereafter LMA) has: Pinner Parish Records (which include churchwardens' accounts, parish rates, vestry minutes, endowments, registers); Middlesex Deeds Registry; St Thomas' Hospital papers; family papers including – Allen/Cooper, Beaumont, Bodimeade, Clarke, Gibson, Northwick (especially for manorial matters), Tooke; and so much more. The court rolls of the Manor of Harrow and of Harrow Rectory, are at LMA, and at Lambeth Palace Library (Estate MSS, 477-8), and run from 1315 to modern times, with breaks. Without the late Percy Davenport's transcription of these manuscripts much of the present work would have been impossible. Until 1742 the rolls were written in Latin, and all translation has been my own. Percy Davenport transcribed many wills and conveyances and I have inspected others in many locations, public and private. The Pinner Local History Society (hereafter PLHS) has many original papers. Its publications are particularly useful for the coach, horse bus, Metropolitan Station, National School, Pinner Hill House, Pinner Park, post offices, public houses, servants, shops, sport, suffragettes, Waxwell Lane, wind and water mills, and the workhouse. Its newsletters are useful in general. The illustrations in Alan Ball's *The Countryside Lies Sleeping* (1981) repay study.

THE EARLIEST TIMES

W.D. Bushell, *Harrow Octocentenary Tracts*, at LBH; P.A. Clarke, 'Anglo-Saxon Harrow & Hayes', *Transactions London & Middlesex Archaeological Soc.* (hereafter *TLAMAS*), 40 (1989); J. Cotton & B.Wood, 'Recent prehistoric finds from the Thames foreshore and beyond in Greater London', *TLAMAS* 47 (1996); R.H.M. Dolley, 'Three Merovingian Tremisses', *British Museum Quarterly*, 20 (1) 1955; R. Ellis, 'Excavations at Grims Dyke, Harrow, 1979', *TLAMAS* 33 (1982);

D.M. Kiddle, 'The Changing Landscape of North West Middlesex – especially Harefield Ickenham & Ruislip' (1974), unpublished thesis at Uxbridge Library; I. Thompson, 'Harrow in the Roman Period', in *Two Thousand Years: the Long Journey*, Stanmore & Harrow Historical Society (2000).

THE MEDIEVAL PERIOD

The series of ministers' accounts for Canterbury at Lambeth Palace; Alecto Historical Editions, *Domesday Book Studies* (1987) (now available separately in paperback as *The Story of Domesday Book* [2003]) and *Middlesex & London Domesday*, 1991; W.D. Bushell, *Harrow Octocentenary Tracts*; Canterbury & York Society, vol. XLV, LII, LIV and LXIV (for the archbishops in Pinner); P.A. Clarke, 'Headstone Manor, Pinner, Middlesex', *TLAMAS* 51 (2000); P.A. Clarke, 'The Church House of Pinner', *PLHS Newsletter* 79; C. Currie and H. Borrill, 'Pinner Village Gardens', *London Archaeologist* Vol.5 no.8 ,1986; F. R. Du Boulay, *The Lordship of Canterbury* (1966).

THE 16TH AND 17TH CENTURIES

LMA Acc.1052 for Lord North's Survey of 1547, with list of customs, leases and other estate papers; North MSS at Bodleian Library; *Chantry Certificates 1548*, by London & Middlesex Record Society (1980); Middlesex Sessions Records; Hearth Tax lists at LMA; A. Howard, 'The Clitherows of Boston Manor', unpublished thesis at LBH; records of the Tallow Chandlers Company; P.A. Clarke, 'Dissent in a Middlesex Parish – story of early Dissent in Pinner', *TLAMAS* 48 (1997) p.157.

THE 18TH CENTURY

Licensing Records for Middlesex at LMA; B. Harrison, 'The Pinner Murder and A Serious Miscarriage of Justice' in *PLHS Newsletter* 70; B. Elliott, 'The Nevills of Nevill Holt', *English Catholic Ancestor Journal*, Autumn 1985, pp.16-17; Isaac Messeder's Map of the Manor of Harrow 1759 at LMA

A PERIOD OF CHANGE

Harrow Enclosure papers, at LBH; Cary's *New Itinerary*, 1798; *Paterson's Roads* 1808; John Middleton, *View of the Agriculture of Middlesex*; Pigot's *Directories of Middlesex*; K. Kirkman, *Pinner Chalk Mines* (1992); Accounts of Overseers of Poor, of Highways, and Poor Rate Assessments – all at PLHS

SUBSEQUENT CHAPTERS

For these periods the records are too numerous to list, and I have singled out only a few. The LBH has a very rich collection of which the following are a starting selection – the records on which is based *Pinner Streets Yesterday and Today*, by E. Cooper and PLHS; Pinner Parish Magazine; directories; the census records; collection of sale particulars; the brochure for Woodridings Estate 1855; brochures of 20th-century developers; *The Villager*, journal of the Pinner Association, from 1938; O.S. maps; and plenty about organisations, activities and personalities. There is much miscellaneous information in the archives of PLHS, including rate books, extracts from Pinner National School log books, and the taped or written memories of Pinner residents. The late Jim Golland's articles for the *Harrow Observer* are invaluable. For North Harrow I have relied considerably on a draft work by Iris Long.

Index

Surnames usually relate to more than one individual. Fuller names refer to people of more than local renown. Illustrations are shown in bold type.